CONTEMPORARY REFORM JEWISH THOUGHT

Edited by

Bernard Martin

Published in Cooperation with
The Central Conference of American Rabbis by

Quadrangle Books/Chicago

SECOND PRINTING

Library of Congress Catalog Card Number: 67-13461

PREFACE

This collection of essays, while sponsored by the Central Conference of American Rabbis, does not represent the official views of the Conference. Including in its membership all of the almost one thousand Reform rabbis in the United States and a considerable number abroad, the Conference embraces many varieties of theological belief and opinion. It could not, even if it wished to do so, present any single theological statement as the authoritative stance of American Reform Judaism, or even of the American Reform rabbinate. The present collection itself bears witness to the wide spectrum of belief that prevails within the Conference.

All of the essays here included were written by rabbis who are alumni of the Hebrew Union College–Jewish Institute of Religion, which is the fountainhead of Reform Judaism in America. Three of the authors serve as professors at their alma mater, one occupies a chair of Jewish Studies at a university, and eight minister to congregations. Most of the essays were written expressly for this volume, though several have appeared, in somewhat different form, in publications of the Conference, its *Yearbook* and *Journal.*

One was previously published in the quarterly *Judaism*, to which grateful acknowledgment is made for permission to reprint it.

It has been my privilege, as chairman of the executive committee of the Special Interest Group on Theology of the Conference, to edit this volume. The common hope that motivated all its contributors is that these essays, in presenting the deepest convictions as well as the reasoned conclusions of their authors on the ultimate concerns of Judaism—God, Torah, and Israel—may not only stimulate further theological reflection and discussion within American Israel, but also deepen the commitment of Jews everywhere to their religious heritage.

BERNARD MARTIN

CONTENTS

CONTEMPORARY REFORM JEWISH THOUGHT

FAITH AND METHOD

IN MODERN JEWISH THEOLOGY

Eugene B. Borowitz

I

My subject is the role of faith in modern Jewish theology. In this context, faith may have three separate though related meanings: faith as commitment to action, faith as commitment to content, and, mostly, faith as commitment to a beginning. Each level of definition has its particular implications for theological method and must therefore be treated on its own.

On the first level, to say that Jewish theology involves faith means, at least, that we expect the Jewish theologian to live what he teaches. Of the philosopher of religion we can demand only that he understand the reasoning of religious thinkers, not that he believe and live by all the diverse systems he expounds. A theologian should be no less academically competent and

This paper was published in somewhat different form in the *Yearbook* of the Central Conference of American Rabbis, 1963.

proficient, but in his case one critical requirement is added which radically changes the context of his scholarship. He shares the faith he expounds, and we expect his life to show his strength of belief in the truths he proclaims.

If faith for us must include both acts and thoughts, it is because of our frequent experience with those whose concepts are persuasive but whose behavior is repulsive. Not all men who think bright thoughts, not even those who are persuaded of their truth, actually live by them—even most of the time. This gap between cognition and decision, between idea and resolve, cannot be ignored. We may not ourselves believe much, but we will judge the man who says he believes more by his performance than by his preaching.

In Judaism, in which action has traditionally been valued above thought, the theologian's life must be the first evidence of his teaching. And for a Jew that must inevitably mean not just his private and familial existence, but his participation in the ongoing activity of the synagogue and of the Jewish people as a whole.

At this level there is virtual unanimity among us. The Jewish theologian should live his understanding of Judaism, and through his Jewish living he should test and refine his Judaism. But Jewish action stems from an understanding of the content of Judaism, and that content is itself established through faith. Surprising as it may seem, that is the almost unanimous conclusion of contemporary Jewish thinkers. Let us take, for example, the absolutely central question: How do we know there is a God? Even those Jewish theologians who are committed to the utmost use of reason acknowledge that at a given point reason will carry us no further. It may prepare the way. It may be necessary for clarification afterward, but reason itself does not lead us to the conclusion that there really is a God. The only way to get to Judaism's position is by faith.

Mordecai Kaplan has said that belief in God "is an assumption that is not susceptible of proof." [1] He has written, "Whence do we derive this faith in a Power that endorses what ought to be? Not from that aspect of the mind which has to do only with mathematically and logically demonstrated knowledge. Such faith stems from that aspect of the mind which finds expression in the enthusiasm for living, in the passion to surmount limitations." [2]

Elsewhere he speaks of it as an intuition or an affirmation of one's whole being.[3]

Levi Olan similarly acknowledges that "the God faith is not subject to proof in the rational or scientific sense. . . . Ultimately, as Judaism learned at the beginning, God is an affirmation and a postulate." [4] What affirmations and postulates involve is made clear by him in another connection: "Faith by its very nature involves affirmations *beyond the rational* [italics added] and the Hebraic spirit is not characterized by a rigid syllogistic encasement." [5] Similarly, Roland Gittelsohn, in the course of his argument for the existence of God, says: "The mind . . . by itself, unaided by the heart, . . . can never provide total answers. . . . We need faith. Man cannot live by reason alone. . . . Of course we need faith to carry us beyond the bounds of reason." [6]

We are so accustomed to hearing these men called "rationalists" that we tend to accept that appellation naïvely. We begin to believe that they are true philosophic rationalists, that if we follow their views we may hope to dispense with the kind of faith which they themselves categorize as "beyond the rational" or "beyond the bounds of reason." But we have only ourselves to blame for this illusion. The thinkers themselves have been far more rigorous and honest. They say plainly: "We need faith." Their claim to the title "rationalist" does not derive from their elimination of faith but from their effort to control faith by reason, as we shall see.

There have been Jewish thinkers in ages past—not only in medieval times, but as recently as Hermann Cohen—who were thoroughgoing philosophic rationalists. These men sought to demonstrate the truth about the existence of God by means of a rigorously logical argument. In this, the simple philosophic meaning of the term, it would be true to say that there are no rationalists among liberal Jewish theologians today.

This description is not limited to naturalists. Leo Baeck, often considered a rationalist by the uncritical, is rather to be found with those who clearly confess reason's inadequacy to establish a Jewish view of God. One might have expected Baeck, as a faithful if independent follower of Hermann Cohen, to restate Cohen's philosophical demonstration of the necessity of the idea of God. Baeck, however, completely avoids this and instead, following Schleiermacher, bases his discussion on inner experience, grounds which would have been repugnant to the neo-Kantian philosopher of Marburg. Thus it is not of God as idea, but of God as Exalted One, as Mystery, as Secret, that Baeck often speaks of Him. Moreover, Baeck does not wait for the end of a long, rationally ordered argument to introduce faith as the means of reaching a triumphant conclusion. God, in all His shroudedness as well as His righteousness, is present from the very beginning of Baeck's discussion. When, in his chapter on "Faith in God," he discusses faith directly, he says:

> In Judaism faith is nothing but the living consciousness of the Omnipresent. . . . This conviction is not sustained by speculation and gnosis, or by facts and proofs. Hence there is in it nothing subtly reasoned out, nothing demonstrated or expounded. On the contrary, it is the opposite of the faith which has to be set forth by arguments or established by victories.[7]

Only Martin Buber, among contemporary thinkers, finds God by knowledge, so to speak, rather than by faith. Buber manages this by positing an epistemology which has two categories of knowing, object-knowing and subject-knowing. The latter is as natural and everyday as the former. It involves no special state of consciousness and is clearly not to be compared with the mystic's special experience. Buber says we know God as we know other subjects, save that He is non-corporeal. Thus faith for Buber is not a way of reaching convictions about God, but the life which comes from knowing Him.

Philosophically, we cannot insist a priori that it is impossible that knowledge is available in two modes, each with its appropriate structures and values. If Buber's categories are right, it would seem just as rational to know subjects by subject-knowing as it is to know objects "objectively." In those terms one might facetiously suggest that Buber is the only "rationalist" among Jewish philosophers today. But the title has now lost all meaning. Though faith has become knowing for Buber, what he has really shown us is that all subjects are known by faith, and that faith is more common to life than most modern men had thought.

Thus, there is almost universal agreement among contemporary writers that faith is basic to Jewish theology, not only on the level of action but on the more fundamental level of content as well.[8]

Once faith has been admitted to Jewish theology, we are led to a third and deeper plane of discussion. Faith brings us to such fundamental Jewish affirmations as the existence of God, His goodness and its eventual triumph. But what else will it bring us of Judaism? As modern Jews are we prepared to accept everything that has been characteristic of believing Jews over the centuries? Admitting faith to our religiosity raises the danger of Orthodoxy and sets the liberal Jew in search of a principle by which to regulate the content that faith may contribute to his liberal Judaism.

The need of a regulative principle is prompted, too, by our knowledge of human history. Summoning the deepest of men's passions, faith may lead to superstition, fanaticism, and oppression, and it has done so among Jews as among other peoples. Perhaps a liberal Jew could somehow reconcile Orthodox Jewish observance with his liberalism, if his personal decision so demanded. But that his faith might bring him into conflict with his sense of morality is as intolerable as it is a realistic possibility. For this reason, even more than because of Orthodoxy, a means of controlling faith must be found.

In traditional Judaism the search would quickly be over. The halachic tradition of authentic interpretation would do this in theory, even as the sanctions of the observant, organized Jewish community would do so in practice. But for us liberal Jews, who have neither a unifying law nor an observant community to channel our faith, but who rather require a firm faith so that we may rally our community and reestablish standards of Jewish living, the regulating principle must be found on the personal, not the communal, level.

How has this need been met over the past one hundred or so years of liberal Jewish theology? For Abraham Geiger, the progress which history displayed in its systematic evolution was the criterion of his Jewish faith. In its name he could abandon the personal Messiah. For Baeck, God's will is always understood as an ethical demand, and ethical monotheism is the test of Judaism. For this reason he makes the Jewish people a means to preserve and foster ethical monotheism, and Jewish observance a secondary

means to preserve that primary means. For Buber, though faith
is a kind of knowing, one is commanded only as one encounters
or is personally encountered. Thus Buber is halachically more
radical than the most radical Reform Jew and rejects any practice which stems from community tradition rather than personal
experience.

For Kaplan, the modern, naturalistic, particularly social scientific, understanding of man and society is indispensable. This,
he believes, requires him to posit an impersonal God. Roland
Gittelsohn's argument carries this view of reason as the arbiter
of faith to its fullest and clearest exposition. Now, let us read
the sentences which follow our previous citation and thus give
his thought his own completion:

> Of course we need faith to carry us beyond the bounds of
> reason. But that faith must be built on a foundation of reason,
> must be consistent with the reasonable and the known, not
> contradictory to them. If the direction of the knowledge yielded
> by experience and reason be represented by a solid line, faith
> must be a dotted line which continues in the same general
> direction, not one which goes off at a capricious and contra-
> dictory angle.[9]

Here faith is strictly bound by reason, and Gittelsohn's reason
can permit him to have faith in only a limited God.

We may, with some hesitation, summarize this cursory survey.
Liberal Jewish thinkers have generally sought to regulate their
faith by finding a universal standard of truth and reinterpreting
Judaism in its terms. This standard has usually been borrowed
from the philosophy current in the theologian's time and place,
though Cohen and Buber created their own. If liberal Jewish
thinkers, excepting Cohen, deserve to be called rationalists,
though they rely on faith and cannot dispense with it, it is
because they have regularly sought to control their faith by some
rational principle.

II

Now let us turn to our own case. What principle is most appropriate to our day?

Before responding to this question, we must make very clear

the responsibility involved in making our decision. The choice of a principle to guide the operation of faith is not a modest technical matter. It involves the very heart of our Judaism. As we select one concept pattern over another we are already committing ourselves to a certain character in our Judaism—not just its beliefs, but the balance and weight of its observances as well. This principle changes the nature of God, alters Israel's character, and reforms the hierarchy of Jewish values, as we have seen above. This is the most fundamental decision we can make with regard to our religion.

For some men the response is relatively easy. They recognize in one or another contemporary philosophic system man's best guide to truth, and they interpret Judaism through it. But for most of us the choice is not that simple, particularly when we look at the views which previous thinkers have espoused.

If we turn to the vaguely Hegelian trust in historic progress of either an Abraham Geiger or a Kaufmann Kohler, we find ourselves in most uncongenial territory. History is not always progressive, and we find it difficult to say with conviction that we know the truth of man and God better and more clearly than did a previous age. We do know, however, that we cannot, as they did, unselfconsciously choose what we wish in history and, by calling it "the highest," "the noblest" or "the best," consider it validated by the historical march of truth.

The rational idealism of a Cohen, even as modified by Baeck, is similarly problematic. We are troubled by the former's relation to the real world. How shall we make the transfer from the philosophically necessary idea to the concretely existing reality? And in both cases, how can we today reestablish a philosophic certainty which derives from the clarity and independence of the ethical demand? We obviously do not wish to compromise the significance or the authority of the ethical. But it is another thing to make ethics the one sure and self-substantiating foundation of all our other affirmations of value. The varying apprehensions of ethical responsibility among different peoples, and even in different social classes within Western society itself, as well as the role education and personal exposure play in determining conscience, all make of the ethical a problem with which to deal, rather than an unshakable base on which to build.

Nor is the scientific naturalism of Kaplan, Olan, and Gittelsohn any less troublesome. Perhaps in the thirties it was possible to hold simply and self-evidently, as Kaplan did, that to be modern necessarily meant to think in terms of naturalism.[10] Today there are clearly other ways of being sophisticatedly modern, particularly since naturalism has floundered in dealing with the key philosophic problem of our time, the identification and authorization of values. One can take a thoroughgoing scientific view of reality and come up morally neutral, as the atomic bomb so dramatically illustrated. Such an uncommitted naturalism is far more "rationalistic," that is, internally consistent, than is Kaplan's theism. His response to this charge is that such a naturalism cannot motivate morality, and therefore must be rejected.[11] Philosophically, if the morality is prior, Kaplan should, like the neo-Kantians, first rationally establish the realm of the ethical, which he never does. Practically it is simply not true that naturalists, agnostic philosophically of God or ethics, cannot be morally active, as the cases of Bertrand Russell and others make clear.

Gittelsohn's more tightly drawn argument from science suffers from a similar difficulty. If scientific reason knows anything, it is that superfluous hypotheses are rigorously to be excluded. To add God to a strictly scientific view of the universe is therefore not to continue in a direction previously established but to add a new and rationally unnecessary direction. It is not just adding a bit of spice to the food, but radically changing the menu.

Of course, if what Gittelsohn means is that God seems a "reasonable" addition to the scientific view of the universe, that is another matter. It is a far cry from the philosophically ordered "rational" to what I personally can believe, the "reasonable." What makes the addition of God so "reasonable" to Gittelsohn is that he already believed in Him before the argument began. Indeed, it would be difficult to explain why Gittelsohn prefers the scientific data and opinions which will make the addition of God reasonable to all those which would not, if it were not that he begins with faith in God. Thus while Gittelsohn claims faith only completes a line which rationality itself drew, it seems clear to me that faith here preceded reason and guided it.

Levi Olan, who has given a similar argument about man's place in the universe, has been far more precise on the matter of presuppositions. While insisting that reason is a fundamental ingredient of truth, he has, in his discussion of faith and reason, frankly noted: "Reason, of itself, is never the source of truth." [12] Thus he correctly calls his evidence from modern science neither proofs nor even indications but resources. In other words, having established by faith that he believes in man, he can then find much substantiation in modern science for such a view.

These previous choices—historic progress, idealism, naturalism—do not easily commend themselves today as means of guiding our faith. Perhaps, then, we should turn to the current fashions in philosophy: linguistic analysis, Tillichian ontology, or one of the varieties of religious (not atheistic) existentialism? Or perhaps, dissatisfied with all the alternatives, we ought instead to begin by creating our own system of universal truth.

Which of these living, if troublesome, options shall we choose?

But considering what is at stake, should we not first ask: *How* shall we choose? On what basis shall we decide whether to adopt one principle or another to regulate our faith? This question may with equal significance be asked of the man who is not troubled by our uncertainty but knows which philosophy he must follow. How does he know it? How did he determine it?

Three possibilities suggest themselves. At one time it might have been possible to suggest that certain truths were self-evident, or so clear and distinct that one could not doubt them. Obviously a philosophy which based itself on them was sound. Such a view could be accepted by only a few in our day. We have learned to doubt everything, not least ourselves, our certainty, and our intuition. To be modern is, to begin with, to be critical.

Perhaps, then, we should prefer to see our choice more as a hypothesis, an educated guess, a temporary venture whose validity we will determine as we experience the results of its use and its application to life.

In many ways that is an attractive suggestion. Surely we do not consider ourselves in possession of absolute truth here and now. We, as liberals, do not want to take up a dogmatic stand, one which is not open to change and the possibility of whose further refinement is rejected in advance.

But while we are determined to remain open to new and keener truth, it is difficult indeed to call the principle we seek but a tentative surmise. Let us remember what is involved in this decision. On this "hypothesis" our whole religion hangs.

What is at stake is simply—*everything*. A commitment of such intense involvement and immense consequence is not merely an enlightened hunch about what might possibly turn out to be right. In all its momentariness, in all its openness to readjustment, I do not see how we can call our choice less than an act of faith.

Indeed, the very structure of the decision itself makes that clear. When we are judging among alternative possibilities of reason (in fact, when we stand before any single system of reason asking ourselves whether we shall use it), we cannot use reason itself as the basis of decision. The criterion of the adequacy of reason cannot be reason itself, for it is precisely reason which is being judged. Or, to put the matter more directly, every philosophy begins with an act of faith. That is what we mean when we say that each one inevitably has its own assumptions. Assumptions are not validated by reason. They are an expression of faith.

On this point, too, Olan has been far more clear and consistent than other naturalists. Beginning in 1947 (as far back as I have been able to trace the matter), he has openly referred to liberalism as a "faith." An essay published in that year is appropriately entitled: "Rethinking the Liberal Faith." [13] And his address to the Central Conference of American Rabbis in 1962 was on the theme: "New Resources for a Liberal Faith." [14] Olan does not seek to prove the rational necessity of liberalism. He rather admits that liberalism is a faith, one which is consistent with reason but clearly not established by it. Faith first establishes a matrix, and then, within its frame, reason is free to operate fully.

In short, choosing a regulative principle involves a paradox. We know we do not arrive at the content of Judaism without faith. But we also believe that we cannot affirm everything to which believing Jews in the past few centuries have been committed. Hence we seek to limit our faith in Judaism by some sort of regulating principle. Only now is it clear that no self-justifying, autonomous principle exists, but that all the possibilities before us themselves involve a prior act of faith. Thus, we can delimit our Jewish faith only by acknowledging that we have a *prior faith*, in whose name we are willing to alter and revise traditional Judaism. This is the third and deepest level of faith on which the Jewish theologian must take a stand, commitment not only to action or to content but also to one particular beginning. Thus the structure of Jewish theology is tripartite, or even reduplicated. It begins in faith, and this makes possible the work of reason, which, in turn, ends with faith—from this point on it is always faith followed by reason followed by faith in infinite, better messianic, progression.

So, to return to our theme, I ask again which approach shall we today choose?

III

From this point on I should not speak of what "we" should choose. Rather, in accord with what I said on the first level about the theologian's thought and life, I should rather speak of what I must choose and of the method which derives from it. If I say "we," it is in the hope that there are others who share my commitment and that I am articulating their views, consciously held or not, as well as my own.

My position is simple. I believe that the general method of Jewish theology over these past hundred years no longer makes sense. It reflects a point of view that may once have been necessary or even desirable but is so no longer. And it is time we consciously confronted this issue and radically altered our course.

Perhaps I can clarify my position by a question, hypothetical to be sure, but not unrealistic. Suppose that we follow the traditional method of liberal Jewish theology and choose an intellectual medium for our faith, say neo-Kantianism or existentialism. We carefully work out the meaning of our Judaism in its terms, adding some insights, on the one hand, but also refusing to believe this or observe that, on the other. Whereupon, over the years, we discover that the philosophy in which we had placed such faith is not nearly so adequate to life as we had thought. Indeed, we now wish to replace it with a better one. But wait. We had based our Judaism on that philosophy. In its name we had both justified and revised our Judaism. Once we have lost faith in our philosophy, do we lose our faith in Judaism as well? Would we, in the face of this intellectual setback, conclude that Judaism itself no longer had meaning for us?

Some men have indeed given up their Judaism under such circumstance, but I would like to believe that I would not and that the majority of Jews would not either. Despite such an intellectual catastrophe we would insist that we knew Judaism was still true. And we would do so despite the crash of reason and the tragedy of this experience, because our belief in Judaism was deeper than our trust in any philosophy.

Let me be blunt. Our theologians in the past century have acted as if they knew a truth superior to Judaism. But I do not know a body of knowledge or a system of understanding God and man and history superior to Judaism. I do not have a faith more basic to my existence than my Judaism. I believe in Judaism not because there are such good expositions of its content and its meaning, but despite all the inadequate and clumsy statements of its substance, including my own. I should be delighted one day to have a philosophically tenable exposition of the truth of Judaism, but I shall not wait for one to believe in it. I want faith in Judaism to come before any other faith, and I want to make this priority of faith in Judaism my methodological start-ing point.

Surely rabbis, students, teachers, and servants of Judaism do not have to be reminded of their commitment to Judaism. But what is of critical concern to me is the level on which that com-mitment is made. This question of primacy is not only crucial to our theological method, but explains the great difficulty rabbis often encounter in dealing with their congregants. Let me take two examples.

Every rabbi has had to deal with intellectuals whose approach to life was genuinely framed in terms of a given mental pattern. When such a man inquires seriously about Judaism, we are eager to tell him of its truth but usually have great difficulty in doing so. The reason is clear. This man has a prior faith. The only way we can make ourselves understood and, we hope, convincing to him, is to translate Judaism into the terms of his prior faith. And that is just the trouble. Often his private faith is so constructed that it does not make possible a belief in God or—to him, worse —an institutionalized religion. But whether he already has a hospitable or inhospitable point of view, we must recognize its priority in his life. We must talk to him in his terms, and that is why we have such difficulty doing so to our own satisfaction.

This task of explaining one's faith to a man with another faith has an old and honorable theological history. Its name is unfortunate. It is called apologetics. Much of our work not only with intellectuals but with our members as well is apologetic theology. And, in general, liberal Jewish theology this past century has been apologetic theology. Perhaps unconsciously, it seems to have assumed that it was addressing nonbelievers. It then took up its argument in terms the nonbeliever could perhaps accept and sought to explain Judaism convincingly in them.

Apologetics is an important practical task, not only for the Jew who does not believe but also for all those men of good will who seek its truth. We have a responsibility to share such truth as we have found. But apologetics cannot be our primary intellectual task today. Before we devise a theology for the outsider, we must clarify what those inside the circle of faith share.

If our faith in Judaism is prior to any other body of truth, then it is entitled to receive our attention in its own right, not just as explanation in terms of another point of view.

More critical to this issue of priority is the case of our more loyal members, those who have some faith in Judaism. Why does their Judaism generally have so little impact on their lives? Why do we so often find it difficult to communicate to them the overwhelming importance of Jewish belief and observance? Here, too, the answer may be found in analyzing the level of their Jewish faith. They do believe in Judaism, but they have other faiths of greater importance. As long as Judaism can be explained in terms of their private world of belief, they will accept it. We win their willingness to Jewish action when we explain it in their terms, say mental health or the image of themselves as good parents, dutiful children, or loyal Americans. But let the demands transgress their private norms—say we suggest mid-week Hebrew, daily prayer, or public agreement to racially integrated housing—and Judaism has become a bore, a chore, a nag.

That is the danger of marketing Judaism in the consumer's terms, of our informal apologetics. We are covertly endorsing the private faith by which our member lives. We never shake him loose from his more basic faith. We never make Judaism the foundation of his faith, and he lives out his days, using Judaism when it suits his purposes, rejecting it when it does not.

Many people are attracted to Reform Judaism for just this reason, not because it is "convenient," but because they know we stand committed to freedom of individual conscience. We will not deny each man's right to spiritual self-determination. The

result in many cases has been that our members believe first in
themselves, their needs, their goals, their image, and only on a
secondary level in Judaism, its God, its commandments, its aspira-
tions. And that is why every sensitive servant of the God of
Israel suffers so as he works with his people. A religion that
takes second place is no religion. Unless we make Judaism primary in our lives and in the lives of our people, we shall not
have accomplished that first step on which all the rest of the
journey depends.

Liberal Judaism is committed both to the self and to the tradition. Previous generations sought regularly to put the self first,
to work from the self back to the tradition. In part they were
right. The individual must always be the foundation of belief
and thus retain the right to disbelieve. Our full respect for his
freedom makes the right of dissent inalienable.

But many of our people have gone one step further. We taught
them that Jewish tradition was not absolute, but that they had
the duty to reach their own religious conclusions. They have
transformed this, mostly unconsciously, into a whole view of life.
They have made their selfhood the ultimate source of their religiosity, and their individuality the determinative principle of
their faith. They confidently judge such truth as comes to them
from without in terms of their goals and their predilections. They
may occasionally find themselves confused and troubled, and
they may then turn to Judaism for help. But mostly they seek
a new fad, a new recreation, for they cannot abandon their operative faith that they personally know more about man and his
destiny than does Judaism. "The anxious shall live by his faith
in himself." This position is a logical outgrowth of liberalism, but
it is at the same time the source of a superior, sometimes patron-
izing attitude toward Jewish belief and Jewish action. As long as
Judaism is not primary to the existence of our people, we cannot hope to see their inertia and apathy disappear.

But can we give primary allegiance to a tradition we cannot
accept as absolute? Can we retain the self's right to judge and
to dissent, without turning it into a rival principle of faith? That
is, indeed, what I am suggesting. By faith in Judaism I mean the
conscious, personal assent to the unique meaningfulness and significance of the Jewish religious tradition for our lives. Such
faith affirms a qualitative distinction between the body of truth

given us about God, man, and history in Judaism and in any other system or structure, without thereby insisting that Judaism is always right or cannot learn on this or that issue. Being founded on individual assent, it likewise guarantees the right to dissent without thereby raising the self to the status of a prior principle.

IV

The faith by which I seek to live as a liberal Jew is therefore a vigorous affirmation of the primacy of Judaism for my life if not of its absolute character. If I am consistently and rigorously to carry on the work of theology in its terms, a fourfold process suggests itself.

First, it should be obvious that such Jewish theology begins not with an idealist, naturalist, ontological, or linguistic philosophy, or an existential diagnosis of the self, but with the tradition and its affirmations. Nor will the disciplined detachment of a Büchler or a Marmorstein, or the quiet appreciation of a Schechter or a Moore, suffice us. They saw the Jewish past as an object of investigation. I see it rather as having a claim upon me and my life reasonably similar to that which it had upon other generations of Jews. Their careful objectivity can only be a beginning for a search which now must also ask: what did it mean once to believe such a faith? What did it mean to try to live such a faith? And, most important, what does it mean for me to join my forefathers in this belief? We begin with the tradition not as an interesting curio from the past or a source of quotations to illustrate some modern view, but as a living content of belief which confronts us in authority and challenge.

Nor can we, in the second place, say in advance that we should limit our attention and concern to just those aspects which are relevant to us. Because we assert no principle prior to Judaism we cannot know beforehand what no longer has the power to speak to us and to guide our lives. We must pay attention to the priesthood as to the other prophets, to the rabbinic apocalypses and mysticisms as to their ethics. And we must, if we would be true to our faith, remain as open as possible to what Jewish tradition can teach us, even if that means we might end up believing it all. The methodological principle here is that we seek to make our faith in Judaism self-regulating. Once prophecy was that judgment-from-within that helped the tradition transcend itself. Our hope is that a living Jewish faith can show the way to an ever truer Judaism.

Third, our openhearted search of the tradition may from time to time lead us to dissent. Because we do not wish to make a faith of dissent, we should not search to disagree nor study to disavow. In our affirmation of the primary value of Judaism we would not easily or peacefully dissociate ourselves from its teachings. When we are in all seriousness moved to disagree, the responsibility now rests upon us to justify that disagreement. Previous generations of liberal Jews often acted as if Judaism had to justify itself to the Jew. I am arguing that making Jewish faith primary calls on us to justify ourselves when we dissent from it.

Nor do I worry that this shift of responsibility will make it difficult for the liberal to remain free and selective. We can rely not only on his decades of autonomy and the influence of the American environment to strengthen his will to think for himself, but also on the instinctive human disinclination to accept duty and responsibility freely.

This affirmation of the right to dissent is the reason we cannot follow the theological methodology of Abraham Heschel. Omitting now all questions of the literary form in which he puts his arguments, the content does seek to be true to the Jewish tradition in its own terms. Heschel's favorite response to the questions of modern thought is to point out how the reverse may be asked if we only begin from within the circle of Jewish faith. But while he is no fundamentalist and makes allowances for the humanity of the channels of revelation, he does not understand genuine dissent. Again and again he asks whether it is believable that a biblical author should lie or misrepresent. Again and again he characterizes possible alternative thoughts as unthinkable, unbelievable, irrational, even insane.[15] We can recognize the consistency of his theology with one variety of Jewish believing, but it is one whose certainty liberals do not share. Perhaps this contrast with Heschel's full-fledged neo-Orthodoxy will make clear why I believe the position enunciated here, with all its emphasis on the priority of faith in Judaism, is yet fully a liberal one.

Fourth, from this dynamic process of confronting the claims of the tradition in its fullness, and working out concurrence and dissent, the individual will come to know himself fully. It is not just that Judaism will teach him what a man is and ought to be. In thinking through his disagreements with the tradition, in seeking to justify and explain his necessary difference of opinion, he will find himself revealed. Both Judaism as accepted guide and as rejected standard will call forth the mixture of person and tradition that should mark the modern Jew.

This living interchange between the self and the tradition can thus provide the base from which the individual can reach out to all that diversity of modern life and culture which the tradition could not know. Again the order is reversed. We do not here begin with psychiatry or democracy and come to find what in Judaism agrees with them. Rather, in confrontation with the tradition we create a matrix of value with which to reach out to modern culture, willing to learn from it where we can, but sufficiently secure that we shall not also hesitate to criticize it. The firmer our roots are in our Judaism the freer we will feel to participate in modern society in its most varied activities. Knowing with reasonable clarity who we are and for what we stand, we can go our way as critics or enthusiasts with quiet confidence.

I have tried to make clear the way in which method in Jewish theology necessarily depends upon faith. The critical question then becomes: What is your primary faith? For some of us that faith is Judaism, and, as a result, we feel that a new methodology is needed in liberal Jewish theology. Men of other basic commitments will take other directions. That is their privilege and their right. If anything can characterize the proposal given here, it is this: for me and for many others the crucial question of our existence has shifted from "How can a Jew truly be a modern man?" to "How can a modern man be truly a Jew?"

NOTES

1. Mordecai Kaplan, *The Meaning of God in Modern Jewish Religion* (New York: Jewish Reconstructionist Foundation, 1947), p. 28.
2. *The Jewish Reconstructionist Papers* (New York: Behrman's Jewish Book House, 1936), p. 98.
3. *The Meaning of God in Modern Jewish Religion,* p. 84.
4. *Yearbook* of the Central Conference of American Rabbis for 1962, New York, 1963, p. 238.
5. *Judaism,* V (No. 2, Spring 1956), 114.

6. Roland Gittelsohn, *Man's Best Hope* (New York: Random House, 1961), pp. 61-62.

7. Leo Baeck, *The Essence of Judaism* (New York: Macmillan, 1936), pp. 118-19.

8. Obviously this does not mean that all the content of Judaism is derived from or reached by faith, but that its major premises, such as the existence of God, His goodness, the ultimate triumph of righteousness, revelation, election, all involve faith.

9. Gittelsohn, *op. cit.*, p. 62.

10. Kaplan, *Judaism as a Civilization* (New York: Reconstructionist Press, 1957), pp. 36-45.

11. *Ibid.*, pp. 309-10.

12. Olan, *Yearbook*, p. 114.

13. Olan, "Rethinking the Liberal Faith," in *Reform Judaism, Essays by Alumni of the Hebrew Union College* (Cincinnati: HUC Press, 1949), pp. 28 ff.

14. Reprinted below, pp. 21-38.

15. Although I cannot associate myself with Ben-Horin's own exaggeration and the dogmatism which he brings to his pragmatic criteria, the reader will find a useful collection of some of Heschel's most disturbing habits in Meir Ben-Horin, "The Ultimate and the Mystery," in the *Jewish Quarterly Review*, LI (No. 1, July, 1960).

NEW RESOURCES FOR A LIBERAL FAITH

Levi A. Olan

I

The general character of all liberal philosophies is a belief in the idea of human improvement through the use of organized intelligence. Specifically, the liberal faith holds that progress is an essential ingredient of the cosmos, that man is educable and therefore perfectible, and that the perfect state, which had previously been reserved for another world, and that through grace only, is attainable on earth.

Despite the wars and revolutions which marked the end of the eighteenth century, it appeared to the men of the Enlightenment that the human creature was improving and becoming happier. Science and technology were not only advancing but were manifested by a flood of inventions and an increase in business enterprise. For the first time in human history it was possible for men to visualize the realization of the day not too distant when

This paper was published in somewhat different form in the *Yearbook* of the Central Conference of American Rabbis, 1963.

these remarkable blessings would be for all the people, not just for the few. Material progress was matched by the promise of a new moral climate, the beginnings of which were demonstrated in the abolition of slavery in America and in the release of the serfs in Czarist Russia. Good causes were popular and they were recording shining successes.

The twin pillars which supported the liberal outlook were nature and reason. Isaac Newton described a world which is naturally good, orderly, beautifully simple, and dependable once it is properly understood. Reason enables man to penetrate from appearances to reality, where it is found that the real is rational and the rational is real. This intellectual formula set science off on a series of promises which looked toward a world free of hunger, disease, and discomfort. Nature was no longer man's enemy; on the contrary, it was designed for man's increasingly satisfying life. Ignorance was the only obstacle preventing man from achieving the best life on earth. Nature was the clue to the good life, because what was natural was good, and the unnatural was bad. Darwin's disclosure of a general theory of evolution was summoned as evidence for the belief that progress is an essential ingredient of life, inspiring Herbert Spencer to affirm the dogma that organic evolution is an inevitable law of progress. This hopeful view of human destiny found expression in a new word, meliorism, the belief that the world can be made better through human effort.

The new weapon against evil was reason, best defined in mathematics and revealed practically in the natural sciences. The laboratory explored nature, and the mind subjected institutions and beliefs to critical analyses. The heavy burdens of man—hunger and insanity, serfdom and war—became subjects for empirical and rational investigations. The evils of social injustice, the painful contrast of slums and palaces, the privileged authority of kings and aristocrats, these and other systems embodied in laws and institutions became proper material for critical investigation and for change. Reason can be used to eliminate the evils of nature and of society equally well. The perfect political and economic order became as much a possibility as a water closet or a steam-driven engine. Liberty, fraternity, and equality awaited man's use of reason, which was the same for all men, and all nations, and all cultures. Reason, for the philosophies of the Enlightenment, became a metaphysical entity which promised to enable man to live in accord with a universal reality of natural harmony and human concord.

Judaism cannot be equated with any philosophic system, past or present; nor is it subsumed under any one descriptive term. It cannot be claimed exclusively by rationalists or mystics, by liberals or existentialists. The Jewish historic experience is unique, and its outlook is eclectic, reflecting the diversity of human needs and talents. The mystic and priest are as much at home in it as are the rationalist and prophet. The complexities of nature and of man, encountered in pain and stubbornness, dissuaded the Jew from accepting the either/or formula as an adequate response. It is in this broad historic frame that the major characteristics of the modern liberal outlook find a significant and natural place.

A belief in progress is central to Judaism, for its faith centers around the Kingdom of God, which is nothing less than the ultimate reality of a perfected world peopled by perfected men. The covenant is understandable only in a setting where men can mature morally and bring nearer the "day of the Lord." In the end of days it shall come to pass that men will "beat their swords into plowshares . . . and none will make them afraid." Time is linear in a universe that is unitary. Contrary to the views of Plato and Paul, wherein the universe is dualistic and static, or to those of Hegel and Marx, whose thought systems are dualistic but in process, or to those of Buddha and Spinoza, which are unitary and static, Judaism understands the universe in unitary terms and at the same time as being in process and movement toward a final victory. Upon the ruins of many shattered hopes Judaism has risen, phoenix-like, to affirm the eventual reality of God's kingdom on earth.

The Enlightenment's dependence upon reason as an instrument of progress is also natural to the Jewish view. Recognizing that there are other means of comprehending reality, Judaism does not give exclusive rights to any one of them. The values of inwardness and mystical sensibility, the meaning of a primary experience as a source of faith, and the significance of the torment of human existence are all respected and given freedom of expression. However, these bear their own dangers when they abandon reason as a cooperative and corrective instrument. The fanaticism like Hitler's are ever present when reason is suspended. possibilities that grossness and stupidity will lead to a malevolent

The experiences in the past and of the present of those who have abandoned the use of the mind are grimly instructive. The ethical can be suspended, the group can be disregarded in favor of the self, history can be ignored and the saving moment idealized, and the Kingdom of God can be rejected for personal salvation. In gnosticism yesterday, as in existentialism today, the despair of man and his destiny leads to the demiurge and to salvation in escape from the world itself. Reason in Judaism is never an "affront" or a "scandal." Having no mysteries which can be understood only because they are absurd or paradoxical, Judaism does not demand anti-intellectualism. The Torah must be studied, understood, and followed—a program which is inconceivable without the proper use of reason. Reason is never an insult to faith, for reason itself is a divine gift. There were anti-Maimonideans who cautioned against reliance on reason alone, but their objection was practical and aimed at preserving the tradition. No Jewish thinker, however, ever suggested a radical incompatibility of reason and faith.

Judaism is more than is described under the rubric of modern liberalism, but the basic characteristics of belief in progress, the perfectability of the world and of man, and the virtue of reason are very much a part of its religious structure. The possibility of a better life for man on earth is a belief common to both, although Judaism is more patient with failure and more tolerant with slowness because it is conscious that beyond what men can see there is God, who "renews daily the work of creation." Despair of the human venture is alien to Judaism because it would defeat both God Himself and man in whom the spirit of God abides.

The liberal vision has been fading for several decades as the faith in progress has begun to dissolve under the terrifying shock of two world wars, the rise of ruthless totalitarian powers, the stench of gas chambers, and the exploitation of scientific intelligence for the preparation of weapons capable of annihilating life itself from the earth. The hope that fraternity, equality, and liberty were being realized through a rational creature who now had science as a perfect tool has ended up in a "murderer's masquerade." Disillusionment has set in and pervaded every aspect of modern culture. The funeral obsequies for the Age of Hope were attended by many in seeming haste to bury the remains of the Enlightenment tradition. A mood of despair has taken hold of artists and philosophers, a mood not unlike the "failure of nerve" of a former age. Its major theme is escape from responsibility, a revival of a belief in the original depravity of human nature, a distrust of reason and the scientific method. The poet Rilke said it for our age: "Because the middle-class world believes in progress and humanity, it has forgotten the ultimacies on which human existence turns; it has forgotten that it is outdistanced, before it starts and forever, by death and by God."

The poet, who, like the prophet, is especially sensitive to the realities of the human condition, is today creating in a spirit of pessimism and nihilism. James Joyce is representative of the modern novelist. He refashioned Homer's Ulysses, who is a god-like hero, and produced an un-godlike Leopold Bloom, who is anything but heroic. In this vein Kafka, Camus, Hemingway, Faulkner, and Salinger write their distinguished novels. Picasso's *Guernica* represents the summation of the loneliness and anxiety of modern man; his hunger for order is constantly frustrated but can never be denied. Looking at a painting by Jackson Pollock one feels the experience of chaos or nothingness. In modern music dissonance is a flight from consonance and absolute tonality. Schoenberg's twelve tones bear no relationship to each other, can be played forward or backward, singly or together, up or down. Dissonance exists for its own sake, and in it one hears the cry of despair, a malediction upon life, indeed what Tillich calls "the experience of the void." The modern creative artist has followed the advice of Joseph Conrad: "In the destructive elements immerse yourself." It is impossible to escape the fact that the major mood of the arts in these last years projects the disillusionment of modern man and expresses repeatedly a feeling of nihilism. Man appears to exist in a fragmented condition, caught between hope and frustration, sunk into intellectual chaos and moral disillusionment. Louis J. Halle, commenting upon modern art, observes that "when the meaningfulness of meaninglessness becomes the theme of serious art and music, it becomes difficult to distinguish such art and music from what represents a meaningless meaningfulness."

A reading of our modern systematic disciplines reveals a uniform subjection of human reason to darker forces and higher mysteries. They are engaged in a revolt against reason, taking their cue from Kierkegaard, who said: "It was intelligence, and nothing else, that had to be opposed." Drawing injudiciously from

Freud's complex psychology, the irrationalist finds support for his position in the unconscious which is supposed to be truly in control of man's behavior and which prevents his ability to think independently or to reason objectively. The physical scientist contributes to the hopelessness of the hour by diminishing man's place in a constantly expanding universe and referring to him as "but a highly temporary bio-chemical episode on a very petty planet." The interpretive disciplines of philosophy and theology have joined the parade of despair. The professional philosopher today is engaged in a highly academic and technical discussion of such matters as linguistics, semantics, symbolism, epistemological niceties, and aesthetic wordplay. Reading modern philosophy, Paul Schilpp told his colleagues recently: "I would never dream that today's handwriting on the wall may spell *finis* to the human race." The theologian of today takes his cue from Kierkegaard, who rejected confidence in man and nature and found salvation in a universe of dread and helplessness. Man is a sinner who is deprived of the freedom not to sin, who is condemned to seek after an impossible victory and adjust himself to an inevitable defeat.

II

Man's disillusionment with the shining promises of the Enlightenment has become, for our generation, a mood of despair which pervades the arts, science, psychology, philosophy, and theology. In such a climate, is it time to put the liberal faith to rest with a pious Kaddish? Only the miracle of a resurrection can prevent it! But, before we lower the body, we ought to look a little more critically at the nature of our disappointment and, what is more to the point, we ought to look at some new resources which are available to man in his hope for a better life in a better world. Nihilism is a form of hysteria wherein a patient who cannot solve his problem moans incoherently in confused defeat. Ours is not the first age in history that has confused change with the end of the world. Our disappointments have been frightfully real, but they are not final. It is a form of masochism to deny that, even though the times are dangerous, progress has been real and impressive. The basic conditions of life have been improved. Man lives longer, is more literate, has more leisure and does less bur-

densome work, is aware of liberty, and is increasingly respectful
of law. These gains may be limited, but it is a form of sickness
not to see them. Our danger, as Charles Frankel has suggested,
is not the disasters themselves, but the "imagination of disaster,
and the attempt to convert an historical circumstance into a
metaphysical necessity." Evil is not a modern invention, and
liberals have confronted diverse forms of it in all ages. Our day
has merely organized them more efficiently. But, as Frankel suggests, "if we have new techniques for organizing stupidity, and
for exploiting fear and ignorance, then, at least in principle, we
also have techniques for controlling or mitigating these things."

There are available today, moreover, new resources which not
only can revive the liberal outlook, but can give it an impelling
urgency. The paradox of our time is that our cultural interpreters
seem to neglect the significance of the new scientific revolution.
The most important fact for us is that the atom has been smashed
and within it were found electrons and protons, and some twenty
or thirty other energy units that have been identified. "If there
is anything ultimate, eternal, and absolute, that something must
be energy," writes Kirtley Mather of Harvard. Whatever else
this means, it shatters once and for all the materialistic interpretation of the universe, and ends once and for all the notion that
the world is a machine. The old dualism of matter and force has
been replaced; matter and force are one and the same thing, a
form of energy. In the long story of evolution, this energy moved
from the inanimate to the animate, from the inorganic to the
organic, from vegetable to animal, and from animal to human.
Reality is not a machine, it is an organism. If man now asks "Is
the universe friendly to me?" the answer must take into consideration some new facts about the universe that the scientific revolution has revealed.

It had been assumed until now that everything had already
been created, and Aristotle's thesis that essence and form moved
toward a predetermined *telos,* or end, dominated man's view of
nature. The whole future was conceived as the unfolding of
what was enfolded, the scientist as a discoverer of what lay wait-
ing to be discovered. The Darwinian thesis first introduced the
idea of chance variations; new forms appeared and were discovered—but not through a careful investigation of cause and
effect, for we cannot know in advance what the form will be.

There is nothing in the properties of hydrogen or oxygen as gases which would enable the scientist to predict the properties of water, had he had no experience with water in the first place. A new form can be traced to a past, but we cannot predict new forms.

A better knowledge of chemistry and physics revealed that these could not explain the life process, although they are an integral part of it. Something new has arisen—an emergent, as Lloyd Morgan calls it—which cannot be predicted by any law, since mutation is a violation of law and is beyond the cause and effect relationship. What seems to occur in the process of evolution is not the appearance of a new substance, but new modes of organization. In the division of the single cell a differentiation does not affect the quantity—it does affect the quality. Thus means and ends are not identical, because the end contains an unknown factor which cannot be predicted until it comes into existence and can be repeated. Not only is something new possible, but it had better occur, for without it life could not continue for very long. "No species in its present form," writes D. L. Miller, "existed five million years ago, and most if not all species five million years ago could not survive under present environmental conditions." Survival, then, depends upon a new emergent, which cannot be predicted in advance.

It is this view of the universe, one with infinite possibilities, which renders obsolete all deterministic and mechanical descriptions of reality. Nature, it appears, has in it an infinity of different kinds of things, an unlimited variety of additional properties or qualities. There is almost no limit to the new emergents which can arise, and in time the universe will reveal an inexhaustible variety and diversity of them, totally different in quality from anything which has ever been. In the last century men were aware of mechanical, thermal, electrical, luminary, and potential energies. Now we know of nuclear energy which constitutes a much larger reservoir. The future of the universe is wide open in time and possibilities.

Man is the most significant emergent thus far, and constitutes a radical break in biological continuity. He is an animal by heredity; his structure is only a little more developed in basic traits. His innate intelligence is not much beyond that of the higher apes. The novelty in evolution which came with man is his ability to use symbols and language; for the first time a creature has had the ability to control the environment by culture. This is what Dobzhansky calls a "third kind of history," a history of culture, superimposed upon cosmic and upon biological evolutionary histories. The use of the written and spoken word opens a vitally new form of transmitting the experience of the race from generation to generation. This is man's distinguishing characteristic. Insignificant as he is in size and duration, measured by the vast space-time dimensions of the universe, "he alone," as Hudson Hoagland writes, "can experience the thrill of imagination and understanding not shared by other forms of life. Man's creative imagination is a magnificent evolutionary emergent of his nervous system."

Man is not an alien in the universe. He is of the earth earthy, and of the animals an animal—yet he is more. There is nothing physically which he has that is not found in the inorganic environment. He is part of the cosmos, he belongs to it, and to a large measure what is inside him is essentially what is outside, duplicating it in substance and often in structure. Let there be no mistake about man; he is no stranger on earth or in the universe.

The process of organic evolution, occurring over a thousand million years, unfolds as a movement toward a higher form, and man is the latest product. When life emerged in the process of cosmic evolution, it overcame its own limitations; and when man arose, the biological development was transcended. In fact, man is the only animal that has broken free from the bounds of biological heredity. He transmits culture from generation to generation outside the biological mechanism of the genes. The emergence of culture introduced a new, unpredictable fact in the evolutionary process, one we may call human evolution, characterized by the interaction of biology and culture.

There are radical implications in this emergent nature of evolution, particularly for the social and historical thinking of our time. The dialectical formulae of both Hegel and Marx are now invalid; the idea of biological heredity implicit in Freudian psychology is no longer adequate. There are no such phenomena as purely inherited or purely environmental traits, since all traits appear as the result of the interaction of both, are applicable to both physical and psychic natures, and their result is not predictable.

Man, however, has one distinctive quality: he can transmit

knowledge to his descendants. The creative influence of scientists
and artists, of philosophers and theologians, goes beyond their
few years of active production and endures as an influence upon
man long after they are dead. Here, truly, the many owe much
to the few. And as a method of transmission, this is more efficient
than the biological process. Once we add culture as a third
determinant in the process of human evolution, we unveil a
vast realm of possibilities for man. Every emergent that has
arisen in the slow development of life has made a profound difference to the world; this latest symbol-making creature points
toward a new direction. This capacity for cultural acquisition
makes possible a greater control of behavior than could be
achieved previously and enables man to aim knowingly toward
new achievements.

Man's control of his destiny is just beginning. The trend is
from a state of "unconsciously nurtured phantasy to one of
consciously forced reason." The new scientific revolution presents
us with a universe of infinite possibilities and man with many
potential natures from which he may choose. There is no law of
self-entelechy, no determined self that man must become. Furthermore, he has the faculty of applying to his activities the accumu-
lated experience of the race in the arts and sciences, in philosophies and theologies. The world is incomplete, the new things
possible are well-nigh inexhaustible, and the symbol-making
creature can, in large measure, help to guide the course toward
a selective goal.

III

The primary question today is no longer whether or not we can
believe in God, but in what sense we can have faith in man.
Our culture presents him, generally, as a hopeless creature unqualified in mind and heart for the arrogant role of creation
that he has assigned to himself. Common sense and a more objective look at some facts can lead us to a more realistic view.
That man is not an angel is evident, but he is not an animal
either. We must see him for what he is and can become, not for
what he once was. While from the animal kingdom, he is not of
it; he is a new emergent endowed with the capacity for con-
ceptual thought. This difference is not trivial, because his dis-

tinction is inseparably associated with his particular kind of body and brain. All living things have an "itch to live"; man has a "zest to live." He has previsioned goals for which he seeks satisfaction, and an active, striving nature busily adopting new means to achieve new ends. Compared to those creatures whose adaptation to change depends upon germinal alterations and in whom stability is overweighted and readaptation almost impossible, man, the cultural creature, has developed instruments for survival which surpass anything that ever existed. Man does not have to do what the rhinoceros does, because he is not a rhinoceros. He is man, born with the instincts of an animal, urges of hunger and sex, a deep feeling within himself of love and fear, impulses to shout and scream, to tear and to run. But he has something in addition to these which enables him to understand and control them.

Man is more than his instincts, a fact he manifests in his ability to see himself from the outside and to be conscious of his own self. This furnishes him with the sense of time so that he can look back into the past and forward into the future. Animals probably do not suffer neurotically, nor are they oppressed by a feeling of guilt; "they do not sweat or whine about their condition," wrote Whitman, "and they do not lie awake in the dark and weep for their sins." But man does, because he is human and aware of time and himself. This self-awareness is also the key to man's opportunities, because it is the foundation for his intelligence and his ability to symbolize and to think abstractly. It is, furthermore, the source of his moral nature, for it enables him to imagine how others feel and to ask himself how he would act in the same situation. Herein lie the roots of his love for his neighbor, the demands of justice, and the appeal of mercy.

Some psychologists suggest that man should adjust to his id, his animal origins. They are in grievous error, for man must be man, not a beast, in order to be himself. Unconscious emotions, the libido, or the death wish, are real enough as factors in man's behavior, but therapy does not lie in concentrating upon the initial error. Man's hope lies in his potential to be human, to realize himself, and to establish a wholesome relationship with his neighbor. Man needs to love himself without egotism and his neighbor without tyranny. The focus must be changed from cause to potentiality. As Karen Horney tells us, "the constructive possibilities stem from man's essential nature, from the core of his being, from what he calls his real self." Man turns to the destructive only if he cannot fulfill himself.

The history of man discloses a process of change from potentiality to reality; from being a primitive creature held in the grip of magic, he has increasingly attained mastery over both physical and animal nature. Through a better understanding of himself he has acquired the beginnings of a self-confidence which enables him to achieve a more cooperative relationship with his neighbors. He is not doomed by what others have done to him, because he can discover what he is doing to his real self and to others. Malinowsky, after studying primitive societies, observes that complexes which are frequent among us are lacking in another social setting. The Oedipus complex does not occur in a society where by custom the father does not dominate the family. There is nothing biological about complexes, and it is suggested that the particular complexes of those Europeans who happen to have been patients of Sigmund Freud are not typical of the whole human race. Psychologically, man must confront himself—the potential human nature inherent in himself—and assume the responsibility of becoming human.

It is now established that the genetic nature of man can be changed, since the human organism is plastic and subject to environmental conditions. The idea of a fixed germ plasm is no longer valid, since genetic control is flexible and permits a wide range of development. The fact that a characteristic is hereditary does not imply that it cannot be changed. What distinguishes modern man from his primitive ancestor, where there is no significant change in the human stock, is not his genetic constitution. The difference lies in the environment, which is responsible for the cultural diversity, permitting alteration without changing the genetic constitution of the race. "As eugenists," writes Julian Huxley, "we must therefore aim at transforming the social system." Man freed of ignorance and superstition, endowed with more knowledge of mutations, can plan for a better human nature which can become the precious inheritance of his descendants.

The belief that human nature cannot change has been rendered obsolete by the development of the biological and psychological sciences. Its lingering presence in our time is what Lewis Mumford calls the work of the "Society for the Prevention of Change."

The members of this society feed upon the ugly facts of history in which men exhibit their lower natures in brutality and lust, in selfishness and meanness. They focus upon this in a posture of resignation and defeat. Had men of the past always focused thus, cannibalism and slavery would still be with us.

A certainly more sensible and surely more realistic attitude is for man to confront the possibility of doing with human nature what he has so wonderfully done with nonhuman nature. He can begin to organize the principles governing the discovery and release of his potentialities. There are limitations here, as in the universe in general: there are some things that, thus far, cannot be done; we cannot turn back time, nor go beyond the existent universe. But we can go very far, and, as Gardner Murphy suggests, "we must always demand proof that the impossible is truly impossible. The alchemist was not essentially wrong in hoping that gold could be made from lead. He was wrong simply with reference to time, knowledge, and physical scope required." We have the tools to enable man to develop the power to control himself and to relate himself cooperatively with his fellow man. It is possible that we may not do it quickly enough to save ourselves from final annihilation, yet if we really wish to do it, we can, because we have the potential and the technique.

"Man," wrote Aristotle, "is the only animal that possesses reason." This classical view of man as a rational creature became one of the bases of the liberal outlook. However, the dreadful world which surrounds us has given us a distrust of man and his reasoning capacities. His behavior is ascribed to atavistic and amoral drives rather than to his rational faculties. Since man has a dual nature, a higher and a lower, it is not surprising that in the process of history one age should stress one side of that nature and the succeeding age the other. Our tendency is to think well of human nature while civilization is prospering and to think badly when things go wrong. Human nature is presumably the same in good times and bad, and we are better advised to follow a detached and objective view. Instinct plays a greater role in human behavior than some are prepared to admit and yet, when man is compared with all other animals, the ratio of the instinctive to the non-instinctive is high for the animal and low for man. An animal will make decisions which may derive from some source other than the instinct but, in the main, reacts by a built-in response. Man's senses give him his encounter with nature, but his reason enables him to interpret what he discovers. Freud was certainly aware of the role of instinct in human behavior, yet he was sure that the intellect must in the end determine his destiny. "Ultimately," he wrote, "after endlessly repeated rebuffs, it [intellect] succeeds. This is one of the few points in which we may be optimistic about the future of mankind."

Modern man has many effective tools to aid him in knowing himself and his relation to other men and to the world at large. Biology, psychology, and the social sciences can guide him toward a comprehension of his purposes and values. In fact, man by his very nature is endowed with a faculty which can resist the irrational forces which are so evident today. Hudson Hoagland points out that one of the neglected qualities of man is his curiosity, the drive to explore for its own sake, which is the source of all learning processes. Aside from the instincts of hunger and sex, the desire to discover is part of human nature, and "man's great cerebral cortex gives him a top billing among animals in his hierarchy of achievement." What is primary is the fact that man is a problem-solving creature who desires the satisfaction of having his curiosity rewarded by discovery—the "a-ha phenomenon," and later, the "a-ha, that's it" experience. Everything we know about man tells us that he has a great talent for using his intelligence to find answers to questions, a talent which is applicable to questions about himself. Passion can blind a man to reason, but it is blindness to conclude that we must trust passion alone. Impulse and desire play an important role in conduct, but they do not provide the principle of organization. Only reason can provide that, and imperfect a tool as it is, it is the only tool we have to guide us. To reject it is to wander in a hopeless jungle.

If we recognize that an absolute objective reality is not available to us and accept the proposition that, by the methods of empirical research and rational interpretation, we can arrive at the best basis for action, we can avoid much of the hopelessness which pervades our modern culture. John Dewey once said that "thought put some portion of existence in peril." Modern man is being told that he does not have to live in peril, for he can, by renouncing his status as a rational creature, find absolute peace in a faith that passes understanding. In place of the risk involved in acting upon an intelligent hypothesis, men are urged to seek a course which, historically, is known as demonism. Demons, whose function is to destroy and annihilate forms, bring in a darkness which defies the mind. When man forfeits the only instrument he has to analyze and criticize, to test by reason and experience, he will soon fill his life with devils. The view of man as a cringing creature, fearful of his own intelligence, appealing for an irrational salvation, has in the past, and probably will in the future, lead to an authoritarianism, whether of the left or of the right. Reason may lead us to error, and it often does; but anything else as a substitute guide is certain to bring confusion confounded into chaos.

The new scientific revolution has produced one other change which radically affects our view of man and his place in the universe. It has extended his freedom from one in which he selects the means toward a fixed goal, to a situation wherein he must choose both ends and means. Until now, the ends were determined by nature, by fate, or by God; man's role was to devise the means. Man's freedom was limited either by natural law or by a divine power. Furthermore, ends and means were clearly separated in this view. Today man is unfettered and charged with the responsibility of selecting goals among alternatives and of manipulating objects and behavior toward his selected end. In the older view, the purpose lay in the object, or in fate, or in God; the modern view puts the responsibility of selecting the goal upon man. Human freedom, then, involves man in choosing the ends and the means of achieving them. He is thus basically an evaluating being whose nature enables him to do what no other entity in the universe can achieve. His freedom lies in his ability to select from alternative possible goals and alternative possible means. Where there are no alternatives, there is no freedom, and the premodern view gave man no choice in the selection of goals. When future events, however, are not determined, then as thinking creatures, endowed with the capacity to use symbols, men can evaluate and choose what they believe to be a better goal. There is, of course, some limitation, since we cannot reach beyond the essential demands of nature. But within the wide range of the given, the possibilities for new ideas and ideals, for new purposes and aims, are many. Man's freedom lies in his capacity to evaluate and choose his direction.

Freedom is inextricably linked to responsibility. If man is not free to choose his goals and cannot direct his energies toward them, then he is not to be blamed when he does nothing about solving his problems. Man today stands free in a universe which has been released from the narrow strictures of Aristotelian physics and from the medieval metaphysics based upon it. Charged with the responsibility of selecting purposes and devising means, he can no longer blame anyone but himself if he fails to achieve a better life. He is free today to change not only nature but himself, and he faces the responsibility which goes with his freedom. "He can choose to develop his capacities as the highest animal," says Carleton J. Coon, "and try to rise still farther, or he can choose otherwise." He alone can make the choice, and his alone is the responsibility. The purpose in evolution becomes man's concern, and his duty is to supply its moral direction. Man must exhibit a will to live, not simply an instinct of self-preservation. Freedom is not automatic; it must be achieved each day, as Goethe once told us: "He only earns his freedom and existence who daily conquers them anew."

The chances that man will overcome the evils which threaten him are better today than they have ever been before in his long history. The universe has been unfettered from determinism and mechanism, and now lies open to unlimited possibilities of new emergents. Man's life is not at the mercy of a fixed and unchangeable cosmos, nor is it bound by the designs and purposes of supernatural powers before whom there is no choice but submission. Man, the latest emergent in evolution, comes armed with the newest weapon for survival—a mind to perceive truth and select goals and the means to fulfill them. Related to the animal kingdom by history, he is not an animal; he is man, free to know the world and himself; and knowing these, he has the intelligence to choose both ends and means, limited only by raw materials and mind. Contrary to the dark and brooding spirits of our day who have made sin and anxiety, despair and defeat, an ontological equation, man is today free to dream dreams for the future that he has never dreamed before. The universe has room for his highest imagination, and he has the capacity to choose his direction and invent the means of reaching nearer to his destination. Confronted at this moment with the threat of annihilating war, man can proceed to apply his intelligence and his imagination, to save himself from the final holocaust.

IV

Many modern theologians will react to this reformulation of the liberal faith by declaring that it is nothing more than secular humanism, entrusting the fulfilment of God's kingdom entirely to man. It does stand in sharp contrast to much of modern theology, which depends only on God and relegates man's role to one of passive submission. The Jewish tradition, never hospitable to the either/or formula, recognized the significance of the roles of both God and man in bringing near the messianic era. The resources available to man in the disclosures of the new scientific revolution strengthen his capacities and give him courage in his spiritual purpose. His God-faith, which gives meaning to his striving and his suffering, is inspirited by the revelation that the universe can respond to his moral effort. The secular humanist robs his hopeful vision of a large part of reality by rejecting the guiding hand of the creative spirit of the universe.

The God-faith is not subject to proof in the rational or scientific sense. Men have arrived at it through the inward experience of the mystic, the metaphysical structure of logic, the prophetic insight of the moralist, or direct revelation as recorded in a scripture. Each of these separately or all of them together are inadequate as universally acceptable evidence. Ultimately, as Judaism learned at the beginning, God is an affirmation and a postulate. The new view of the universe disclosed by the modern scientist does challenge some descriptions of God which have had a long traditional acceptance. The attributes of omnipotence or omniscience are called into serious question, and the religious thinker is challenged to find a more adequate understanding of the nature of God. But this ought not to surprise the Jewish theologian who learned from Solomon: "In all thy ways know Him"; it is never said: "In all His ways know Him." What is of significance in the new view of the universe and of man is the support it brings to the God-faith. For the first time in history the universe is revealed as an organism alive and growing, endowed with thought, and disclosing in its evolutionary process a direction from lower to higher forms. The modern Psalmist can sing with a new rapture: "The heavens declare the glory of God, and the firmament showeth His handiwork."

The vision of what was once called the "liberal imagination" has been replaced today by the "imagination of disaster." The modern liberal seems to have lost the unique characteristic of liberalism—the ability to fill the imaginations of his time with programs which are daring and attainable. Frightened by the disasters of recent history, he has relinquished the stage to prophets of despair and to totalitarians who exploit the utopian vision in order to maintain a society of slaves. The evils of our time are real enough, and science has armed them with a dreadful power. But it is equally true that men of vision and will are armed today with tools to match them and overcome them. The liberal hope of a better world brought about by better men is more valid today than ever before in history, and has a fighting chance for realization. Two immediate steps are urgent if men are to rescue themselves from the torpor which has settled upon their hopes. The cosmic hypochondria needs to be shaken off, and the imaginative leadership recaptured from the prophets of doom.

The Jewish people have stood many times in the past where men despaired of the Kingdom of God and retreated into philosophies of the "failure of nerve." Early in their own history, painfully tried in the wilderness, they bitterly watched their vision of the promised land fade into nothingness. They wanted very much to retreat from the faith of the prophet. The divine command which Moses then received has been heard by Israel in every crisis of its historic experience. Judaism, as the oldest spokesman for the Kingdom of God, is called upon today to give witness to it with increasing loyalty and fervor.

"Tell the children of Israel that they go forward."

ON GOD AND THEOLOGY

Arnold Jacob Wolf

It is curious that the *Shema,* which the Talmud specifically says "may be recited in any language," [1] is always spoken in Hebrew. Even in those Reform congregations where almost nothing else is said in Hebrew, the *Shema* is. Is it only nostalgia that irrationally retains a Hebrew *Shema?* Is it not rather that, since the *Shema* cannot be understood adequately even in English, it might as well be recited in Hebrew? Is this not the lesson of the controversy over the new Jewish Publication Society translation of the Torah which gives us the fresh rendering: "Hear, O Israel! The Lord is our God, the Lord alone." Following Ibn Ezra and the Rashbam, the new translators diverge from the customary translation, "The Lord, our God, the Lord is one." But both translations are nearly correct or, what amounts to the same thing, are incorrect. We do not know what the *Shema* "really" means. In the seventeenth century, the Sabbatian "prophet" Heshel Tsoref de-

---

This paper was published in somewhat different form in the *Journal* of the Central Conference of American Rabbis, 1966.

voted more than three thousand pages to the mysteries of
the *Shema*.[2] It is overdetermined. Every translation betrays it by
oversimplification.

The rabbis tell us that the *Shema* proclaims the "yoke of God's
kingship." (That must be why they introduced the further obfus-
cation of the *Baruch Shem* as antiphon.) But, as we know from
Kafka, if not from Kabbalah, a King is altogether mysterious. It
is of the essence of a subject to be unable to understand his king.
He feels the royal yoke; he cannot ever know the king. God, the
King, is even more mysterious than earthly rulers. He is *hativah
ahat b'olam*—uniquely numinous in the cosmos.[3] The *Shema*
warns us not to expect intellectually to comprehend Him whom
we are bidden to love with all our mind and self and power. The
Shema is, accordingly, a proem to commitment. Theology in
Judaism is always and only introductory. The *Shema* requires
kavanah, cosmic other-direction, *davke* because man can only face
God, not understand Him.[4] What the *Shema* means to educe is
neither more nor less than love.

Hence, the word *Adonai* in man's mouth is more precious than
in the angels'.[5] For angels, theology is scientific. Standing in the
presence of God, they describe what they see. They say what they
experience. But the Jew is to love a God he cannot see. His love
comes from trust, not from cognition. It is an expression of God's
power over him and not of his own unmediated experience of the
divine. His prayer is risky; the angels have nothing to lose. His
Shema is all mystery; their *Kedushah* is superlatively factual. He
cannot fathom what he says; they only say what they see. His
theology is understatement (Heschel); theirs is perceived and
exact. They take God for granted; man alone assumes the terrible
yoke of the unseen King.

The Psalmists sing of the Master of the World: "He made darkness his covert" (18:12); "Clouds and darkness are around Him"
(97:2). *Koheleth* confesses: "I have tested all this scientifically. I
said, 'I must know (God), but He was far from me. How can
anyone find Him Who is far off and very deep?'" (8:23 ff.) How
can anyone expect to? God is, at the least, infinitely Other. He is
not less than absolutely unique. Man can perceive only by way of
similarities; he can understand only classes. Science enlightens,
but God is covered in darkness forever. Reason tests and systematically discloses false assumptions. God's truths are the

hidden and the unreachable.[6] Man longs for light, but God remains nonetheless impenetrably dark.

Moses, Judaism's primal rationalist, sought to know the Name of God, i.e., His nature. All he learns is the tautology: "I shall be what I shall be." [7] My Nature is none of your business; all you can hope for is to sense My presence. Earlier, neither Abraham nor Isaac nor Jacob had known any more, for the Mystery is itself the Ancestral God. Had not Jacob gone lame trying to wrestle God's secret from Him? And all he got was a mixed blessing.[8] Israel did not need to know God's name to flee from Egypt. Jacob did not require the intelligence he sought in order to become Israel in the first place. God tells us as much as we need to know. His mystery empowers, but His Kingdom is not of our world-view.

The Talmud consistently forbids exaggerated or unstructured praise of God. In T.B. Meg. 25a, for example, we are reminded that ecstatic interruptions of the order of service are not permitted. A certain fellow prayed in front of the ark while Rabbi Haninah was present: "O great, mighty, aweful, majestic, strong, powerful God." Haninah asked him finally if he had finished describing the King. Haninah then said: the only reason we are permitted to recite even the first three attributes is that Moses wrote them in the Torah and the *Anshe Knesset ha-Gedolah* fixed them. Anyone who multiplies attributes is like someone who praises a millionaire by saying he is worth a thousand dollars. You insult God.

Such principled suppression of theological originality is fascinating. Not only may we not add information about God, but even the attributes we presume to apply are allowed only because we have been so instructed. We have no right to go beyond Torah (written or oral) because we have no new data. What is more, we know what we may say of God not from direct contact but only from authoritative tradition. If Moses had not told us, we should not even be able to say God is great.

T.B. Meg. 18a renders halachically the decision to refrain from too much talk about God. Simeon the Pakulite had reformulated the order of prayer after it had been forgotten. "Beyond this, we are forbidden to praise the Holy One, blessed be He. Rabbi Eleazar recalled the rhetorical question of Psalm 106:2: 'Who can express the mighty acts of the Lord, or make all His praise heard?' Only a man who could make *all* God's praise heard should try to express God's mighty acts. Rabbi ben Bar Hanah said, quoting Rabbi Yohanan, 'A man who praises God too much is uprooted from the world' . . . Rabbi Judah cited Psalm 65:2 (which we translate 'Praise waiteth for thee'): 'For you is silence best!' The best cure is silence."

Theology inevitably involves us in blasphemy. Because we cannot say enough, our saying is a betrayal of God. The distinction made in modern Protestant theology between presumed knowledge of God-in-Himself and a mere description of God-Who-Acts is not satisfactory. Even as we cannot know all of God Himself we do not know all the "mighty acts of the Lord." What we do learn is always partial and misleading. This is true because of Who God is and because of what we are not.

Maimonides, standing at the center of the scholastic tradition, was surprisingly reticent in describing God. In his excursus on *Perek Helek*, designed to enumerate exhaustively all that a Jew must believe in order to merit the future world, the Rambam asks us to believe very little about God. Of the five articles dedicated to Deity, none is problematic because none says very much. The first principle is that God exists but in a way utterly different from the existence of any other existent. This is not claiming much. It is practically the equivalent of asserting God's nonexistence. Everything we know exists contingently; only God is Being Himself. But if that is so, we cannot know Him in the ordinary sense at all. The second fundamental principle is that He is One, but here again His unity is the unity neither of a set nor of any individual we can know. "A oneness like no other oneness" is, in a sense, not one at all. The third principle only denies God a body either essentially or accidentally. The fourth denies that He is limited by time. The fifth is only indirectly about Him. It forbids us to pray to anyone who is not God. It tells us that "we are obliged to know His greatness and to do His commandments."

The quantitative bulk of the Thirteen Principles is not about God at all but about Moses. Maimonides takes great pains to tell us that Moses saw God. He wants us to know what Moses did and to impress upon us that we are not Moses and can never again do what he did. Which is to say that we reach God only through the Torah. We should know precious little about God were it not for the Mosaic Torah. Though categorized as a rationalist, Maimonides does not expect the unaided mind of man to connect with God. The mind can barely discover what God is not. No mind since Moses can find out Who God is. Therefore we require the Thirteen Principles to activate ourselves in a way raw intellection could never achieve. We do not ultimately have to know much about God; we must do His commandments. The rationalist Maimonides is unexpectedly suspicious of reason; he remains humble before the mystery.

It is curious too, how little the classical Reformers say about God. Though for them the trinity of God-Torah-Israel had contracted to God alone, they did not say much about that God. They talked a lot about history, about aesthetics, about sociology. Yet they, God-centered as they claim to be, had not much interest in theology as such. The rubric "God" does not even occur in the index to Gunther Plaut's fine survey of European Reform. The synods did not debate, much less enrich, the idea of God. Kohler, by far the most theology-minded of the Reformers, is somewhat more ambitious. But his description of God in Part I of the *Jewish Theology* is a collection of citations rather than a *summa* that can be argued or even refuted. Who could dissent from the Table of Contents of a hymnal? What, in fact, Kohler did, as his successors at the Hebrew Union College were also to do, was to substitute, systematically, historical theology for systematic theology. This is to admit that we cannot form clear and distinct notions of God and that our function is to trace the history of the idea of God in Jewish tradition. Since we cannot know God, we must strive to know Judaism.

The reticence of classical Reform is less graceful than its biblical or medieval precedents. Moses was not to know God because God is too big for man. But the early Reformers often acted as if God were too small to be worthy of their attention. They were more interested in getting along with the job (of traducing Zionism, of Christianizing the service, of Germanizing the Hebrew language, of systematizing the gorgeous chaos of earlier times, of increasing at any cost their own movement's success) than in finding God. The darkness of God is agony to the Psalmist; it breaks the biblical Moses' heart. But one has the feeling that while Maimonides retired to secret speculation and code-writing (Leo Strauss), Abraham Geiger and Isaac Mayer Wise were relieved to discover how little they had to say about God. For many years it

was possible to graduate from our American rabbinical schools
without ever having wrestled with the problem of God. One feels
this was not to save the students pain, but merely to avoid rocking
the theological boat.

There are, however, signs of change. On the left (or is it the
right?), humanist proclamations by Jews of the death of God
bring us up to date with the latest in post-modern Christian
theology. We are told by some leading liberal Jewish theologians
that God is a process or an immanence or just a uniquely useful
word. Leftist rabbis agonize in print over the hypocrisy of their
having to recite the same old prayers, to bury the dead with the
same old comforts, to read an old Torah which talks about an old
God in Whom they no longer believe.

On the right (or is it, because I would wish it to be, the left?),
neo-Orthodox and existentialist post-liberals assure us that all the
old lies are true. That God is a Person, a Father (it is our own
sublunar fathers that we are no longer so sure about), a Transcendent Power available to all who call upon him in truth, i.e.,
with the appropriate Barthian formulae. Some would even read
out of what remains of our movement both dissenters and ignostics, because their idea of God appears too dangerous.

But the truth is that we do not know the truth. Dogmatic
humanists are much too sure that God is not something-or-other.
We on the traditionalist side are much too ready to commit the
Master of the universe in writing to one or another of our own
pet projects. But God is, whatever else, a Mystery. And Judaism
must be, whatever else it may be, humble before Him who spoke
and theology came to be. We put too much stock in sincerity and
not enough in patience, too much emphasis on our being right
and not enough on God's being superior to our idea of God. All
of us, I believe, are too dogmatic, some about the process God,
some about the scholastic Cause of all causes, and some about the
revealed Truth. Such dogmatism is incompatible not only with
searching but more especially with finding the One who searches
us.

Consider again the nineteenth chapter of the Book of Leviticus:
One after another, our pretentions are there flayed off by the
biblical command. Do we think we create with mind and body?
Then observe that Sabbath in which all creation is forbidden, and
a man must not even look into the mirror of his own mind. Would

we make a god (all ideas of God are idols)? Then we are told
not to create or inspect the image of God but rather to become
it. Would we offer sacrifice even to the true God? Then it must
be on a certain day according to His order which is an order that
surpasses our understanding. Ethics merges into mystery. Law
emerges from the transcendent. "Let go" of your wealth, do not
exploit your brother man whom you would like to exploit. And do
not exploit God's "Name" either. The rabbis interpret the Levitical
command to include "any Name which is His." The truly spiritual
is not committed to us; we can dispense no Name; we are empowered by no charisma, no sacrament, no self-serving power at
all.

The idea of God belongs to God and not to man. *Kedushah* is
always and only *Kiddush ha-Shem*. Holiness is letting go.

Nor is science the accumulation of truth that some of its non-
scientific idolizers believe. It is, in the most literal and precise
sense, the production of ignorance. Reason is the invasion of
mystery by which, every year, less is known because more seems
to be. Mind cannot complete the work it is not free to desist from
altogether.

Theology cannot imprison God's selfhood in our categories. It
is only the continual regrouping of foolhardy armies doomed to
defeat. It is not the final solution of ancient problems but the
recovery of perennial questions. At best it promises not the
knowledge of God but the transformation of man. Its "holy, holy,
holy" is submission to the Unknowable. Our knowing means
loving our crooked neighbor with our crooked hearts, and our
far-off God with our libidinously contaminated apperceptive mass.
It means caring less about whether we are only sincere and more
about whether we are honest. It means caring less about ourselves and more about Him.

What Moses could not know we cannot know. What the Rambam gave up we shall not come to possess. What the Reformers
bypassed is no longer available to their successors. God will not
become the image of our image of Him. He will be what *He* will
be. In humility undesecrated by intellectual pretension and dogmatic self-congratulation we pray before the Immeasurable. Our
questions remain unanswered; all serious questions are. But we
who bow and ask and bow again are now different. We have been
in the very presence of the God we have sought. We still own

nothing, especially not certainty, but we have become able to obey. As Leo Baeck told us, we are to be both humble before the unsearchable and also reverent before what is manifest and definite—the commandment, the task, which alone is always clear and always binding. Humility and reverence equal holiness.[9]

Perhaps our new interest in theology is only a "cop-out" from the commandment. Neither ignostics who know for sure what God is not, nor scholastics who know what He is, are implicated. But the believing Jew, eschewing all ideologies and above all his own, seeks humbly to do the commandment nevertheless. Our reason is almost always rationalization; it is our ambivalence that intellectualizes. But "if we help the holy spiritual substance to accomplish itself in that section of Creation in which we are living, then we are establishing, in this our place, a dwelling for the Divine Presence." [10] That is a task not for the theologians alone but for men. The Presence burns our theologies to a crisp, but it suffers men to suffer, praise and live.

A SUPPLEMENTARY STATEMENT

I am told that I elucidate a dooming theology. But I understand the meaning of death to include more than the threat of extinction for my personality. I understand it to signify the extinction of my idea system, the utter transiency of my reason, and the utter doom of everything I create. Perhaps that takes death too seriously, but it seems to me only to reflect what the Jewish religion has meant by death. Nothing I am is permanent, nothing I say is true and nothing I know can be known forever. Now, if that is so, it will not do simply to say "that cannot be right because it is a sad story"—if it is true, the sad story *is* the true story. If you read the great scientists, the great artists, you find a mood of doom hanging over everything they write. Think of Shakespeare's *Tempest* with its sense that everything we are, everything the world is, passes and is gone; think also of Freud's penultimate essay called *Analysis, Terminable and Interminable*, in which he says that the process of healing is an infinite process and, therefore, man is condemned to permanent illness—this from a great physician and, I think, a great scientist, who understood that everything man is and has and knows are, in the most specific and literal sense, doomed. Now, for me, there is hope, but hope comes in another way. Hope is a theological category. Hope can never be extrapolated from the facts. News is always bad news. Hope intervenes—it does not emerge.

I am told that there is a danger in what I permit my critics to call my irrationalism and, of course, there is. But it is not certain that more atrocities have been committed in the name of unreason than in the name of reason. If I understand the greatest atrocities —the concentration camp and the atomic bomb—they were very rational. Hannah Arendt has said, in *Eichmann in Jerusalem,* that evil is banal. Perhaps one could even say that evil is scientific. Or, to put it in a slightly different way, there is no escape from the problem of evil, neither with reason nor with unreason. There is no criterion a priori to distinguish *deus* from demon. That, I think, is the sense of one of the profound stories of the Bible. Shortly after Moses meets God at the burning bush, God seeks to kill him. In the confrontation with the Divine, the demonic is wholly present; there is no escape from that danger. One of the mistakes of Reform Judaism has been its attempt to build a wall against reality, hoping thereby to save itself from demonism. There is no solution that way. The only way to avoid madness is not to give up on madness but to enter into it and to move beyond it. The criteria therefore are all a posteriori, not a priori. They are not criteria which can be given in advance of a situation. There is no escape from death; there is no escape from madness. One of the lessons of the theater and literature of the absurd is that all that we are, besides everything else, is pretty ridiculous.

What are the criteria, if there are no standards, at least a priori? The answer is complicated, and I am not sure that I can explicate it with sufficient clarity. Standards are inherent in, though partly hidden by, the situation. Let us use psychoanalysis as an example and, here again, try to take it very seriously. If a person is sick and goes to an analyst because he has a symptom that he acts out in some way or other—let us say he drinks—the analyst does not give him advice. (Leo Baeck once said "God does not give advice.") The analyst does not set for him rules of reason, nor does the analyst give him an anthropological framework, a description of the human personality. In fact, some analysts will not even let their patients read such books—because those principles, abstractions, scientific guides are evasive. They are, ultimately, verbal tricks. They do not effect cure; they prevent it. What the analyst does is to offer himself without reservation or, at least, without inappropriate reservation; and out of the dialogue between physician and patient, Torah emerges. The analyst never judges or prescribes, though he may interpret. The analyst is only present, and out of the dialogic relationship something happens. The patient, if he is wholly present also, no longer can drink, because drinking is incompatible with dialogue. Drinking prevents relationship. In a much more complicated way, the same thing happens in marriage. There is no advice that can be given a priori, but law emerges out of marriage, if it is a real marriage.

The same thing happens with religious experience. The mind of man often serves to prevent relationship, but it cannot effectuate relationship and cannot substitute for it; but relationship is not wholly irrational, because the relationship of God and man incorporates everything that man is. It incorporates his reason, too, but reason no longer abstracted and defensive, rather reason integrated with all that he is and with all that he confronts. And out of the dialogue with God, both historical and personal, there emerges a way. Now, this way is different for different people. I think, though some may disagree, that this was always true in Judaism, that the way was never a single way. It certainly is no longer a single way. Rosenzweig said that the great throughway is blocked and now we must have a few highways, a great many byways, cloverleafs, and bridges; each man has to walk the privacy of his interior journey. But each is part of the same landscape and, what is more, the experience to which he gives himself is normative. It does not permit just anything in the world —it permits what is permits. Without surrendering itself, his subjectivity connects with God's subjectivity; and God surrenders no subjectivity either. No idea of God fully incorporates God himself. But experience, which I take to be more than emotional or rational or even existential, which has the power to transform, therefore gives a criterion to me personally, to Judaism, and, I think, to mankind. It is not enough to say that God is both transcendent and immanent, because even the immanence of God is darkly mysterious. The immanence of man is also mysterious. And the erosion of mystery, it seems to me, forecloses the possibility of dialogue. All that I have sought to do is to make visible again that mystery into which we enter wholeheartedly. But Leo Baeck was right: mystery educes commandment. The man who comes through the mystery is not mad, nor, indeed, quite sane—he is, God willing, at last a man.

NOTES

1. T. B. Ber. 13a.
2. Gershom Scholem, *On the Kabbalah and Its Symbolism* (New York: Schocken Books, 1965), p. 131.
3. T. B. Ber. 6a.
4. T. B. Ber. 13b, 16a.
5. T. B. Hul. 91b reminds us that the *Shema* pronounces the Tetragrammaton one word earlier than the angelic *Kedushah* does.
6. Deuteronomy 29:28.
7. Exodus 3:14 ff.
8. Genesis 32:27 ff.
9. *God and Man in Judaism* (New York: Union of American Hebrew Congregations, 1958), pp. 40 f.
10. Buber, *To Hallow This Life* (New York: Harper, ed. Jacob Trapp, 1958), p. 3.

THE GOD OF NATURE AND
THE GOD OF EXISTENCE

David Polish

I

Of our world it might properly be recorded, "In the beginning was disbelief," and with disbelief we shall begin. The refusal to acknowledge God under any terms or any definition cannot be gainsaid as long as it is a personal decision rather than an intellectual conclusion. Denial can be a sort of commitment, or even a tenet of faith. But when it presumes to claim the authority of reason, it is subject to the same inadequacies and refutations as are the wholly rational appeals to the existence of God. This should not discourage the unbeliever, but he should not assume that denial is somehow armed with less vulnerable weapons than affirmation. For example, the insistence upon intelligible definition of terms requires of us greater linguistic care, but it does not

This paper was published in somewhat different form in the *Journal* of the Central Conference of American Rabbis, October 1965.

make negation credible. It is a necessary corrective to careless-
ness, but it is sterile in supporting its own denials. All that it can
do is expose the inadequacy of my definitions. But this inadequacy
does not begin to make a case for blanket rejection. Definition,
except perhaps in scientifically controlled situations, is at best
proximate and often symbolic. Unless I undertake a vow of silence, I must communicate as adequately as I can, risking misunderstanding but generally expecting a comprehensive response;
I risk even more if I fail to speak. Knowing, as I do, that centuries
ago "pistol" was a word meaning a dagger, I am not prevented
from referring to a pistol as a weapon which shoots rather than
stabs. I must, of course, revise my conception of the word, but I
am not bound to discard it.

Terms much less difficult than God, and not only terms but
actualities, are so defiant of acceptable interpretation that we can
only be silent if we must define them beyond all possible misunderstanding. What is truth? What is freedom? What is justice?
What is existence? Does my inability to offer more than a proximate definition invalidate or demolish truth and justice, or does
it rather indicate my own incapacity? "The Torah speaks the
language of men," says the Talmud. The intuitive awareness of
the rabbis that human speech is a tenuous rope cast across the
abyss between man and eternity reminds us that we are not
absolved, by virtue of our inadequacy, from voicing what is beyond articulation. We do not, strictly speaking, employ words. We
use symbols for reality; and when the symbols fail us, we rage
and gasp, like the mute who wants to be heard, who knows what
he wants to say. You may taunt me, God's mute, with my frenzied,
angry inability to say what I mean by "God," but you can refute
only me, not God. Once you invalidate God because of my inept-
ness, then the very instruments which you wield must be turned
upon you, and we face one another in cold silence, immobilized
in a catacomb of proliferating definitions which demand their own
definition.

The disbeliever must demand no less of himself than he does of
the believer. He must be no less scrupulous in weighing his
assumptions, testing his data, and torturing himself to discover his
motives. He cannot purchase negation simply by parrying his
opponent's thrusts. It is not enough that he deny God. He can do
no less than make an earnest search for the Void which he affirms.

And the way to the Void is as heartbreaking as the way to God.

But what is it that the believer affirms? I do not see how he can begin affirmation without asserting God as the Creator. It is becoming theologically acceptable to circumvent the creative deity and to assign Him, so to speak, another role. Whatever that role may be, if God is not to be identified with *maaseh b'reshit,* then integrity will demand that we declare Him irrelevant or, certainly, less than God. Once we assert that there is no need for a cosmic deity, with all of the implications about life and about man as creature of God that follow, then it would be more honest to assert man's freedom within the Void and to ascribe to man, and man alone, the issues of his existence than to introduce God as the factor giving special meaning to human existence. To abstract God from Creation is to reduce Him to an idol created by our own cleverness and theological acuity, and nothing more.

By a logic of its own, our tradition affirms the creative God. The stress in both the Tanach and the Siddur upon the God by whose will the universe came into being and by whose will creation is recurrent should not be dismissed as mere antiquarian dogmatics. Without at this point invoking science, we must recognize that the chain of cosmic history from the first infinitesimal atom to the emergence of a universe, to the inexplicable leap of life, to consciousness, to man, is the most compelling manifestation, though not proof, of God. If this is not so, appeal to any other kind of justification for the reality of God becomes futile. Man is capable of ultimate concern without the necessity of giving it a theological label. In such a manipulation of our preferences and our needs, it is clear that we reach into ourselves for help. When we bypass the immense possibilities implicit in our relationship to the universe, we destroy the one true source of belief in a deity (God or process) which is not of our own making.

If we are earnest, not about concepts but about realities, we cannot, except as a casuistic exercise, abandon a belief in a *Bore ha-olam,* a creator of the world, without jeopardizing all belief. All things else—revelation, covenant, moral law, redemption—are precluded as theological factors. They may play a role in man's sanctification of life and in self-sanctification, but only as an aspect of mythology, not as theology.

In the last analysis, dependent as we are on creation for the living God, we are ultimately driven to an act of personal decision and not to a compulsion of proof. We do not dismiss science. Quite the contrary. We invite it and are enriched by it. The new cosmology talks about a definite beginning of the universe, about its origin with a single electron or a pair of neutrons, and its expansion ever since. The new cosmology also believes that there is a continuous process of dying and new birth in the endless reaches of the universe. As one writer says, "Creation is an essential feature of the material universe." Another writes, "The law of evolution is a kind of converse of the second law of thermodynamics." "A conviction, akin to religious feeling," says Einstein, "of the rationality or intelligibility of the world lies behind all the scientific work of a higher order. This firm belief, a belief bound up with deep feeling, in a superior mind that reveals itself in the world of experience, represents my conception of God." William F. G. Swann, a physicist, states: "Viewing the universe as a whole, I cannot escape the fact that it is of intelligent design . . . It is not so much the failure to comprehend completely the universe which fills the man of science with awe, but rather the fact that in what he does understand he sees a plan akin to his own way of doing things, but one with enormous cleverness."

Science brings evidence, not proof. There is no proof. The scientific world is at odds in its diverse interpretations of the phenomena of the universe. The same factors which compel some to acknowledge more than inexplicable chance drive others to reject or at best declare irrelevant the problem of causation. Some even question the validity of universal law in the new world of contemporary physics where, according to one scientist, "a law is a trial balloon that hasn't been exploded for ten years." Sometimes we wonder whether the need for vigorous terminology is not as important for science as it is for theology. What can Julian Huxley possibly mean when he says that evolution represents a "trend" in the universe? A random universe could hardly support a cosmic "trend" in respect to an evolution whose origins are mystifying and whose goal is inscrutable.

Thus, while we look to science for truth, it can supply us only with data, indispensable to truth, yet not synonymous with it. What is more, science is far from united on the religious issue. This confronts us, on the one hand, with a harsh disappointment, and on the other, with a frightening, yet awesome mandate— to make a personal decision, predicated on everything we can intellectually embrace. Faith is not knowledge. It is decision. In another idiom, this idea is presented thus by a scientist: "If then we consider a world entirely devoid of consciousness (as we not infrequently try to do), there is, so far as we know, no meaning whatever in discriminating between the worlds A and B. The mind is the referee who decides in favor of A against B. We cannot describe the difference without referring to a mind. The actuality of the world is a spiritual value. The physical world at some point (or indeed throughout) impinges on the spiritual world and derives its actuality solely from this contact."

We stand in the presence of a cosmic Teacher who requires that we, and we alone, affirm or deny. The true teacher, the *moreh*, is abstemious in revealing the truth. He is profligate in posing questions and, above all, in challenging the individual, not the collective, to discover truth for himself. If the truth cannot be packaged and placed in our grasp by the most competent of all the masters of the cosmic mystery, why not fall back on the faith of tradition or of Torah and circumvent science or reason altogether? First, because tradition, at least within Judaism, has not been contemptuous of reason. "The heavens declare the glory of God" is a poetic manner of saying that there is demonstrable evidence of the presence of God in the universe. Second, faith must not be acquired cheaply. It can be transmitted only in part, and its uncritical acceptance reduces it to a lifeless idol.

Can the recourse to inwardness or to ontology, as alternatives to cosmology, lead us to certainty and truth? Wherever we begin, whether with cosmology or inward discovery, the final answer is not objective but faith-demanding. One scientist finds God, and another the absence of God. Kierkegaard, reaching into his own being, confronts God, while Sartre, affirming God's absence, confronts only his own human freedom.

Thus the issue is not necessarily one of rationalism against existentialism. I suggest that for some of us it must be both an intellectual struggle which we cannot escape, and a personal decision which we cannot avoid—a decision which is not so much a leap as an option, based upon a weighing of two sets of factors which appear equally convincing and equally compelling. I cannot escape this responsibility and when I choose God, I do so only after I have negotiated the rope of reason as far down the mountainside as it will take me. I can choose to go the rest of the

way on my expectation that I can make it safely, or else climb
up again to the safety of the ledge. In either event, there is risk—
the risk of faith and its consequent anguish in God or the risk
of noninvolvement and the anguish of alienation. No body of
reason has emerged which can enable me to stand aside from a
decision or which can make the decision for me. The rabbinic
statement about man's moral condition applies to his spiritual
condition as well: Each man should live as if the world were
weighted evenly in the scale between good and evil. His conduct
can tip the scales. "I place before you good and evil. Choose
good." Note that this admonition is addressed not to the community but to the individual.

It is I who must choose. The question is not, "What is truth?"
but, "How do I cast my soul's ballot?" The universe demands that
we enter into the mystery and choose whether we are for God
or for madness. Both claims to truth cancel each other out and I
am left with an awesome decision. This, too, is religion. I can
no longer leave my ultimate decision to experts. I turn to Israel's
hymn of faith, *v'acharei kichlot ha-kol l'vado yimloch nora:* "and
after all has passed away, He alone will reign in awe."

II

For a Jew, there is a false option between the faith deriving from
cosmology *or* the faith nurtured by inwardness. From whatever
source we begin, we must eventually arrive at the other destination. The universe acts upon the human spirit. The soul of man
reaches out to the cosmos, like a foundling always seeking its
absent mother. The cosmic God who does not address our inward
parts is too austere and forbidding, too remote to be relevant. The
inward God who is not also the *Ribono shel Olam* is only a thread
which the human spider spins out of his own being, a thread
which can never bridge the Void. Only when we accept the transcendent universe are we warranted in turning to being, to per-
sonalism, to inwardness. If we cannot live with the eternal, how
can we live with the transient?

I am suggesting that our estrangement becomes all the more
intolerable unless we make our peace with the universe. But once
we have achieved this, we can turn inward not in flight nor in
illusion, but in truth to the place where man meets God most

authentically. Here the tension necessarily engendered by the dialectics of reason is shattered. Here God discloses himself in the pathos of the soul. Here God shares man's loneliness. Here prayer is most anguished. Here the moral law makes its greatest demands. Here all restraint is dissolved and the soul is inundated by God.

I believe that further thinking may shatter the untenable tension between the rational, or naturalistic, approach and the existential. I offer this clue. Our traditional Siddur, which once was the theology of the people, contains the magnificent ethical declaration, *Elu devarim she'ein la-hem shi'ur:* "these are the things that have no limit . . ." This is as rational and ethical a religious pronouncement as we can find anywhere. It is followed by *Elohai neshama*, as personal and faith-laden a prayer as we can find anywhere. This juxtaposition is not accidental; it suggests that the rational discipline of ethics must lead beyond the deed itself to the disclosure of the expanses of our personal spiritual resources.

The Nineteenth Psalm represents the synthesis of cosmology and inwardness: "The heavens declare" and "the fear of the Lord." It matters little that this may be an inadvertent union of two psalms. Our tradition's acceptance of the unity of this poem is what really matters.

Just as we would seek to overcome this dichotomy, we would seek to transcend the conflict between naturalism and supernaturalism. Nature, uninformed by a creative deity, is at best morally neutral, at worst predatory. In its raw state it gives no indication that it is equipped wtih a guidance system making for salvation. The moral element is not inherent in nature, nor does it necessarily derive from nature unless the universe be so constituted—a condition which would require cosmic intent. Both terms, naturalism and supernaturalism, are open to misunderstanding. On the one hand, a built-in moral law is either logically untenable or it is another way of saying that God functions within nature rather than beyond it. On the other hand, the idea of supernaturalism is so vague that it contains both belief in biblical mythology, the miraculous which assails our credulity, and belief in a God who is beyond nature. To believe in the latter is not necessarily to be committed to the former. The God who acts *within* the cosmic process also acts *upon* the cosmic process. Much of our difficulty stems from attempting to verbalize a physical situation within which God stands. The terms "outside" and "within" are altogether inadequate, and in fact confuse the issue. The religious naturalist need not say that God is coeval with nature. This would render God superfluous. He says that God is a process within nature that redeems nature. The supernaturalist, in the context of my remarks, insists that the very activity of a process must be predicated upon an antecedent. God is the process-server of the universe. What is there in the cosmic process which bridged the abyss from the inorganic to the organic? God is identified with nature, but not identical with it. Nor is He removed from nature, but He enters into it. Yet note: He *enters* into it. He is in the wick that comes alight, but He is also the flame that comes to kindle the wick.

Some will accompany me to this point, but no further. If, on the one hand, the God who is stripped of creative powers becomes anthropomorphized, then on the other hand, the God of nature *and* beyond is inaccessible to man. Man may pray to God, but what sense can it possibly make to say that God responds? Are we not keening outside the locked door of a child genius who has barricaded himself against his family's pleas? Is it not cold comfort that God created a universe in which He stands mute? We are God's mutes. Is He also man's mute? Job was comforted not because he learned that God created the universe but because it was God who told him so. If God had told him that his wife was going to give him breakfast, he would have been comforted. Let me suggest, then, that creation is more than an act out of the past. Its continuity, its renewal, its pervasiveness, make us witnesses not to history but to a continuous process in the universe. It tells us that God lives. But, and here I borrow from Teilhard de Chardin, it tells us that the very stuff of the universe is consciousness. Consciousness is implicit in the cosmos.

Perhaps the new translators of the Torah should have left the verse alone. "The *spirit* of God hovered over the face of the deep." In a way not yet explained by science, out of inert dead matter, a leap occurred at some point in the history of the universe and life came forth. Out of the primeval lifelessness of the cosmos, a spark was ignited in the swamps and rivers and a miracle occurred: life emerged. Life came out of death, if the absence of life can be called death. The universe and life were implicit in the first hydrogen atom; not only life but consciousness; not only consciousness but man; not only man, but a Moses, a Gandhi, as well as a Pharaoh and a Hitler. There are rigid laws in the universe, but there is also freedom. God allows us to choose. This is the distinction between the orbiting of a planet and the wavering of a man. But this choice, too, comes out of a cosmic process by which blind matter awoke to life. The Torah represents this in the way in which it describes creation. When the world is created, we are told, *Eleh toldot ha-shamayim v'ha-aretz:* "these are the generations of the heavens and the earth." When man is completed, we are told that *Zeh sefer toldot adam:* "this is the book of the generations of man." Because the God of creation is the God of life, the God of man, He is the God of the moral law as well. The God who disclosed Himself with no witnesses at Creation, disclosed Himself to Israel at Sinai. The God who gives us the universe is the God who gives us His Law.

Before we touch on revelation, let us try to understand that the force which makes for life also endows life with all the conditions out of which the issues of life and death emerge. The moral law is implicit in creation itself. It is more variable than physical law, and hence subject to doubt concerning its exalted origin. But it must be considered not against the laws of physics, but rather against the laws of life which reveal much greater variability and mutability. The moral law reflects man's own wavering condition. But it is a derivative, like man himself, of the creative process.

It is thus possible for man to address God. But does God respond to man? If man is a creature of God, he never ceases to stand in relationship to his Creator. God's self-disclosure to man is both a manifestation and a response. It is also a summons. The response is not to our requirements for the fulfilment of our generalized needs. It is in response to our greatest of needs, the conviction that God is. When we arrive at the faith that God is, we no longer ask whether He hears prayer. Whatever exists, responds to us. The flower responds to my touch. The violin responds to the bow. The tide responds to the tug of the moon. God responds to man. How? By disclosing Himself to us. God hears prayer not by satisfying our needs, but by making Himself known to us as a living reality in our lives. When I pray, I become aware that God "is what He is." Yet even more important than that I should hear is that I must address myself to God. Not that He needs it, any more than He needs sacrifice, but I need it. I need to feed and nurture my soul. I need to feel awe. I need to be aware of my finiteness and the wonder of my existence. I need to be reminded of this daily. More important, I need to affirm, to say yes.

One aspect of prayer that has been overlooked is not only that men refuse to pray, but that often we must not pray. When the human spirit is so corrupted that its every utterance is a blasphemy, it is wrong to pray. Perhaps this is a clue to our presumed inability to pray when in fact our own situation refuses us the privilege of prayer. But when, at last, I call, it can be that God will make Himself manifest. Not always; in fact, rarely. Even a poet in an age of belief cried out, "Do not hide Your presence from me," but another another poet wrote, "I called and God responded." God, too, says "Here am I." For some, this is not enough. For others, it is.

Just as creation cannot be circumvented without reducing God to a captive prince in a tiny domain, so creation flings us out to an unbridgeable distance from God. We are removed from God by every infinity we can conceive. Yet we are given a measure of access to Him by the conviction that the Will which willed a cosmos obedient to law also willed that man, product of the same cosmos, composed of the same stuff, conform to law as well. I digress to ponder on Karl Jaspers' assertion that God does not necessarily require the survival of the human race and therefore it is permissible to blow ourselves up if it becomes an inescapable necessity. In Judaism, this is not the issue, although we would append the question, "Why would you die?" The issue is that as long as man does exist, the mandate of the moral law is inescapable.

I do not believe that this law or that is God-given, but I do believe that submission to the principle of moral law impels men to search endlessly for the most effective ways by which they can comply with it. What is given is "I am the Lord"; what is derived is "You shall not murder."

This enables me to accept revelation and yet not to be bound to the Torah's conception, or conceptions, of it. For me, revelation was not a spontaneous moment at Sinai, but a culmination which could not have occurred without the Exodus. The path to Sinai had its beginnings at Pithom and Raamses. Only slaves could receive the revelation, and it was embodied in a collective awareness of God. What was the nature of the awareness? We cannot guess. But it did take place on the way from Egypt, and it was recalled as a self-identification by the God "Who brought you out of the house of bondage." It represented a deepening of human comprehension that the Creator is the Lawgiver as well, and that the Law, however any age may cast and recast it, is a human embodiment of a divine purpose, however dimly we perceive it. When I say *asher kid'shanu b'mitzvotov,* I translate—"You have made life sacred by letting me know that I am subject to You. I can manifest this subjection in the manner prescribed by my tradition, or in a manner which my own generation may yet devise." Some of the *mitzvot,* like reciting the Kiddush, are symbolic of this relationship. Others are the commitment of the whole being to the moral imperatives of social existence. We know what they are. The laws of nature are revealed when man discovers them. Man unearths them. God reveals them. The twilight zone between discovery and revelation is dusky and obscure. The moral law is not so clear-cut or so absolute. Yet it, too, is not merely an invention, but a discovery, however tentative, of what the creative act had flung into the world when life began. The Torah understood this when it envisioned God as telling man: *milu et ha-aretz v'chivshuhah u'redu b'degat ha-yam:* "fill the earth and subdue it, and have dominion over the fish of the sea." First the mastery of nature, then the mastery of life. But from this derives ultimately mastery of the inner being. It is from this position that the man of faith can respond to the issues of justice and of evil in the world. It is here where man can become aware not only that God is but that He loves.

Jewish thought rejects bifurcation. There is *havdalah* but, even more, there is *ichud.* If Jewish theology can make a special contribution to contemporary thought, it lies in its classical capacity to reconcile dichotomies. We can find an analogy outside of Jewish thought. Kierkegaard saw redemption in the human soul and nowhere else. Karl Marx saw it in society and nowhere else. Each, by ripping a limb from the quivering body of a greater whole, distorted and disfigured reality. Hillel was authentically Jewish when he reconciled this inauthentic dichotomy: "If I am not for myself, who will be for me? And if I am for myself alone, what am I?"

In the same spirit, we should be on guard against isolating theology from Jewish experience, Jewish history, and the Jewish people. The specialized study of theology is one thing. The equating of it with Judaism is quite another. The intricate balance of God, Israel, and Torah has been upset by the separation of one component from the rest. It is historically unsound. It is Jewishly inauthentic. The current extraction of Chassidic thought from Jewish history attenuates the thought and trivializes the history. The Science of Judaism without a living people is not Torah. The people without God is not Israel. Pure theology which does not interact with a living experience of the people can become sterile. What is the channel through which all of the components in our trilogy can interact? It is the covenant of God with Israel. Through the covenant, Jewish theology becomes sacred history, and Jewish history becomes popular theology. We need to expand our studies of the covenant, beginning with God's initial bond with all men and continuing down to the present meaning of human experience as well as the meaning of Jewish history. In this way, theology will avoid going off into a deviant orbit.

Let none boast of the exclusive authenticity of his position. Falseness is the mark of any such claim. What is the meaning of *zaddik be'emunato yichyeh:* "the righteous shall live by his faith"? Let me suggest that the stress is on *"his* faith." Each of us lives by his own faith, hewn out of his own experience, his own search, his own pain. Not that he lives by faith as against deed, but that the faith by which he lives is his own. We inherit, we borrow, but, if we are to live, we must make faith our own.

GOD AND JEWISH THEOLOGY

Alvin J. Reines

I

A mode of consciousness has become widespread that rejects the concept of deity which for centuries has been identified by the popular mind with Judaism and even with religion itself. I say that this identification has been made by the "popular mind" because those who engage in the scientific study of Judaism have long been aware that this concept is not the original concept of deity among the Jews, and it is certainly not the only one that has been subscribed to in the Jewish continuum. This concept, which is commonly called theistic absolutism, is the notion that God is a transcendent, omnipotent, omniscient, and omnibenevolent person who is directly concerned with the individual and collective welfare of man. This concern of God's is supposedly expressed by a providence which guides and controls the affairs of man both through ordinary (natural) and extraordinary (miraculous) causation.

The rejection of theistic absolutism is prevalent among clergy and laity alike. In the case of the former, it is made expressly and self-consciously, and has become increasingly explicit of late. The rejection by the laity is subtler but even more significant. It is the rejection, as it were, of silence, the ordering of one's life and the resolution of its difficulties without recourse—other than nominal—to the God of this concept.

The problems raised for institutional Judaism by the rejection of theistic absolutism seem to many, both within the institution and without, to be insuperable. However, I believe that the critical nature of these problems is more apparent than real and rests upon the acceptance of certain dogmatic and a priori beliefs which are, in fact, fallacious. These beliefs may be formulated as follows: (*a*) the word "God" properly refers only to a being defined by one concept, theistic absolutism, so that if this concept is rejected it follows that there is no God, or, as some have put it, "God is dead"; (*b*) religion is to be understood only as *belief in theistic absolutism,* so that if theistic absolutism is false it follows that all religion is false; and (*c*) every Jewish religious system is intrinsically committed to belief in theistic absolutism, so that if theistic absolutism is refuted or rejected it follows that every form of Judaism is refuted or rejected.

In the course of the following discussion, I shall attempt to show that these beliefs are fallacies. Not that I think that the rejection of theistic absolutism is a trifling matter in the history of religion, or that all religious systems are consistent with the mode of consciousness that rejects it. On the contrary, it is fairly clear that neither Orthodox Judaism, Roman Catholicism, nor normative Protestant Christianity is consistent with such thinking. But there is, in my opinion, a system of Judaism—namely, Reform Judaism—which can be shown to be fully consistent with the mode of consciousness that rejects theistic absolutism, and which is also coherent with the nontheistic theologies proposed by many contemporary religious thinkers. I propose to develop this thesis by an analysis of the three terms basic to any Jewish theology—"theology," "Jewish," and "God."

The most prominent feature of the terms "theology," "Jewish," and "God" is that none of them enjoys an absolute meaning. Thus these terms, when employed without extensive qualification, can neither communicate knowledge nor provide understanding. The most obvious of the several reasons for this situation is that the use of these terms is not, for the most part, indigenous to the religious experience of the Jews. The very word "Jew," *Yehudi*, whose adjective "Jewish" is taken generally to describe the totality of this experience, refers in part to people and events of a time long preceding the post-biblical period in which the word is first found. Moreover, until recent times, Hebrew was almost the sole language of Jewish religious expression, and it is a very problematic enterprise to attempt to discover the Hebrew concepts and expressions that the term "God," derived from the Gothic *guth,* and the term "theology," taken from Greek philosophy, may be held to connote or translate. As for the use of "theology" by Jews in whose native languages the term appears, this has occurred only in the most recent period, and then in a bewildering variety of senses.

Hence the subject may be pursued from the point of view of history, in which the many usages of the past, which in no way lays down authoritative or univocal meanings, are defined and catalogued. However, my concern is not with instances of past usage, but with advancing selected and even new meanings of these terms for present acceptance. In short, I shall offer a theory of God and Jewish theology that is appropriate to the philosophy of Reform Judaism.

The phrase "appropriate to a philosophy of Reform Judaism" requires clarification. As employed here, the word "philosophy" is understood as "the science or study of the principles, pervasive characteristics, or essence of a subject." The subject is Reform Judaism, and the philosophy of Reform Judaism is the science which precedes the study of any part or element of Reform Judaism. Concepts of God and Jewish theology constitute such elements, and no definition of these terms relevant to Reform Judaism can be given until the nature of Reform Judaism is itself first determined. The philosophy of Reform Judaism provides knowledge of this nature. By abstracting the general and pervasive characteristics of Reform Judaism the philosophy of Reform reveals to us its essence, which, in determining the nature of Reform Judaism as a whole, determines the nature of its parts as well. The many meanings which the terms "God" and "Jewish theology" admit prohibit their use in significant discourse without clear and univocal definition. In proceeding to such definition, we shall reject some meanings, select others, and create new ones. The principle of selectivity and creativity is in all cases "appropriateness to the philosophy of Reform Judaism," which limits our freedom in two ways. One directly, in that no definition of "God," "Jewish," or "theology" relevant to Reform Judaism can be given which is inconsistent with the essence of Reform Judaism; and the other indirectly, in that, of two or more definitions of these terms all of which are consistent with the essence of Reform, the definition most coherent with its essence and spirit is to be preferred.

It is not my intention here to present a philosophy of Reform Judaism.[1] However, inasmuch as the concepts of God and Jewish theology later to be offered will presuppose certain principles of this philosophy, it is necessary to summarize these principle briefly before proceeding further.

The first principle is that the community of Reform Jews denies the existence of an authoritative body of knowledge or beliefs whose affirmation is obligatory upon the members of the community. The rationale behind this principle may be analyzed into three points. The first is the denial that Scripture in its entirety is the literal word of God. This denial must be made, otherwise some form of either Sadduceeism or Pharisaism is true, and Reform Judaism clearly rejects both. Thus this denial is the proximate cause which brings Reform Judaism into existence and the ground upon which it stands. The second point is the presumption that if Scripture is not in its entirety the literal word of God, there is no authoritative way, other than through a subsequent prophecy, to establish what the actual word of God is, whether in Scripture or elsewhere. No one, to the satisfaction of the Reform Jewish community, has established that he has received such a prophecy, that is, a direct and literal communication from the divine mind. Evidence satisfactory to the Reform Jewish community would consist in such verification as Scripture and the Jewish continuum generally require for prophecy, for example, miracles and the prediction of future events whose occurrence is naturally unknowable. The third point is the presumption that knowledge or belief which is the product of finite minds is fallible and therefore not obligatory upon Reform Jews. Since the existence of prophecy has not been established to the satisfaction of the Reform Jewish community, there is only fallible knowledge, and this may be accepted or rejected as individual preference dictates.

The second principle of Reform Judaism is that Reform is a polydoxy. A polydoxy is defined as a religion that admits as equally valid all opinions on the great themes of religion, such as the meaning of God, the nature of man, etc. The only beliefs disallowed are those inconsistent with its polydox nature, for example, belief in an authoritative revelation or an orthodox doctrine. The polydox religious institution as such is committed only to the affirmation of its members' individual freedom. The recognition of Reform Judaism as a polydoxy flows from the first principle. The only mode of religious organization coherent with the doctrine that no person possesses the right to impose his beliefs upon others is one that affirms the radical freedom of its adherents. In a polydoxy the religious institution does not prescribe the total religious life of its followers. Membership in the community, viewed from the total religious commitment possible, constitutes in itself only a state of potentiality. Through the dialogues its followers pursue with one another, the possibilities of religious choice are presented and realization through decision invited. Persuasion through suggestion, not indoctrination by promulgation and interdiction, is the form of instruction and communication proper to a polydoxy.

II

In developing a theory of God and Jewish theology appropriate to the philosophy of Reform Judaism, we must first engage in an analysis of the term "theology." This word as such possesses no significant or clear history of usage in the Jewish religious past. Perhaps this is the reason, in part, that its use among Jews today reflects such varied and even contradictory meanings. It should be noted, however, that almost from its inception in Aristotle, "theology" has been employed by religionists and philosophers to represent many meanings, so that usage today in Christianity and philosophy shows a similar variety and ambiguity. The many uses of the word theology do not concern us per se, except to note that the word is a general problem. Our interest is in arriving at a meaning suitable to Reform Judaism. We will, therefore, limit

ourselves to the following points in this order: the basic or classical definition of theology; a definition appropriate to Reform; an
analysis of the major forms theology has taken; and, finally, the
forms that are possible in Reform.

The classical definition of theology is "the science or study
which treats of God, his nature and attributes, and his relations to
man and the universe." This definition, I maintain, is not entirely
suited for Reform Jewish use. Appropriateness is determined by
the twofold rule laid down above: (1) no part of a religion, such
as theology, can be inconsistent with its essence; and (2) where
a part admits of two or more consistent definitions, the one most
coherent with the essence and its spirit is to be preferred. Polydoxy has been described as an essential characteristic of Reform,
which means that the members of the Reform Jewish community
are affirmed in their freedom, and that all opinions of Reform
Jews on such subjects as God are, therefore, equally valid so far
as the institution of Reform Judaism is concerned. In the classical
definition of theology as "the science or study which treats of
God, his nature and attributes," the clear implication is that there
is an *ens reale* of which theology is the study. However, theology
in a polydoxy, particularly one respectful of scientific method,
cannot proceed in this closed and uncritical manner. There are
those in a polydoxy who, out of their freedom, will deny a reality
reference to the term God, yet whose study in arriving at this
conclusion is their investigation of God. A definition of theology
appropriate to Reform should include their activity. Moreover,
the term theology applied to their study is apt in that it conveys
the nuance of approval for the activity it designates, and the
study of God pursued by those persons has the same institutional
approval in polydox Judaism as the study of those whose conclusions are ostensibly more congenial with past theologies of the
Jewish continuum. Hence the definition of "theology" I would
offer as coherent with the essence and spirit of Reform Judaism
is the following: "the science or study which treats of the meaning of the word God."

This definition satisfies both the polydox and scientific needs of
Reform: the former, in that a Reform Jew who studies the possible meanings of the word "God" engages in "theology" whatever
his conclusion about this meaning may be; the latter, inasmuch as
a Reform Jew who theologizes is not committed beforehand to

any conclusion and may pursue his investigation in a scientific manner without presuppositions. Furthermore, this definition requires no change in the classical meaning of theology, since it continues to include all the activity that the term has otherwise denoted. Its usage is merely extended to cover all the activity of our present age. This definition makes of theology an open enterprise, with the capacity to serve the Reform community's often expressed feeling that knowledge and religion are progressive and continually advance.

The forms of theology are those general procedures which have been followed in establishing the meaning of the word "God." We will concern ourselves only with those forms which serve to establish the meaning of "God" as reference to a real existent. These forms may be classified as follows:

1. *Theology which proceeds on the evidence of an authoritative revelation.* An authoritative revelation is one that a religious community or group of persons accepts as possessing absolute right over them. This is usually because the revelation is understood to come literally from God and therefore to be infallible. This form of theology is the primary means of establishing a reality referent for God in such religions as Pharisaic Judaism and the fundamentalist types of Christianity. Such a theology is inappropriate to Reform, since it is inconsistent with the first principle of the philosophy of Reform Judaism discussed above—that there is no authoritative body of knowledge or belief whose affirmation is obligatory on the members of the Reform Jewish community. No theology can bring as evidence for its truth that which must itself first be proved true. Therefore, a Reform theology which assumes the style of an authoritative, systematic theology may give the appearance of theology of this (first) form, but it belongs in actuality to theology of the fourth or the fifth form discussed below.

2. *Theology which proceeds on the evidence of certain and irrefragable natural knowledge.* Examples of theologies which claim to proceed in this manner are Aristotle's *Metaphysics,* Spinoza's *Ethics,* and probably the system of Maimonides. If such a theology were to be demonstrated, it would, of course, compel assent and through reason be

authoritative over man. However, so far as I know, no present claim to such knowledge exists.

3. *Theology which proceeds on the combined evidence of infallible authoritative revelation and certain natural knowledge, and which seeks to reconcile whatever conflicts or contradictions appear to exist between them.* This form is often taken, erroneously, as the model and basic meaning of theology. Philo and Saadiah, among the Jews, and Thomas Aquinas among the Christians, are representative exponents of this mode of theologizing, which was prevalent throughout the Middle Ages. Theology of this form is inappropriate to Reform Judaism for the reasons given in evaluating forms (1) and (2) above.

4. *Theology which proceeds on the evidence of subjective experience.* This evidence is subjective—*so far as the total religious community is concerned*—because the experience occurs privately to one or several persons of the community, and is not or cannot be shared or verified by the other members. Reported examples of such experience are: prophetic visions, the apprehension of a presence or power taken to be God, mystic union, the solitary witnessing of a miracle, and (more recently) the Buberian "I–Thou." This form of theology is, in principle, appropriate to Reform Judaism, for the evaluation of theological evidence as subjective has for its corollary the judgment that the theology is fallible and without authority over others. There is no sensible reason why the members of a religious community should accept the beliefs of a fellow-religionist on the latter's unverifiable assertion that there exists private evidence for those beliefs. History is replete with the tragic consequences of subjective theology. Hence such a theology is consistent with Reform Judaism only when a renunciation of authority is understood to accompany it.

5. *Theology which proceeds on the evidence of objective experience.* The basic characteristic of objective evidence is that it is apprehended publicly. Generally speaking, evidence is objective to a community of religionists if, given ordinary conditions, every member of the community can experience it. Since new members are continually entering

a community, objective experience must be repeatable at will. Experiences that are unique, for example, the reported cleavage of the Red Sea, are objective only to the persons who witness them. Since such events cannot be reproduced at will, the testimony of those who witness them, or the tradition that reports this witness, is subjective evidence to those who have not observed the event directly. Theology based upon the evidence of repeatable objective experience, like all natural knowledge critically considered, is uncertain or probable. Since this theology is open to error, it is not authoritative so far as the community as a totality is concerned. Such methods of determining truth as pragmatism, coherence, and empirical verifiability are employed in this form of theology.

In concluding this discussion of the word theology, I should like to point out a significant corollary of the foregoing analysis. This concerns the phrase "Reform Jewish theology," which is often taken to refer to some one kind of study into the meaning of God and some one conclusion resulting from such study. Added to this is the vague implication that this one theology is obligatory on all Reform Jews. The fact is that many theologies are consistent with the essence of Reform Judaism, and the phrase "Reform Jewish theology" is capriciously or erroneously used in referring to some putative "only possible" theological system in Reform Judaism. Only if Reform as we now know it undergoes essential change can such an authoritative theology be established. Either the nature of Reform as a liberal religion or polydoxy will be arbitrarily subverted, or the entire community will share in an experience which conclusively and irrefragably establishes such a theology as true. Yet the phrase "Reform Jewish theology" is not entirely without present meaning. It may refer either to the aggregate of particular Reform theologies, all consistent with the essence of Reform Judaism, or to the general discussion that lays down the conditions which a theology must meet to be appropriate to Reform Judaism and as such refers to no single method of theologizing or to any particular conception of deity.

III

The word we next turn to is "Jewish." What characteristic or quality must a theology possess so that the name Jewish is properly given to it? What, in other words, is meant in Reform Judaism by the phrase "Jewish theology"? At first it would seem that only that theology is properly called Jewish which is identical with the theology which has been called Jewish in the past. We may term this the static use of the term Jewish, and the criterion of identity with the past, *the static rule.* The simplicity of the static rule is obvious and appealing. Unfortunately, the static use of the term "Jewish" is impossible as regards Reform Jewish theology. For at least three reasons, each of which is decisive by itself, the static rule cannot be applied to give meaning to the term "Jewish" in the phrase "Reform Jewish theology." The first of these is factual, the second essential, the third practical.

First, Reform Judaism, in denying literal and infallible revelation, is the first religious system (excepting, perhaps, systems of individuals like Maimonides, which differ otherwise from Reform) of the Jewish continuum to do so. Hence if the static rule were to be followed, there would be no Reform *Judaism* and Reform *Jewish* theology at all. Thus Reform Judaism, by the very fact of its existence, repudiates the static rule.

Second, any meaning of the word "Jewish" appropriate to Reform Judaism must be appropriate to the essence of Reform. This essence implies that there are no authoritative theological beliefs or dogmas obligatory on Reform Jews and that Reform Judaism is a polydoxy affirming every Reform Jew's radical freedom. Therefore, if "Jewish" is properly applied only to a belief identical with that of the past, we have the absurd result that this word in the phrase "Reform Jewish" contradicts the whole of which it is a part. The phrase "Reform Jewish" would expand and affirm freedom, the term "Jewish" would constrict and deny freedom.

The third reason is that it is not possible in actual practice to apply the static rule. The static rule calls for the name "Jewish" to be applied to a theology in the present which is identical with a theology called "Jewish" in the past. A *sine qua non* of this rule, then, is that there *be* a past theology called Jewish to serve as the criterion of application. However, the past as investigated by the science of Judaism does not give us *a* Jewish theology; rather, it gives us many theologies and God-concepts that have been called Jewish, not a few of which differ substantially from one another. What is the criterion we will use to determine which of these many past Jewish theologies will serve as the criterion for our use of the term Jewish? Will it be the theology and God-concept of Amos, based upon direct prophetic experience, which differs greatly from the theology of the Pharisees, based upon the tradition of a perfect and finished revelation to Moses? Yet both differ radically from Maimonides' concept of God, based as it is on negative theology and the primacy of reason. These examples can be multiplied tens of times. What has the theology of Mendelssohn to do with the Kabbalah, although both are called Jewish? Hence it is impossible, except arbitrarily, to select a past Jewish theology which will define our use of the term Jewish, and serve as the paradigm for application of the static rule.[2]

One further observation concerning the static rule: there is a procedure which masquerades as the application of this rule but which, on inspection, turns out to be just the contrary. This procedure, abstraction, attempts to bring in the static rule through the rear door. The argument is given that all theology called Jewish in the past has an essence which can be abstracted, for example, theism, and that "Jewish," therefore, is properly applied only to a theology which has this theistic characteristic. But the static rule requires *identity* between a past and present theology. If someone abstracts a concept like theism from complex religious systems such as those of the Jewish continuum, and says theism is their essence, he does not apply the past, he violates it. He introduces subjectively, on personal say-so, an entirely new element. Take the following case as an illustration. To the Pharisee and his descendants, the name "Jewish" is not applied to a theology because it is theistic; the theologies of Christianity and Islam are theistic too. "Jewish" is applied to a theology which *consists of a particular kind of theism* and accepts a *particular revelation.* Hence to deny the revelation and generalize away the specifically Pharisaic theism is not to keep the past and apply the static rule, but, on the contrary, to repudiate the past and change the very essence of Pharisaic Judaism.[3]

Moreover, abstraction as a name-giving principle does not work. If we say that the word "Jewish" is applied merely to a theology that is theistic, then Christianity, Islam, and many other religions are Jewish. Surely, this is absurd. We were seeking a principle that would enable us to apply the name "Jewish" more accurately; instead we find that abstraction destroys whatever meaning "Jewish" may reasonably be understood to have. In other words, a rule based upon abstraction or "essence" that would be broad enough to include the entire Jewish continuum would be so general that theologies would be included which plainly are not Jewish; at the same time, this rule would be so arbitrary that theologies which are patently Jewish, such as those held by many Reform and Reconstructionist Jews, would be excluded.

Inasmuch as the static meaning of "Jewish" cannot be applied in Reform Judaism, I should like to propose another meaning for the word in the phrase "Reform Jewish theology." This meaning, which is open to development and progress, is, I think, implicit in some instances of past usage but not identical with any meaning of the past consciously given. We may term this meaning the *dynamic* use of the word "Jewish."

The dynamic meaning is derived from an understanding of the word "Jew" as an ontal symbol, a symbol that points to the problematic structure of man's being (*ontos*) and summons him to respond to finitude with authenticity. This understanding is based on a phenomenology of the human person which finds man to be a "problem" existent. The sense of the term "problem" as employed here is indicated by its etymology. *Problema* in Greek means "something thrown forward," that is, a question that is proposed for solution. The existence of man is not given to him as a thing, fully and at one time, but is thrown forward to him as a question of anxious interest demanding solution. Man cannot refuse to ask this question, although it engenders anxiety, for he is the question he asks. This question, bluntly stated, is, "I am finite, I crave infinity; what can I do, what should I do, what shall I do?" The conflict between the finite being of the human person and the infinite strivings of his will is sharp, penetrating to the core of his personality and constituting a threat to its unity and integrity. Finity entails aloneness and death, whereas the finite person longs for unlimited relation and eternity. Man's response to the conflict between what he is and what he wishes to be, in other words, his response to finitude, is the definition I give to religion. The ontal symbol has the power of calling to being; it directs man to constitutive decision and genuine religion. As an ontal symbol, the word "Jew" turns the one whom it names to the essential demand of his being, but, as an ontal symbol, *it summons merely to authentic response, not to any one particular response.* In a religious situation such as Reform Judaism, where the evidence for response is admittedly fallible and the autarchic individuality of each member affirmed, response is determined as authentic not by its agreement with dogma, but by the capacity of the response for resolving the individual finitude of the one who makes it.

The symbol "Jew" brings before man past and present possibilities of response. The possibilities produced by the past are evoked by the intrinsic association of *Jew* with the history that produced it: shall it be decided with the *Jew* Job that no Infinite disrupts the structure of finite being and that human existence is radically bounded by the limit of death, or shall it be decided with the *Jew* who is Pharisee that relation to an Infinite breaks the limits of finitude? The possibilities of the present are evoked by "Jew" as the name of a "now existent" whom it calls to authentic response. For the response of the "now existent" takes place in a concrete, present reality to which, if the response is *authentic,* it must be true.

Thus the meaning of the word "Jew" as ontal symbol is dynamic, not bound to the past as the static meaning is; it is heuristic, furthering investigation into the nature of man and his universe.[4] Here lies the relation between the word "Jew" and theology. As ontal symbol, *the word "Jew" creates theology,* and the creation is therefore properly named after that which begets it. The ontal symbol creates theology by inducing the one over whom it has power to search for authentic response to his finitude. Authentic response is based on reality, and the concept of God, the product of theology, gives to man the characteristics of the real ultimately relevant to his finitude. Finitude, it may be said, raises the question of the infinite; theology provides the answer; religion is the individual's engaged response. "Jewish theology" in Reform Judaism is therefore defined as "the study of the meaning of the word 'God' produced by the finite being named 'Jew' who is called by his name to give authentic response to finitude."

IV

We come now to the third and final word of our subject, "God." Inasmuch as no authoritative or dogmatic definition of God can be laid down in Reform Judaism, and more than one concept is consistent with the essence of Reform, the discussion which follows is to be regarded primarily as an explanation of why I personally take the position I do rather than as a polemic against positions to which others are committed and which possess great value for them. Of course, in explaining why any position is taken, it is inevitable that reasons should be given why other positions have been rejected. Negation is an aspect of affirmation. Negation, however, is not the purpose of these remarks.

All inquiry into the reality and nature of a supposed existent begins with an examination of the ways of knowing. Even our brief investigation, therefore, cannot proceed directly to a statement about the reality and nature of God. Rather, as (I believe) all theology must, it starts with a consideration of the nature of evidence and the justification of belief. What is the evidence, if any, that is necessary to justify belief in a reality called God?

To begin with, let us consider the possibility that no evidence at all is to be required. It is evident that no proof can be brought to determine the question of evidence, inasmuch as that which constitutes proof is itself dependent upon the same question. No proof, therefore, can be brought that evidence is necessary; the choice of evidence is a starting point of inquiry. He who so wishes can state anything, affirm anything, or believe anything, without evidence. Such is the way of *ipse dixit* theology. After I have conceded this, however, it is my choice and conviction that evidence must be given to justify whatever reality reference is to be assigned the word "God." I have no quarrel with anyone who uses his freedom to deny that evidence is necessary, provided that he affirms my freedom to withhold serious consideration from any proposed reality meaning of God for which no evidence is given.[5] The word "theology" literally means "science or knowledge of God" and, though the heart may not wish to know, thought must have its reasons. As Maimonides says in laying down the rules of evidence and the definition of faith which preface his inquiry into the nature of God:

Bear in mind that by "faith" we do not mean that which is uttered with the lips, but that which is apprehended by the (rational) soul, the conviction that the object [of belief] is exactly as it is conceived. If, as regards real or supposed truths, you content yourself with giving utterance to them in words, without conceiving them or believing in them, especially if you do not seek certainty, you have a very easy task, as, in fact, you will find many ignorant people who retain (the words of) beliefs (in their memory) without conceiving any idea with regard to them . . . belief is only possible after a thing is conceived; it consists in the conviction that the thing apprehended has its existence beyond the mind (in reality) exactly as it is conceived in the mind. . . . Renounce desires and habits, follow your reason . . . you will then be fully convinced of what we have said.[6]

Without evidence, there is no genuine conviction possible for man, the existent who, perhaps *malgré lui,* is committed to reality and endowed with reason.

The decision having been made that evidence is necessary to establish a reality reference for God, we must now weigh which of the two kinds of evidence generally accepted is to be required, subjective or objective evidence. The outstanding characteristic of our age regarding theological evidence is that the objective evidence which has in the past been employed to justify faith in a reality reference for the word "God" is now generally rejected, and particularly so among liberal religions. This is primarily the evidence described above under the first form of theology, infallible and authoritative revelation. But repudiated as well is the evidence of infallible and authoritative natural knowledge, described above under the second form of theology. The most striking consequence of this development is that the evidence which traditionally provided substantiation for that concept of God which I have called theistic absolutism has been discarded. Theistic absolutism, which, in the Jewish continuum, is subscribed to in its most rigorous form by Pharisaic or Orthodox Judaism, is the theory that the referent of the word "God" is an omniscient, omnipotent, omnibenevolent Being who reveals Himself to man.[7] Those who reject the traditional evidence and wish to retain theistic absolutism must now resort to subjective evidence, which constitutes theology of the fourth form, since no theology of the fifth form satisfactorily makes a case for this concept.[8] Hence those theologians who vigorously affirm the validity of subjective evidence are primarily the ones who are committed to the concept of theistic absolutism. Owing to this present, intimate relation between subjective evidence and theistic absolutism, it is difficult to evaluate subjective evidence without touching on the latter as well.

A good description of the mode of subjective evidence predominantly subscribed to today is given by a prominent theologian:

> The new and more empiricist apologetic that is replacing the traditional theistic proofs focuses attention upon the state of religious faith, and claims that this is a state which it is rational to be in, but which philosophical reasoning cannot put one in.
>
> The state of faith, in its strongest instances, is that of someone who cannot help believing in God. He reports that he is conscious of God—not of course as an object in the world, but as a divine presence. In the Old Testament, for example, the prophets were aware of God as dealing with Israel through the vicissitudes of her national history. In the New Testament the disciples were conscious of God as acting towards them in and through Jesus, so that His attitudes towards the various men and women whom He met were God's attitudes towards those same people. And the contemporary man of faith is aware of existing in the unseen presence of God and of living his life within the sphere of a universal divine purpose.
>
> Having thus pointed to a putative religious awareness, the new apologetic argues that this is no more in need of a philosophical proof of the reality of its object than is our perception of the physical world or of other people. The rationalist assumption is no more valid in relation to religious cognition than in relation to sense experience . . . the believer does not reason from his religious experience to God but is conscious of God Himself . . . the central claim of the new type of apologetic is that it is rational for someone who believes himself to be aware of God, and who finds himself linked in this belief with a long-lived community of faith, to trust his religious awareness and to proceed to base his life upon it.[9]

Inasmuch as the points usually made in favor of subjective evidence as the basis of theology are ably summarized in these comments, an analysis of their contents will serve as a critique of

subjective evidence generally.[10] If subjective evidence is found
wanting by this critique, as I believe it is, then no alternative is
left but to select objective evidence of the fifth form as the justification necessary to establish a reality reference for the word
God.

It appears to me that there are four major difficulties with
subjective evidence. First, once the principle is affirmed that such
evidence is valid, then the subjective evidence of any and every
person is validated. If everyone's subjective evidence is valid, how
is a choice to be made between two conflicting statements on
the nature of God and religion, both of which are supported by
subjective evidence? How does one choose between the God and
religion of the pre-exilic prophets, which knows of no Trinity,
Messiah, resurrection, and immortality, and a religion such as
Christianity which affirms the Trinity and a Messiah, and makes
afterlife the goal and purpose of human existence? Surely, unless
reason and the law of contradiction are to be dismissed, these
religions cannot both be true. It is possible, I suppose, for a person to claim that his own subjective evidence testifies to its own
validity and tells him as well which other subjective evidence is
valid. But this seems arbitrary and unconvincing. It resembles, in
fact, a claim to prophecy. Subjective evidence, then, does not
seem to provide a much better criterion for determining truth
than no evidence at all. One of the principal reasons for requiring
evidence is to judge among truth claims, but the theology of subjective evidence seems to serve this purpose no better than *ipse
dixit* theology.

Second, if the believer "is conscious of God Himself," how is
it, for example, that the pre-exilic phophets' and Jesus' concepts
of the nature of God differ so? And why does the Muslim experience Allah; the Christian, Jesus; and the Hindu, Brahma? The
analogy between religious cognition and sense perception is surely
farfetched. Few will disagree, I am sure, that the tree the prophet
sees will answer to Jesus' notion of a tree and to ours as well, yet
for people ostensibly experiencing the same "presence," their
notions of deity and religion differ greatly indeed.

Third, one of the conclusions of Sigmund Freud's investigations
was that the experience of "presence" which some report as confrontation with the deity is actually to be understood as an experience of self objectified and projected outward. How, in this

Freudian age, can it be considered "rational" to accept "presence" *ipso facto* as consciousness of "God Himself"? It would appear, rather, that one of the prime methodological principles in a theology acceptable to our time would be the recognition that "presences" per se are to be presumed projections of the unconscious.

Fourth, the concept of God which the experience of "presence" is usually taken to substantiate is theistic absolutism. This is the concept of a Being whose nature has consequences for the world we experience. A universe created and governed by an omniscient, omnipotent, omnibenevolent Being may be expected to display the marks of its perfect source. Thus the apprehension of "presence" is clearly not adequate by itself to demonstrate the truth of this concept; it must be proved coherent with the facts of the universe as well. We all grant, I suppose, the existence of "presences"; the great problem is the world of brute fact. Many of our experiences are incoherent with theistic absolutism; the most critical of these is, of course, the experience of surd evil. If the facts could be brought into harmony with the concept of theistic absolutism, "presence" theology would have no difficulty in finding acceptance.[11] Yet the medievals, who considered their concept of God supported by indubitable evidence, gave more attention to the problem of its congruence with the external world than many theologians of today whose primary evidence is the ambiguous "presence."

My conclusion from these considerations is that subjective evidence is not competent to establish a real Being, that is, a reality reference for the word "God." Before leaving the matter of subjective evidence, however, I should like to stress three points. First, to repeat my opinion stated earlier, theology based upon subjective evidence is appropriate to Reform Judaism only if such theology is understood to be non-authoritative. Second, the use of "presence" to which I object is as primary evidence for a concept of deity; I have no objection to the use of "presence" as corroborative evidence for a divine reality established by other than subjective means, or as a symbol referring to a reality so established. Third, not all forms of theism are established by subjective evidence; the exponents of theistic finitism, for example, appeal in the main to objective evidence.

V

The form of theology to which, I believe, we now must come is the pursuit of a reality reference for God based on objective evidence of the kind earlier classified as the basis of theology of the fifth form. For many, the primary difficulty regarding this form of theology is that the objective evidence presently available does not substantiate the concept of theistic absolutism. Their disappointment is understandable but, to the objectivist, constitutes no rebuttal of truth. The objectivist employs a strict standard of evidence precisely because he is aware of man's infinite strivings and the screen they place between him and reality. Genuine religion, as he understands it, is to have God shape his inner life and not the contrary. Thus, far from being that which religion should avoid, reality objectively determined provides the basis of true religion and the source of salvation. For authentic response to finitude, which constitutes true religion, must be based upon reality; salvation is nothing other than the state such response produces.

Moreover, while subjective theology is consistent with the essence of Reform Judaism, objective theology is more than consistent, it is also coherent, fitting naturally with the origins and spirit of Reform. Reform Judaism came into existence as a result of the conclusion that Scripture is fallible, the work (at least in part) of man. This conclusion was reached through critical and objective study, the science of Judaism applied to Scripture. Is it not natural to apply this same method to the theology of Reform Judaism as well?

There are several theories of truth based upon objective evidence. Since it would take us far afield to enter upon the intricacies of reflection involved in selecting one theory over another, it will suffice for my purpose merely to indicate the one to which I subscribe. This is the theory that a proposition concerning the external world is true if it is empirically verifiable. I do not believe—unlike those who generally subscribe to empirical verifiability as the criterion of truth—that there is no direct knowledge of one's self. That I believe such knowledge is possible is clear, inasmuch as it is the knowledge on which the ontal symbol and authentic response to finitude is based. However, I accept empirical verifiability as the arbiter of truth concerning the external world, and, seeing that God understood as a real being is a fact of the external world, our theory of truth must be one that pertains to knowledge of this world. A brief (and general) formulation of the notion of empirical verifiability can be stated as follows: "A proposition or series of propositions concerning the external world will be true if there are predictable and observable consequences of such a proposition or propositions." Hence the test that a reality definition of God must meet is empirical verifiability. If there are empirical consequences of the proposition "God exists," the proposition will be true; if there are not, the proposition will be meaningless or false.

The definition of "God" I propose, in accordance with the foregoing, is: "God is the enduring possibility of being." Inasmuch as being is analyzable without remainder into sense-data and self-data, the existence of God is verified whenever sense-data and self-data are experienced, and the existence of God is disproved when, under equivalent conditions of personal normalcy, self-data are experienced and sense-data are not. God is the enduring possibility of being rather than of sense experience alone because the person (that is, the continuing self-consciousness that is constructed out of self-data) is evidently dependent upon the external world (sense-data and the unobservables reducible to sense-data), and with the annihilation of the external world, the annihilation of the person would necessarily follow.

The concept of God as the enduring possibility of being belongs to the class of theologies that may generally be subsumed under the heading of "finitist theologies." Quite different theologies are grouped together under this heading, but all possess the common characteristic that God is not regarded as perfect, "perfection" being defined by the largely imaginary standard of "having every desirable attribute." For the most part, the imperfection attributed to deity in finitist theologies relates to the divine power, that is, the inability of God to overcome the force of evil, which may originate within the Godhead or outside it. In the concept of God as the enduring possibility of being, the divine imperfection goes beyond this, to the essential nature of the divine existence.

Two classes of existence, each with its distinctive nature, can be distinguished: the possible and the actual. Possible existence is defective in that it lacks actuality. As possibility, it is neither a sense-datum nor a self-datum. Yet if the divine existence is to be infinite in duration, it can be this only as possibility. For the actually existent is always limited; nothing unlimited can be sensed or imagined, let alone conceived. To be actual is to be finite. While the finity of every actuality is present in all the spheres of its existence, it is temporal finity that provides the definitive boundary. The actual is finite in time because, as an actuality, it is finite in the power of endurance and destined, therefore, as an individual, to annihilation. Being thus breeds nothingness; indeed, *nothing* has no meaning except in relation to being. Accordingly, if God is to be infinite in duration, the divine existence must forego actuality for possibility. We find therefore that God is infinite in duration but possesses only possible existence, whereas being is finite in duration but possesses actual existence. Metaphorically speaking, existence, the act of overcoming nothingness, lays down conditions on all that would possess it. As a consequence, nothingness is never entirely overcome. Actual existents temporarily overcome nothingness at the cost of future and total annihilation. God overcomes nothingness by incorporating it into the divine existence and, in so doing, is emptied of actuality and must forever remain possibility. The divine existence, so to speak, is a compromise between being and nothingness; the ground of being overcomes nothingness to exist as the enduring possibility of being, but in the uneasy victory defect is assimilated into the Godhead.

The understanding of God's existence as the enduring possibility of being leads to a further consequence: God cannot exist without the world. God has no meaning without being; being has no endurance without God. God's existence is not absolute; the enduring possibility of being exists as a correlative of being. The world was not created by an absolute God who arbitrarily willed it so; rather the world exists because the divine existence is unconditionally dependent upon it. Of creation *ex nihilo*, we have no knowledge. In experience, God coexists with finite entities in a process of continuous interaction. In this process, as we are justified in concluding from the regular and orderly nature of causal sequence, the possibility of future being is derived from present being. The existence of God is, so to speak, derived from every present moment of being and realized in every future moment.

A further consequence of God's nature as possibility is the relation that obtains between God and man. In this view of God, where the divine is subject to the conditions of existence, it is the nature of actual entities, by virtue of the finity or encompassing boundary that gives them their existence, to be cut off from the ground of their being. To be actual is to be alone. To be finite is to be severed from the infinite. Hence the relation between God and man is one of muted communication. Accordingly, as Reform Judaism teaches, there exists no infallible or verbal revelation nor can there be such revelation, because man, necessarily and substantially separated from the ground of being, has no sure relation to this ground. Equally, the perfect providence of theistic absolutism, its Messiahs and magical eschatologies, have no place in a world where the infinite exists only as possibility, and the actual world is always finite.

Yet if God cannot overcome man's finity, man is not powerless. The possibilities that constitute the Godhead can be influenced and even altered by man. Every individual decision that resolves the pain of finitude increases the possibility of pleasurable being in the future; every social decision that helps resolve the pain of injustice and poverty increases the possibility of social betterment in the future; every scientific discovery becomes a power for the future. If man wills it, God conserves all the value that is possible. This relation of action and passion between man and God may be viewed symbolically as a covenant, an ethics of hypothetical necessity: "If man acts, then God reacts" or, "As man acts, so God reacts." In the words of the prophet Amos:

> Seek good, and not evil, that ye may live;
> And so the Lord, the God of hosts, will be with you, as ye say.
> Hate the evil, and love the good,
> And establish justice in the gate;
> It may be that the Lord, the God of hosts,
> Will be gracious unto the remnant of Joseph.[12]

This covenant, in which man must do the good to receive the good, is to be sharply distinguished from magical covenants with deity, in which man is required to perform some act irrelevant to the good—ritualistic, emotional, or otherwise—and God, without prior and competent causes, miraculously produces the good.

The absence of an infallible and verbal revelation is only part of the larger problem of evil, the great complex of events and conditions that beset and anguish human existence. Evil comes both from events outside man and from conditions within him. The human person, relative to the problems the world presents him, is not only inherently deficient intellectually, lacking certainty in his knowledge and absoluteness in his ethics, but is constitutionally deficient emotionally and physically as well. These deficiencies keep man from perfect and permanent solutions to any real problem and provide a constant threat to the very meaning of his existence. In no way can evil be accounted for satisfactorily by theological absolutism. This includes not only theistic absolutism, but pantheistic absolutism as well, such as we find, for example, in Spinozism. The Whole that is Substance cannot contain the evils of the world and be meaningfully pronounced perfect, any more than the omniscient and omnipotent Creator can be meaningfully pronounced perfect. The Whole exists in and through its parts and cannot escape the defects of their nature, just as the absolute Creator is responsible for his creatures and cannot escape the consequences of their acts. In the theology of divine possibility, there is, I feel, a coherent explanation of evil. Evil is the inevitable result of the nature of God and the nature of man. Evil is not willed into existence, it is a necessary concomitant of existence. The choice, figuratively stated, is not between a world with evil and a world without it, but between a world with evil and no world at all.

Two principles in the theology of divine possibility primarily serve to explain evil. The first is that all actual being is necessarily finite. Every actual thing will in every way be limited; nothing real endures eternally. This does not mean that meliorism is unrealistic and melioration cannot occur; it can and does, but melioration is all that can occur. No final triumph over limitation and nothingness is possible. The second principle is that God, the divine possibility, can offer only for realization in the future the possibilities that reside in the being of the present. God, in other words, is not an independent absolute agent who can miraculously produce the good *ex nihilo;* the divine existence can present for realization in the future only that which has been made possible in the past. Together, these two principles, that the "present" or world of actualities is always limited, and that the future can be created only out of possibilities derived from a present that is limited, offer an explanation of the pervasive presence of evil in the world.

The theology of divine possibility is offered as a theology appropriate to and coherent with Reform Judaism. Out of his freedom a Reform Jew may accept or reject it. However, a theology is to be rejected on valid grounds, and there are two kinds of objections that I feel are not valid. The first is the objection which argues that a theology must satisfy the infinite wishes of man and provide him with unlimited consolation. This argument is invalid, not only because it is historically unsound so far as the Jews are concerned, but because it is based upon a misconception of theology in particular and religion in general. The purpose of theology is truth, and the purpose of religion is to enable man to live authentically with that truth. Hence truth is the only relevant and necessary justification of a theology. The second objection bases the value of a theology upon the number of divine mysteries it reveals, as though the adequacy of a theology resided not in its quality as truth but in its quantity. As Maimonides so profoundly taught, a theology is as important for that which it negates as for that which it affirms. The worship of false gods is idolatry, and if a theology should serve to keep men from idolatry, even though, as in the case of Maimonides' theology, it should tell him nothing of the essence of God, then it will have accomplished a great good. Throughout history, there has been a special fury attached to the deeds of those who have acted in the name of false gods, and who have rationalized, through idolatry, despotic and tyrannical urges that were solely their own. The theology of divine possibility as a negative theology serves the moral role of denying divinity to anything finite, regardless of the basis upon which the quality of divinity is claimed, whether through revelation or incarnation.

We should note, although we cannot fully develop the point here, that the theology of divine possibility holds significant beliefs in common with important Jewish systems of the past. Its affinity with the negative theory of Maimonides, and with Amos' covenantal concept of God's role in the conservation of the good, has already been mentioned. Moreover, since we find that God alone as possibility is permanent, and that all actual being is momentary and limited, the response to finitude that is pointed to is the response of all biblical Jewish systems: that we accept death and the inevitable cessation of all being. The fact of evil, resulting as it does from the necessary limitations of existence, should bring us, as symbolically it brought Job, not to despair but to the meaningful awareness that the divine possibility reacts to acts of value and conserves all possible good. Yet there is a stern overtone to the concept of God as possibility. As possibility God cannot produce the concrete realization of human good; this, of necessity, is left to man. Should man in this strange age fail, then we must agree with Amos and the author of the story of Noah that God does not require for his existence any particular people, species, or world. While it is true that God without a world has no meaning or existence, the infinite divine temporality does not require any particular class of finite beings for existence. The awesome choice, whether man is to be included in this class, is left to man himself.

Still, in conclusion, I must confess my belief that we are tending toward an excellent time in the affairs of men. Radical novelty lies ahead. Man stands at the dawn of the post-Christian, post-Orthodox era in religion. Compelling evidence for these religious systems is now gone, and the effects of this loss should continue to be felt more and more generally. The recent bursts of theological irrationality, as exemplified in aspects of Christian existentialism, the various neo-Orthodoxies, and the fantastic "Death of God" school, are not only telling evidence of what occurs when disciplined and objective evidence for faith is not employed, but the usual *fin de siècle* sentiments expressed when an era dies. Reform Judaism as a polydoxy offers a prototype of the religious structure that is possible in a world given to objective evidence and scientific method. In a world from which poverty is banished, in which sickness of mind and body is diminished and man is politically free, a religion will be accepted not because men are afraid, nor in extreme need of consolation, but because it is true. Inasmuch as there is no way now or in the foreseeable future to determine truth absolutely, man will need freedom to find his religious truth. This Reform Judaism affirms and allows. True to its polydox essence, Reform Judaism is the religion for tomorrow, as it is now the religion for today.

NOTES

1. I have epitomized such a philosophy in *Meet the American Jew* (Nashville, Tenn.: Broadman Press, 1963), pp. 29 ff.

2. It is interesting to note that the totality of the Jewish continuum as revealed by the science of Judaism is itself polydox, containing varied and mutually exclusive theologies. Only a polydox Judaism in the present can offer the entire past (within the broad limits set by the logic of polydoxy) as possibilities for choice and decision. This is accomplished through the word "Jew" as ontal symbol.

3. If anything may be abstracted as an "essence" or abiding characteristic of the Jewish continuum, let me suggest the rational ethical principle that authority over other persons must be based on infallible knowledge objectively demonstrated. Therefore, only on the basis of a revelation publicly and perfectly received from the creator God who, *ipso facto,* has power over all creatures can you have orthodoxy and obligatory belief. If this characteristic is taken as the "essence of Judaism," then the same "essence" is present in Reform, when we say that without such infallible knowledge we can have only polydoxy. See my article, "Polydoxy and Modern Judaism," *CCAR Journal,* January 1965, and "Authority in Reform Judaism," *CCAR Journal,* April 1960.

4. The meaning of the word "Jew" as ontal symbol can, and perhaps in fact always will, coexist with other meanings, aesthetic, cultural, political, and so forth. The point here is that it must be the fundamental meaning in Reform Judaism. The other meanings are subsidiary; either instrumental or accidental "handmaidens," so to speak, that serve this meaning. The word "Jew" without the meaning of ontal symbol collapses into comparative triviality. The threat of triviality is, I believe, the central problem of Reconstructionism.

5. Without the affirmation of such freedom, the arbitrary and anti-rational nature of *ipse dixit* theology lends itself to tyranny. It is also difficult to see how dialogue can be established with someone who has no reasons to offer for his faith.

6. Maimonides, *Moreh Nebukhim,* I, 50.

7. Revelation is, I think, implicit in the most rigorous form of theistic absolutism but, strictly speaking, theistic absolutism does not entail revelation.

8. Neither does all evidence of the fourth form verify theistic absolutism, e.g., the Buberian "I–Thou" does not, neither does mystic union.

9. John H. Hick, *Saturday Review,* February 6, 1965.

10. The Buberian "I–Thou" is subject to similar (as well as other) criticism, but requires special consideration which cannot be given here.

11. "Presence" theology has on its side the fact that the concept of God it wishes to establish allows the most "pleasurable" response to finitude.

12. Amos 5:14 f.

THE HALACHA OF REFORM

W. Gunther Plaut

"Halacha" is by its very nature a historical term, and so is the
appellation "Reform Judaism." Strictly speaking, halacha * is the
way of the Fathers applied to our time and, without stretching
the terms in any way, we may also so define Reform Judaism.
Indeed, when the Liberal movement was still young it was the
objective of its founders to reform halacha rather than reform
Judaism itself. The fact that today halacha and Reform seem to
be disjoined is an indication of the serious and—I will say it right
at the beginning—calamitous drift to which Reform Judaism has
yielded. The reason for this lies in the genesis of the movement
and is reflected in the far-flung misconceptions which are held
about it.

I

Reform Judaism began as a movement to reform halacha. During

* For the sake of uniformity this spelling (rather than *halakhah*) is used
throughout this essay, including all quotations.

the first fifty years the Liberals were concerned primarily with the effort to bring such legal reform about. Only in the second (post-classical or radical) phase did the leaders of the movement attempt to reform (or, better, restore) Judaism per se. Roughly from the days of the Pittsburgh Platform on, their interest shifted away from a reform of halacha. They now rejected it, in form if not in principle, and focused their interests on other aspects of the ancestral faith. When they did this, they awarded the palm of victory to the Eastern reformers led by David Einhorn and made Isaac M. Wise drink the cup of defeat.

It is almost paradoxical that Wise is today installed as the father of American Reform Judaism. He was, indeed, the father of its institutions, but these institutions became filled by a non-Wiseian, anti-halachic spirit. If anyone deserves the title of father of American Reform—at least as it expressed itself in its dominant phase from 1885 to 1948—it is Einhorn and not Wise. For Wise was the spiritual heir of Abraham Geiger, and Einhorn the disciple of Samuel Holdheim. While in Europe Geiger's historicism remained at least nominally in vogue and continued to acknowledge the concept of halacha as vital, in America Holdheim's radical exaltation of the *Zeitgeist* swept the field, with the result that today halacha, in practice as well as in principle, appears to have lost nearly all relevance for Reform Jews.

While the victory of Einhorn's radicalism meant the demise of halacha, it turned out that in the long run his non-halachic Judaism had little viability as Judaism. It became transmuted into ethical culture, flourished as a Jewishly spirited Unitarianism, spread as a broad and pleasant middle-class establishmentarianism, with American or Canadian banners gaily affixed to it—but it had lost its moorings in Jewish history, and no amount of quotations from the Prophets could halt its rapid metamorphosis into the Jewish segment of the new North American religion. All this would have come as an unpleasant surprise to Einhorn and as a shock to Wise, but we can hardly blame them for not having been prophets.

Meanwhile the average Reform Jew, like the average Reform rabbi, considers any mention of halacha or its equivalent as the expression of Orthodoxy or Conservatism, and only because so many people are ignorant of the foundations of Jewish life has the real split which runs through the fabric of North American

Jewry not yet become frighteningly obvious. But the gulf between Reform and Tradition is widening. Anyone who reads
Noam, the Israeli magazine concerned with halachic questions,
and asks himself how Reform Jews in North America would react
to these discussions, must realize that the public to whom *Noam*
is addressed and the membership of Reform congregations no
longer speak the same language. That, of course, is in part due
to the narrow legalism which continues to characterize much of
the Orthodox position; yet one cannot escape the concomitant
conviction that Reform Judaism in its present non- or even anti-
halachic form does not possess the key to the total Jewish future.
If the movement does not now turn decisively away from its post-
classical, radical phase, then indeed its critics will probably be
right: it will have no future.

The remission and even new vitality which we were granted in
the post-Hitlerian years will wear off with increasing rapidity and
we shall shortly be where we were thirty and forty years ago—
struggling for a sense of identity, defining that which is Jewish
in Reform, and taking refuge in a host of ancillary activities
which are Jewish only by Procrustean *force majeure.* Without a
recovery of the sense of halacha, Reform Judaism will dissolve
into a shallow post-Einhornian ethicism. We may not go as far as
Einhorn's son-in-law Emil G. Hirsch and remove the Sifrei Torah
from the ark, but we will be assisting at the final surgery which
removes the marrow from Jewish existence. We must do what
the early Reformers meant to do in the first place and attend to
a reform of halacha. In terms of the mid-twentieth century, this
means that we must spend some portion of our energy on the
recovery of the *sense* of halacha in order to reform it and have it
reform us.

II

From Jacobson to Kley and Salomon, from Zunz to Geiger, from
Bernhard Wechsler to Samuel Adler, the theme of Reform as the
reform of halacha was unambiguous and unmistakable. This became most explicit in the Sabbath discussion at an early rabbinic
conference in 1846 at Breslau. The argumentation was entirely
halachic and, although the later *poskim* were rarely quoted, the
Tur, the Rambam, and the Shulhan Arukh, to say nothing of

Mishnah and Talmud, stood in the centre of the learned debate. Few Reformers then doubted, or appeared to doubt, that a valid development of Judaism had to take place on the basis of halacha. Samuel Adler's Hebrew responsum on the rights of women and the question of whether they could be counted in a *minyan* was, in its Hebrew original, appended to the proceedings of the Breslau Conference. The essay fulfils the most rigid requirements of traditional argumentation and gives the whole volume its special stamp. Twenty-three years later Adler had not changed his point of view. In a major address to the first Synod in Leipzig the future rabbi of Temple Emanu-El in New York had to admit, however, that the reform of halacha was in difficulty. For this reason, he said, the Synod had been called to reestablish halachic authority and to put an end to the *hefkerut* of Jewish practice (or non-practice) which had already set in.

"Gentlemen," said Adler, "there are people who make it very easy for themselves. They have cast off all halacha and have easily managed to bring Torah into line with their lives: by giving up the Torah and enjoying life. Well, everyone may have to settle this with his own conscience, but when such persons appear in our congregations and want to maintain their old reputation as 'pious' people, then we must all together make every effort to minimize such pretensions which cause fragmentation and decay." The synodal assembly applauded.[1]

But the applause was hollow. The spirit of classical Reform was already in retreat in the congregations or at least in the lives of their members. The Synod, in its convocation and its resolutions, officially reinforced the position of the Adlers, Geigers, and Lazaruses—to no avail. The rationale, if not the spirit, of Holdheim was becoming pervasive. In Europe it did not gain control of the Liberal institutions, but in America its ascendency was complete.

Holdheim's position was in fact fundamentally different from most of his confreres'. In his discussion on the Sabbath he stated that while he basically agreed with the definition of the biblical concept of the Sabbath as put forward by the Conference Committee, he had to disagree with its reasoning and therefore was forced to draw different conclusions. His philosophy was encapsulated at once in his thesis: "In order to determine more succinctly what Sabbath rest meant in the Bible and in order to learn what its significance may be for the present, *we must find the original idea of the Sabbath which Mosaism held;* then we must investigate its formulation by subsequent historical developments in Judaism and from this judge for ourselves how far the latter agree with the religious understanding of our time." [2]

Holdheim's opponents had held that biblical *and* post-biblical Judaism *together* were a valid foundation for determining the philosophy and actions of a contemporary Jew. Holdheim on the other hand proposed a radically different approach: he agreed to the validity and authority of biblical halacha, but reserved the right to judge all post-biblical Judaism in the light of contemporary values. It was in effect a Karaitic view, but with one difference. The Karaites were nomists; they believed in and were willing to observe most rigorously the legal precepts of the Pentateuch. Holdheim and his followers were willing to listen to talmudic discussions (Holdheim, being a learned man, was rather good at it), which was more than the Karaites were ready to do; but while Holdheim too harked back to the biblical writings, he had at bottom no taste for Karaitic legalistic observance. He and his followers appeared in principle as biblical purists, but they were eclectic in their practice. They were aiming to uphold "the spirit of Torah" rather than follow its every law. In that sense the Holdheim reformers might be called noumenists rather than nomists of the Karaite stripe.

But even where the Holdheim faction was serious in pledging allegiance to the Torah they were building on shifting sands. Solomon Freehof once phrased this aspect most memorably:

> With our early shouts of independence, when we slammed the door and walked out, we thought that for the purpose of the true Jewish religion the Bible and the Prophets, especially the Prophets, would be quite sufficient. Little did we know then that the progress of biblical science would take even that away from us as a sure and reliable religious foundation. But aside from the insufficiency of the fragmentized Bible, we are coming to see that we cannot hope for an integrated religious personality if we are permanently alienated from 1500 years of the supreme Jewish intellectual effort. I do not mean that we are alienated from the entire rabbinic literature. We have always used the Haggadah and the Midrash. But the real in-

tellectuality of our people, their real brilliance, their full sounding of the depths of human ability to think and to reason, is in the Halacha.[3]

Freehof's analysis is in fact an admission that the ship of Jewish destinies, steered by Holdheim and his disciples, has run aground. The absence of halacha from which the Reform movement is suffering today is the consequence of its early and essentially empty bibliolatry.

We are all the heirs of this radicalism. Its spirit pervaded the Pittsburgh Platform. The movement had come a long way since the days when the young Einhorn had rendered his halachic judgment in the Geiger-Tiktin matter.[4] So have we all.

To quote Freehof again: "The time is at hand when we should attempt to rediscover our inherent kinship with the Jewish legal system. Such an attempt at new harmony requires special justification, since it is precisely the old legal systems against which we as a movement have most vehemently fought." [5] For in a sense we are still fighting the battle, even though our heart no longer is in it. The intransigence of Orthodoxy, especially in Israel but also increasingly in the United States and Canada, has nettled our not-so-dormant anti-nomistic impulses. We properly and prudently shy away from what has been called the "halachic mentality." [6] Also, the failure of the Conservative movement to define its own position with regard to halacha and the principles of historical Judaism—first broadly enunciated by Zacharias Frankel at the Frankfort Conference in 1845—has prevented us from using a ready yardstick with which to measure our own progress.

Yet somehow the revitalization of halacha in Reform terms seems especially pressing today. Perhaps this is the case because our generation went through the Holocaust and saw its effect upon Jewish life—a temporary re-intensification of loyalty and a consequent growth of Jewish institutions—and now has also come to see that the effect is not lasting, that loyalties are waning once again, and that a new basis must be found for that which halacha always was and always will be at heart: a way which tells the Jew what he must do. For Judaism implies the need for such a way, that is to say, some form of halacha. "There is no Judaism without it." [7]

What is it then that Reform Jews must do in our time?

III

There have been several Reform "platforms" which contain general principles in semi-creedal form, and there have been many
expressions by leaders of Reform favoring the creation of a code
or guide which would remedy the breach which the movement
has suffered. Leopold Stein of Frankfort, Germany, was the first
of the creators of a Liberal guide and he has had a number of
successors.[8] To these official platforms and individual guides one
must add the responsa which the Central Conference of American
Rabbis has issued and which constitute a fair body of Reform
halacha. But despite their often great erudition, there seems to be
no clear basis on which they were issued. One seeks in vain for
a common ground on which Jacob Zvi Lauterbach and Israel
Bettan stood, and even the redoubtable Kaufmann Kohler frequently gave us merely his own opinion, leaving us on some
occasions with the suggestion that in his scholarship he had
surveyed the field and then, much like Maimonides, had come
to his present opinion.[9]

Solomon B. Freehof, Reform's most significant searcher after
halachic foundations, is a special case. His contributions lie both
in the works that bear his name and also in the *teshuvot* which he
has issued in the name of the Conference. Yet with all his reference to, and insistence on, the importance of Jewish tradition,
Freehof ends by calling it merely *advisory*. This may indeed be
the farthest he could go, but it gives even the most careful student
a shaky foundation for decision and ultimately leaves it to the
individual Reform Jew to do "that which is right in his own eyes."
In the introduction to his most important work, the two-volume
Reform Jewish Practice, Freehof specifically states that "it is not
the purpose of this book to be, even in the humblest way, a
modern Shulhan Arukh. It does not aim to lay down the norm
of practice except in two or three disputed situations where some
preference must be made. Its chief purpose is to describe present
day Reform Jewish practices and the traditional rabbinic laws
from which they are derived." [10]

But others would go further. Chief amongst these are Frederic
A. Doppelt and David Polish, who so far have provided the only
attempt to create a *systematic* basis for Reform halacha. They

were not satisfied with listing or even demanding certain Jewish practices or describing their rabbinic background as others have done with much scholarship.[11] In the introduction to their small volume, *A Guide for Reform Jews,* they analyze the nature of halacha in the context of Reform and come to the conclusion that Reform Jewish practice must be restructured on the basis of three distinctive levels.

The first is that of *mitzvah* which may be called the essential or principle. *Mitzvah* is not ritual and neither is it primarily related to the moral character of God or His ethical demands. Rather, *mitzvot* are related "to historic experiences in which the Jewish people came in contact with His moral nature and came to grasp with His ethical will. They are to be obeyed, not because they are divine fiats, but because something happened between God and Israel; and the self-same something in history continues to happen in every age and every land." The *mitzvah* of circumcision is an example of this category, as is the *mitzvah* of eating matzah on Pesach. "Without *mitzvot* there simply is no Judaism as a unique spiritual force in the world." [12]

The second level is occupied by what the authors call halachot in the narrower sense. "The makers of the halacha were concerned with the extension of *mitzvot* into concrete life situations; and without halacha *mitzvot* remain extended in the atmosphere hovering like souls disembodied and there remains only an emaciated and emasculated Judaism which cannot long abide." Thus, out of the *mitzvah* of circumcision arises the halachot regarding the time and the method of performing the *mitzvah.* Out of the *mitzvah* of the Passover matzah arises the halachot of the Seder.

The third level is occupied by *minhagim,* "folk customs and folk ways which have their source in the creative activity of the people themselves and not directly in any deliberative and organized body. They flow not so much from the mainstream of *mitzvot* as around and about them. They are therefore subsidiary to them. In different parts of the world and in different periods of Jewish history there emerge from among the masses of the Jewish people certain group rites and group manners—often no more than adaptations from popular customs prevalent in the social, cultural environment surrounding them—which attach themselves to certain *mitzvot* and *halachot.* In the course of time, by the sheer weight of tradition and pressure of popular appeal, these *minha-*

gim dig deep roots in Jewish life and rise to the plane of regular observances.' [13] Thus out of the *mitzvah* of circumcision arose the *minhag* of appointing a godfather.

While the Doppelt-Polish analysis was not designed to explore the full range of the halachic problem, it nonetheless is distinguished by the fact that it resolutely returns to what may be properly termed the classical period of Reform, setting up norms for present-day life while at the same time maintaining a meaningful link with our past.

IV

When the basis of traditional halacha is examined, it becomes at once evident that two of its major premises are no longer held by Reform Jews. One is that the traditional ways of Judaism have their origin in God, and the second is that the tradition which has developed the human expressions of God's will is authoritative. Opposed to these premises has from the very beginning stood the Reform belief that, whatever divine incursion halacha may *represent,* in its immediate expression it *is* but another aspect of human development, and that its force lies in this developmental or historic (Freehof would say, advisory) capacity which can instruct but does not necessarily compel the contemporary Jew.

The traditional trilogy of "God, Israel, and Torah" is no longer operative as a Liberal consensus. As for Torah, the early Liberals excluded from it the oral law, and the latter-day Liberals, because of eclecticism abetted by biblical criticism, reduced Torah to a symbolic accoutrement of the service and little else. As for God, Reform Jews continue to render lip service to His existence but generally deny Him any compelling force when it comes to moral or practical commandments. These latter have been further reduced by relativism and by the general inability of our movement to translate "the demand of God" into more than a philosopher's concept. In addition, it is probably safe to say that an increasing number of Reform Jews do not believe in God at all; many of them will not deny the possibility of His existence, but they simply will refuse to take Him seriously as a force influencing or compelling their own existence. I have no statistics to bear me out, but I would not be surprised to find that more than fifty per cent of all Reform Jews may be classified as deists, if not as outright agnostics or even atheists. For this reason, much as I regret it, it becomes essential to devise a basis for halacha which includes this important segment of Jewry (for the phenomenon is by no means restricted to Reform).

Of the trilogy, therefore, only Israel remains as an effectively operative element in halachic formulation. Mordecai M. Kaplan recognized this long ago when he suggested that the only way in which Judaism could persist in the modern world was by stressing the survival values of the Jewish people. A large portion of Jews, inside and outside of Reform, are in this respect philosophical Reconstructionists, whether or not they know the term. But again, not all of them are, and a Liberal recapturing of halacha must take into consideration that the range of belief or nonbelief is in fact much wider than Reconstructionist theology would allow.

This essay is not the place to examine the possible foundations of Liberal theology. One needs but to stress that such foundations must be fairly broad. They must include Israel and deal with the God of Israel, the question of Jewish survival and Jewish purpose, and they must relate all of these to the possibility and need of worship. They must speak of man and his relation to the world, to nature, and other human beings, that is, man in his relational aspects which again include his wrestling with God or His absence. Finally, they must deal with the self and again search out the deepest meanings of one's own existence, the nature of truth, of faith, of prayer, of saying yes to being.

In other words, in the traditional trilogy "God, Israel, and Torah," neither God nor Torah can be considered as universally commanding sources for Reform halacha. Rather, the trilogy must be supplanted by a spectrum that ranges from Israel to man to self, a spectrum in which the light of God may or may not be perceived by the individual, but where all who count themselves as part of this fellowship agree that, through Israel, individual as well as human uniqueness is validated in a special way and that whatever Judaism has to say must speak to and of and through this uniqueness.

The grounding of Reform halacha must therefore lie both in history and in the present. Its compulsion may arise, for some, from the demanding presence of God, while, for others, it will arise from what they perceive to be the unique destiny of Israel. "The question of the hour is this: to determine what are the spirit and the teaching, the doctrines and the duties of life peculiar to Judaism and inherent in it." Geiger said that; it still applies.[14]

But whatever Reform halacha will be, it will not be *law* in the old sense. The talmudic definition is crystal clear. The biblical phrase, "All the laws which the Lord has spoken" (Lev. 10:11), is its proof text, and the rabbinic conclusion is: "'which the Lord has spoken'—that is halacha." [15] From the revelation at Sinai and the law of Torah to the law represented by halacha runs a straight line. But with the demise of the operational quality of Torah law in our liberal world, halacha as *law* has become a skeletal term.

Still we salvage the word, as do most writers on the subject, because as always we are hesitant to break the thread of tradition. Indeed, little more than terminology remains—but it remains only among the scholars, for the bulk of Reform Jews have never heard of halacha. Reform rabbis do not use this term, mainly because halacha as law would have no relation to the reality of congregational life. One might seriously consider therefore whether another term—such as *halicha*—would not describe more adequately the revalidation of obligation for liberal Jews. If halacha can be called "practice-become-law," then *halicha* may be called "practice-by-consent."

The word *halicha* has biblical and talmudic standing [16] and in modern Hebrew denotes, among other things, behavior and usage —but of stronger connotative value than *minhag*. Halacha denotes the compelling function of formal tradition; *halicha* speaks of the compelling nature of common practice made operative by personal consent. One may not depart from halacha; one may depart from *halicha*. Halacha is effective without personal commitment, *halicha* is not.

If nonetheless, in this essay, I have maintained the term halacha, it is done for the sake of maintaining a link with prevailing custom and discussion. But it should be kept in mind that in a liberal sense *halicha* is in effect the substance of Reform halacha.

V

Where can we start? We start from where we are. It will become at once apparent that the *sense* of *mitzvah* is still strongly alive, although it is not necessarily grounded in theology. Most Reform Jews would give assent to the proposition that they *must do some-*

thing to remain Jews, that they have an obligation to Israel as a historic continuum, and that Judaism had and continues to have a purpose in this world, a purpose that may or may not be related to the will of God. The Jew placing himself consciously into the vortex of this life force becomes a part of its obligatory structure. In this sense circumcision remains a *mitzvah* as do Jewish education, *tzedakah,* social justice, the support of Jews in every part of the world, the existence of the synagogue, the institution of basic holy days. These *mitzvot* are principles, guidelines experienced as compelling life forces. How they are to be translated is, as Doppelt and Polish properly point out, the function of halachot and *minhagim.*

However, a restatement of these halachot—essential as it is— can at present be little more than an important scholarly exercise and, hopefully, an educative device. For on the whole, halachot are only weakly operative and lack the element of obligation. On the other hand, *minhag* has greater compelling force than was assigned to it by Doppelt and Polish. Precisely because the sense of peoplehood and community is much alive amongst Reform Jews and in many instances fills the larger area of their Jewish consciousness, *minhag* must become the channel through which halachot can be redeveloped.

Minhag is that which Jews "customarily" do. Technically it was and still is a local refinement or idiosyncrasy, often nebulous in origin and questionable in value or taste. But people did it and do it this way and that has been enough to entrench the custom as near-law in the community. In the light of our present situation, *minhag* is of crucial importance. For it is what Reform Jews *actually do* that must be the starting point for a practical program of reestablishing a sense of Reform halacha.

In other words, a program of halachic re-formation has both a philosophic and a pragmatic aspect: It must bring to the Reform Jew the urgency of *mitzvah* as a demanding principle of living Jewishly and develop the readiness to make commitments for such principles; and it must select those old and new *minhagim* which may be considered authentic Jewish practice, and boldly raise them to the status of halachot. ("Not only *are* you doing this, you *ought* in fact to be doing it.") *Mitzvah* is the theoretical, *minhag* the practical, lead-in to Reform halacha: *Minhag hu halichah la-mitzvah.*

We have but a few instances which indicate that Reform Jews still have a sense for halachot. They do not get married or buried on the Sabbath, for instance. I do not believe that the observance of such halachot is more than rudimentary and that practically speaking they might not be better classified as strong exponents of workable *minhagim*. *What we are left with is a recognition that Reform Jews do certain things in a certain way*—these are the *minhagim* of Reform. In classical terms their origin may indeed be *minhag* or it may be halacha in the wider sense: *hoq, mishpat, mitzvah,* or *din*—it does not matter. What does matter is that here we have a concrete basis for beginning. What is needed now is to establish within the movement the sense that *minhag* qua *minhag* is an ultimately meaningless form of survivalism, that rather *minhag* must be related in its essential quality to *mitzvah*. *The Reform Jew must again be made to feel that what he does is, at least in part, what he ought to do.* The "ought" is the *mitzvah*.

As we invest various *minhagim* (not all, to be sure) with the sense of *mitzvah* we will begin to reestablish a viable body of halachot. This must be the goal of all efforts in this direction. All guides which have been proposed so far are therefore valuable contributions, but they must base themselves not only on viable goals, but also on viable foundations. They must recognize that the sense for the ought needs yet to be developed. They must recognize that Reform cannot accept the old principle that all *mitzvot* are the same, that there is no essential distinction between the small and large *mitzvot,* and they must, most important of all, accept the fundamental principle of Liberalism: that the individual will approach this body of *mitzvot* and *minhagim* in the spirit of freedom and choice. Traditionally Israel started with *harut*— the commandment engraved upon the Tablets—which then became freedom. The Reform Jew starts with *herut*—the freedom to decide what will be *harut*—engraved upon the personal Tablets of his life. A guide for *mitzvot* and *minhagim* and the development of halachot therefore becomes an opportunity rather than a code—it becomes *halicha,* truly a way, a going, and thereby habituation and obligation.

Before the Reform movement can proceed to the creation of a guide it must engage its membership in a reeducation of *mitzvah* and *minhag,* with a hope that a sense of and for Reform halacha may thereby be developed. I have no doubt that the members of the Reform movement are ready for this, for there is a vague apprehension amongst Reform Jews that Liberalism is heading into a cul-de-sac, that its present direction spells noble idealism, but ultimate loss of identity and hence dissolution. Perhaps here the people are ahead of the rabbis.

Instead of merely studying the Bible and having interminable classes on sociology, psychology, and history, every Reform rabbi must now examine with his people the possibility of Reform halacha. I believe that the Reform movement by doing this can make an invaluable contribution to the existence of the Jewish people as a whole, for while I have in this essay been strongly critical of Reform I have not thereby excluded the possibility of equally strong criticism of non-Reform movements. The vital and experimental qualities which in its best periods have distinguished Reform must now be brought to bear upon this problem. At the beginning must stand a recognition of the seriousness of our present situation.

We will need a guide, but before we can come to its creation we must establish the foundations on which a guide will be effected. The enormous interest elicited by the study of the Sabbath and the presentation of its opportunities, as well as the creation of a liberal commentary on the Torah—these are more than straws in the wind. It may be well for rabbis to learn again to trust the people as Judah Ha-Nassi advised long ago.

Yet the responsibility falls squarely upon the rabbis. They have largely looked away and occupied themselves with questions and activities which seemed more immediately amenable to demonstrable success. But the empty pews which confront the rabbi Sabbath after Sabbath should by now be a telling reminder that none of his lectures, however properly conceived or constructed, and no gimmickry or advertisement, will repair the breach. People will return to the Synagogue either when they feel they need it because of external or internal calamity, or when they have rediscovered their sense of obligation. Since we are not purveyors of calamity, we are left with the task of reestablishing a sense of obligation. It would be well for Reform rabbis to eschew many of the things which they now do, for this one purpose: to build a bridge from *minhag* to *mitzvah*. Nothing less will do and little more will be required. *Amar Rabbi Eleazar: Sheluhe mitzvah enan nezukin lo be-halichatan ve-lo be-haziratan.*[17]

It is probably true that not all Reform Jews nor certainly all Reform rabbis will be ready or willing to undertake this task. They will continue to emphasize what they choose to call the "non-ritualistic" aspects of Reform: its prophetic stance, its communal verve, its commitment to social justice. Far be it from me to denigrate these high intentions. We need them, they are part of our movement, they have given it its special flavor. But I must repeat that the flags of social justice and prophetic concern can fly only when held up by an army that marches out of a sense of obligation and destiny. Otherwise there will be no staffs to hold the flags and no Jews to carry them.

Ideals are conceived when the soul engages in generous thought, but they are executed through the everyday. The Jew who believes in Jewish education must ultimately proceed to the bothersome detail of going to class or reading a book or listening to a lecture—in other words, to the time-consuming, hour-absorbing process of study. Without this, "education" is merely a meaningless (and, worse, deluding) slogan, and of these we have enough. When we come face to face with this and tell our members the truth, we may have smaller congregations—but better ones. We will have more *havurot* and perhaps smaller buildings, we will have more self-motivation and less of the prevalence of vicarious exercise of Judaism through professional expertise. We will then, *mirabile dictu*, have congregations which will ask for more than the payment of dues, congregations that will be able to tell their members that Judaism demands more than the transmission of dollars. A parent who registers his child in religious school will not be able to sublimate his own obligation by simply sending his child, for along with his child's registration there will be a demand made on him as well. He too must study—else his child cannot be educated in our school. It is to these halachot that Reform Judaism can address itself better than any other movement, for it is in this bold experimentation that we will find the building materials for tomorrow's Judaism.

The *sense* of *mitzvah* exists, and it must be identified as *mitzvah*. *Minhag* is a viable force everywhere in Jewish life and no less in Reform Judaism. Now to make *mitzvah* more pervasive, to strengthen the strands between it and *minhag* and thereby to develop the reality of halachot in the lives of our people—this is the next task to which Reform Jewish leadership must address itself. We must say, as did the people in a similar time of crisis and chaos: *Ve-he'emadnu alenu mitzvot,* "And we voluntarily assumed *mitzvot* for ourselves." [18]

If we fail to attempt this, there may be no further tasks; if we begin, we will once more see the vision of the founders of Reform, a vision that was blurred for seventy-five years. Reform's return to the "bridge of *halicha*" can become Reform's decisive turning to a meaningful future.

NOTES

1. *Verhandlungen der ersten israelitischen Synode zu Leipzig* (Berlin: 1869), p. 44.

2. *Protokolle der dritten Versammlung deutscher Rabbiner . . . 1846* (Breslau: 1847), p. 59. For a survey of the Sabbath discussion at that conference see W. Gunther Plaut, *The Rise of Reform Judaism* (New York: WUPJ, 1963), pp. 185 ff.; *ibid,* pp. 90 ff., for a discussion of the synodal idea; *idem, The Growth of Reform Judaism* (New York: WUPJ, 1965), pp. 236 ff., for a discussion of Reform and halacha.

3. *Reform Judaism and the Jewish Tradition* (Tintner Memorial Lecture; New York: Association of Reform Rabbis, 1961).

4. Reproduced in part in *The Rise of Reform Judaism,* p. 119. See there also pp. 112 ff. for a discussion of "Authority and Tradition" among early reformers.

5. *Loc. cit.*

6. See the trenchant analysis of current Israeli orthodoxy by Jack J. Cohen, "The Religious Climate in Israel," *Reconstructionist,* XXXIII (No. 5 [April 28, 1967]), 7.

7. Eugene Mihaly, *loc. cit.,* p. 217. Note the great efforts Wise made for the creation of a synod which would establish Reform halacha; see James G. Heller, *Isaac M. Wise* (New York: UAHC, 1965), p. 572.

8. On the Pittsburgh Platform, see *The Growth of Reform Judaism,* p. 31; on the Columbus Platform, *ibid.,* p. 96; on the German guide lines, *ibid.,* p. 67.

Leopold Stein's Guide (1877) is reproduced in *The Rise of Reform Judaism,* pp. 260 ff. In America a number of individual guides have appeared; amongst them are: Abraham J. Feldman, *Reform Judaism* (New York: Behrman House, 1956); Frederic A. Doppelt and David Polish, *A Guide for Reform Jews* (New York: 1957). See also *A Guide to Jewish Ritual* (New York: Reconstructionist Press, 1962); Morrison D. Bial, *Liberal Judaism at Home* (Summit, N.J.: Temple Sinai, 1967). In Israel, Meir Ydit has published his ambitious *Moreh derekh linevukhe ha-dat* (Jerusalem: Merkaz la-yahadut ha-mitkademet, 1964).

The matter of a guide has been on the agenda of the Union of American Hebrew Congregations and has of late been frequently before the Central Conference of American Rabbis. See, e.g., *Yearbook;* LXV (1955), 124; LXVI (1956), 239; LXIX (1959), 263.

The subject of Reform halacha has been treated often in recent years. See, e.g., these references in the *Yearbook*: LVI (1946), p. 288 (Solomon B. Freehof); LXIV (1954), p. 214 (Eugene Mihaly); LXVIII (1958), p. 246 (Alexander Guttman); LXIX (1959), p. 212 (Jakob J. Petuchowski). Mention should also be made of Jacob Z. Lauterbach's famous "The Ethics of the Halakhah" (*Rabbinic Essays*, Cincinnati: HUC, 1951, p. 262), and of Emil L. Fackenheim's "The Dilemma of Liberal Judaism" (*Commentary*, XXX [No. 4, October 1960], 301).

9. To know Kohler's attitude toward the whole problem, one should read his essay, "The Four Ells of the Halakhah," *Hebrew Union College Annual*, I (1924), 8.

10. S. B. Freehof, *Reform Jewish Practice*, I, 15 (Cincinnati: Hebrew Union College, 1944; vol. II, 1952); see also his *Reform Responsa* (1960) and *Recent Reform Responsa* (1963).

11. Note, e.g., that Ydit in his detailed and documented guide (see above, note 8) merely refers to the passage in Lev. 18:5 ("You shall keep My laws and My norms, by the pursuit of which man shall live: I am the Lord") and the discussion in *Yoma* 88a: man is to *live* by God's law and not to die by it. Hence the law must allow the Jew to be alive to his world and time. The author does not give any further theoretical foundation for his decisions and suggestions. Bial's book contains a brief introduction, "The Criteria of Reform Jewish Practice." He ends by stating that the final authority for deciding what to do and what not to do is the individual himself, "a sense of *K'dusha*, of holiness, if truly meaningful" (p. 6). Beyond this, no other foundations are offered for the Reform practices which the book describes or suggests in considerable detail, incidentally without ascribing to them the term Reform halacha.

12. Doppelt and Polish, pp. 36-41.

13. *Ibid.*, pp. 44-45.

14. Quoted by Herbert Waller, *CCAR Yearbook*, LXVI (1956), 252.

15. Ker. 13b.

16. E.g., Neh. 2:6; Prov. 31:27; Hab. 3:6 (*halikhot olam*, the ways of old); Meg. 28b.

17. Pes. 8b. *Halikhah* is of course here used in a different sense.

18. Neh. 10:33.

PROBLEMS OF REFORM HALACHA

Jakob J. Petuchowski

I

Recent attempts to foster ceremonial practice in the ranks of American Reform Judaism, or even to take seriously such concepts as *mitzvah* and halacha, may appear to many Reform Jews as a contradiction in terms. Historically, Reform Judaism has committed itself to certain theological propositions, involving the concept of revelation and the role of science, which would make the acceptance of *any* form of halacha something of a revolution (not to say retrogression), rather than an evolutionary development of the status quo in Reform Judaism. Difficult as the problem of a Reform halacha is, it is yet further complicated by a number of fallacies included, or implied, in many a formulation of the Reform position. In clearing the ground for a more fruitful discussion of our topic, it will, therefore, be our first task to analyze some of these fallacies.

This paper was published in somewhat different form in *Judaism*, Fall 1958. It is reprinted by permission.

The "fallacy of primitivism" is, no doubt, the most common of this kind. According to E. S. Brightman, this fallacy is committed by the person who is so obsessed with beginnings that he supposes the first stage of the development of any process to reveal what the process really is.[1] Suppose, for example, that a Reform temple is appealing for funds in order to erect a new building. Suppose, furthermore, that one of the members, on receiving a copy of the appeal, argues in the following manner: "Making contributions toward the erection of a sanctuary is something described in Exodus 25. It is all bound up with the priestly element in religion, which is antithetical to the prophetic faith. Reform Judaism is prophetic Judaism, and, in the name of prophetic Reform Judaism, I refuse to contribute to the building fund."

The members of the board of trustees and the rabbi will fail to be impressed by the cogency of this argument. Nor, we may safely assume, is this argument likely to be presented by our hypothetical member. Nevertheless, this hypothetical member, in the company of his board and his rabbi, may very easily justify his disregard of the traditional dietary laws by an argument of analogous, if not identical, structure. "The dietary laws," we can hear him say, "are an aspect of priestly religion. They are bound up with the Levitical concept of holiness—if they do not indeed go back to even more primitive notions of totem and taboo. Such being the case, our Reform convictions militate against the observance of such food taboos."

By and large, this is the type of argument used to defend disregard of any traditional Jewish law. Prima facie, the people who object to the dietary laws may, of course, have a case. The question remains, however, whether the *methodology* is right. Are we really justified in doing away with *any* observance merely because its primitive origin has been found and demonstrated? If so, then the member withholding his contribution to the building fund is fully vindicated. But, translated into such terms, the "fallacy of primitivism" will be recognized for the methodological error which it really is.

The "fallacy of primitivism" is so deeply entrenched in Reform Jewish thinking because of the historical relationship between Reform Judaism and the scientific study of Jewish sources. It will be recalled that Leopold Zunz wrote his *Gottesdienstliche Vortraege* in order to justify an innovation (i.e., the German sermon) which the Reformers had already made. In this instance, *Wissenschaft* in the service of a *constructive reform* can hardly be held responsible for the "fallacy of primitivism." On the contrary, the underlying idea was rather that the primitive represented the pristine purity of Judaism, that only the later accretions had soiled the genuine article. It was, therefore, the task of Reform Judaism —as of any other "reformation"—to revert to the purity and genuineness of the original.

The next step, however, was to employ *Wissenschaft* in the service of a *destructive reform,* of a reform that had as little use for the "primitive" as it did for the status quo. The theory of evolution had made it impossible to look for the ideal in the past. The primitive and the ideal were now considered as antithetical. Evolution meant progress away from the primitive, and toward the ideal! The past can merely illustrate for us the operation of the laws of evolution. It can never serve as the model on which we are to pattern ourselves. To demonstrate this was the lifework of Abraham Geiger. He understood *Wissenschaft* in terms of historical criticism, and regarded its results as a justification for his program of abolitions.[2]

The Reform movement, as a whole, followed in the footsteps of Geiger. Henceforth, the conclusions reached in the scientific study of Rabbinic sources were understood as a justification for the disregard of talmudic law, while the Higher Criticism of the Bible was taken as a dispensation from the observance of biblical law—at any rate, in its so-called ritual and ceremonial aspects.

In a certain sense, of course, the results of critical investigations into origins have never been ignored in the history of halacha. A glimpse of what later generations were to call "religious evolution" was caught by the rabbis when they commented on the fact that the Deuteronomic law prohibits the erection of a sacred pillar (*mazzebah*), even though the Patriarch Jacob, to take but one example, did not incur the slightest condemnation for having done just this (Genesis 28:18). The rabbinic comment on this discrepancy was that the *mazzebah* was *comme il faut* for the Patriarchs but unacceptable in the case of later generations.[3]

But for the rabbis this was primarily a case of reconciling two apparently contradictory statements of Scripture. Where a real historical approach was used in traditional Judaism, it led to quite different results. Well known is Maimonides' treatment of the

origin of the biblical sacrificial system.[4] Not so well known is
the fact that Maimonides was merely elaborating a view already
expressed in the Midrash[5] that the sacrificial system was a
"concession" on the part of God to Israel. What is often completely disregarded is the very significant fact that Maimonides
devotes two whole books of the fourteen books in his *Mishneh
Torah* to the sacrificial service.[6] Now, Maimonides did not write
his code as a contribution to archaeology. If he includes legislation not relevant to his particular time, he does so because, as
Zeitlin has shown, he envisages his *Mishneh Torah* as the "constitution" of the messianic state. In other words, even though Maimonides exercises his critical faculty in investigating the origin of
the Hebrew sacrificial system (and of other observances, besides),
he does not commit the "fallacy of primitivism." His knowledge of
the origin does not have as a consequence his rejection of the
particular institution. In fact, he looked forward to its restoration.

Maimonides could do nothing else because, in addition to his
knowledge of primitive origins, he also knew that the sacrifices
were a part of the Torah. And the Torah, for him, was divine
revelation. Unless, therefore, God indicates that this particular
part of the revelation is no longer valid—which to Maimonides
would have seemed unlikely—the sacrifices must be considered
part of the divine will, and performed as soon as circumstances
permit. Officially, this is still the Orthodox position. The different
position of Geiger and of subsequent Reform Judaism is supposed
to find its justification in the role ascribed to the Higher Criticism
of the Bible and to its conclusions.

It is generally held in Reform circles that the Higher Criticism
has irrevocably destroyed the authority of the Pentateuch. The Jew
in the past held that the Five Books of Moses were dictated by
God to Moses. Modern scholarship is said to prove that this could
not have been so, that, on the contrary, the Torah is a compilation
of documents composed during several centuries.

If these premises are accepted, we can draw from them the
logical conclusion that the Jew in the past was mistaken in his
view about the authorship of the Pentateuch. What does *not* follow logically from the findings of the Higher Criticism is the
widespread notion that, because Moses did not write the Torah, it
can no longer be the authoritative rule of Jewish life.

Let us be clear about this: the Jew in the past lived by the dictates of the Torah, not because Moses had written it down (although he was firmly convinced of this), but because the Torah was divine revelation, because God had made known His will in its pages. The information that it was not Moses, but J, E, P, and D, who wrote the Torah merely shows—if the claim can be fully substantiated—that the Jew in the past was not too familiar with the literary history of his own people. It does *not* necessitate the conclusion that God could not have made use of J, E, P, and D in the same way in which, at one time, it was thought (mistakenly, it is now said) He had made use of Moses.

Again, the question of whether or not a certain ritual is a divine commandment cannot be settled with a reference to archeological findings pointing to a non-Israelite or pre-Israelite provenance of the particular rite under discussion. No Reform Jew would insist that the prohibition of murder is *not* a commandment of the God of Israel—merely because murder is also discountenanced in the Egyptian *Book of the Dead*. Yet the Reform Jew's disregard of the strict laws of *hametz* and matzah on the Festival of Passover will often be rationalized by a reference to archeological findings which prove the eating of matzah to have been part of a pre-Israelite nature festival in the land of Canaan. This is an interesting piece of information, but it can hardly rule out the possibility, on logical grounds, that God used this pre-Israelite raw material and incorporated it in His Torah. Does every worthwhile religious ordinance *have* to be a *creatio ex nihilo?*

After all, according to the view of the Higher Critics, and of Reform's own Julian Morgenstern in particular, each "code" now contained in the Pentateuch was accepted at a specific historical occasion by the people as a whole, in a solemn covenant. Accepted as what? As the definite demands which the covenant deity made upon his partners in the covenant. If we follow this line of reasoning to its logical conclusion, we must arrive at a point in Jewish history when the Pentateuch as a whole (in the form in which it left the hands of its last redactor) was accepted as divine revelation by the people. This would be the "canonization" of the Torah. Tradition ascribes this "canonization" of the complete Pentateuch to the time of Moses. Modern scholarship would set the date at about 400 B.C.E.—that is, a good 700 or 800 years *after* the time of Moses. Inasmuch as the findings of modern scholarship clash with the traditional notion, it is very much a question of temperament and training as to which of the two dates a modern Jew will ultimately accept. But, as we shall endeavor to show, the question of dating the Pentateuch has very little to do with the authoritative or non-authoritative character of that book.

For it is not the province of literary criticism to declare what is, and what is not, divine revelation. If, on philosophical grounds, I deny the very possibility of revelation, I shall refuse to regard the Torah as "revealed" even if a thousand Higher Critics ultimately come around to the view that the Five Books of Moses could not possibly have been written any later than the time of Moses. But if, on the other hand, I am convinced that God can, and does, reveal Himself to man, then it makes very little difference whether the documents purporting to contain this revelation are a few hundred years more or less recent than was believed to be the case in my grandfather's time.

Inasmuch, therefore, as Reform's lack of traditional Jewish practice is justified, or, better, rationalized, in terms of primitive origins, *Wissenschaft,* and the Higher Criticism of the Bible, we have seen that Reform is moving in the realm of fallacies. While the modern disciplines may radically alter our picture of early Jewish history, they cannot be considered competent to determine whether or not a given tradition is part of divine revelation—a commandment (*mitzvah*) which is binding (halacha) on all generations of Israel. This is a theological, rather than an archeological or historical, problem and must be dealt with on a different level altogether.

II

Unencumbered by the "fallacies" which have so often been the stock-in-trade of Reform apologetics and polemics, we may now address ourselves to the "Problems of Reform Halacha" in terms of the Reform concept of revelation. This juxtaposition must be stressed in view of the fact that attempts are being made—notably in some Conservative circles—to deal with the problem of halacha quite apart from the theological problem of revelation. Where this is done with logical consistency it leads—as it does in Reconstructionism—to an affirmation of the *content* of halacha and, at the same time, to a transmutation of halacha into "folkways." This enables the humanist to observe the dietary laws with a clear conscience, but it also involves a frank and honest breach with the halachic tradition in Judaism.

Historically speaking, halacha was the norm of Jewish life—either found in the Scriptures or deduced from them by a universally accepted system of hermeneutics. Where, as in the case of the Karaites, the hermeneutics or the authority of the interpreters was rejected, an attempt was made to base Jewish practice on the literal meaning of the Bible. But both Rabbanite and Karaite Jews submitted to their respective versions of Jewish law, because they believed that in observing it they were fulfilling the will of God, and that this will was expressed—directly or indirectly—in the pages of the Hebrew Bible.

No doubt, Jews always enjoyed and derived aesthetic pleasure from such rites as, for example, the kindling of the Sabbath lights. But these aesthetic effects were mere by-products of an act primarily performed in obedience to God's will (*vetzivanu lehadlik ner shel shabbath*). Judaism was, as G. F. Moore called it, "revealed religion," and where belief in "revelation" was given up, as the case histories of Uriel da Costa and Spinoza show, the practice of the totality of Judaism could no longer be maintained.

What, then, has been the relation of Reform Judaism to this traditional concept of "revelation"? The very first Reformers, it would seem, were blissfully unaware of this whole problem. They were eager to prove that their departure from the traditional liturgy and their innovation of instrumental music were in perfect harmony with the Talmud itself! [7] When it was ultimately realized that Reform did mean a definite break with Rabbinic Judaism, Reform passed through a quasi-Karaite stage in which it was maintained that God's revelation is contained in the pages of Scripture alone, while the Talmud is a mere human invention of no binding character.[8] Again, there was no doubt that God had actually "revealed" Himself. Where strict observance of the Mosaic Code clashed with the practical demands of life, a compromise might be reached by either restricting the actual "revelation" to the Decalogue, with the rest of the Torah forming its "commentary" (the ultimate position of Isaac M. Wise), or by stressing the theocratic setup of the ancient Hebrew commonwealth, with the corollary that the purely "national" and "political" aspects of the Torah have lost their validity with the passing of the Jewish state (Holdheim).

Article 3 of the Pittsburgh Platform (1885) sums up this position by saying: "We recognize in the Mosaic legislation a system of training the Jewish people for its mission during its national life in Palestine, and today accept as binding only its moral laws, and maintain only such ceremonies as elevate and sanctify our lives, but reject all such as are not adapted to the views and habits of modern civilization."

But Article 2 of that same Platform already contained the germ of an idea which could transcend Holdheim's and Wise's simple belief in "revelation." It reads in part: "We recognize in the Bible the record of the consecration of the Jewish people to its mission as the priest of God, and value it as the most potent instrument of religious and moral instruction." An Isaac M. Wise, believing in the Sinaitic revelation of the Decalogue, could, of course, subscribe to this statement. But so, too, could those Reformers who did not believe in "revelation" at all. As "a record of the Jewish people's consecration to its mission," the Bible could conceivably be regarded as a purely human document. Even an all-out humanist could bring himself to subscribe to that. For man might reach for the divine, and consecrate himself to that task, without necessarily obtaining an authentic response.

But on either count halacha had become impossible. If only the moral laws of the Bible were valid, then the Jew was in no need of his own halacha. The law of the secular state took care of that. And if it sufficed for the rejection of a ceremony to demonstrate its not being "adapted to the views and habits of modern civilization," while the criterion of acceptability was its power to "elevate and sanctify our lives"—then the standard was much too subjective to permit of any crystallization of rules and regulations.

It is, of course, hard to imagine that the framers of the Pittsburgh Platform *really* believed that God was behind the so-called ceremonial law at *any* time. Otherwise, a certain amount of casuistry would have been inescapable. One just does not trifle with what one believes to be the Word of God. But, then, what was *God?* The Pittsburgh Reformers did not say. Thus the concept of "revelation" had to remain ambiguous, for the idea of commandment (*mitzvah*) implies a commander (*metzavveh*). Either one without the other is absurd.

Nor has official Reform Judaism ever clarified the matter. In the Columbus Platform of 1937, God was indeed defined as the One in Whom "all existence has its creative source and mankind its ideal of conduct." He is said to reveal Himself and that "not only in the majesty, beauty and orderliness of nature, but also in the vision and moral striving of the human spirit." Revelation is said to be "a continuous process, confined to no one group and to no one age. Yet the people of Israel, through its prophets and sages, achieved unique insight in the realm of religious truth."

The statement is vague enough to be acceptable even to those who happen to believe in a direct divine revelation. Yet it does not rule out that view of God which cannot conceive of Him as actually revealing Himself in the form of direct commandments. Of course, the Platform could not be more definite. Like all such undertakings, it represents a compromise between divergent views, and full justice cannot be done to any single one of them.

In marked contrast to the Pittsburgh Platform, however, the Columbus Platform is emphatic in its demand for "the preservation of the Sabbath, Festivals and Holy Days, the retention and development of such customs, symbols and ceremonies as possess inspirational value." However, the marked contrast to the earlier Platform is in the formulation rather than in content. We have here an emphasis on what the Reform Jew should do, rather than on what he should not do. But there is no attempt in the Columbus Platform to link the "customs, symbols, and ceremonies possessing inspirational value" with the concept of revelation and with the idea of a God who commands. Consequently, neither the Columbus Platform nor the Pittsburgh Platform can serve as the basis of a halachic development within Reform Judaism.

Thus, with all the "change of heart" that Reform Judaism has undergone in preparation for, and as a consequence of, the Columbus Platform, it is no nearer now than it was eighty years ago to a linkup with the halachic tradition of Judaism. An upsurge of interest in "ritual" and "ceremonies" there has undoubtedly been, and attempts have not been lacking to standardize Reform Jewish practice to conform to what may superficially appear as a Reform halacha. Symptomatic in this context is the recent attempt made by the National Federation of Temple Brotherhoods to determine statistically what is, and what is not, observed in Reform Jewish circles.

A little reflection will, however, show the unsuitability of this particular method to get anywhere near a concept of halacha.

Thus, the statistics indicate that there are actually more Reform Jews who have Christmas trees in their homes than Reform Jews who fully observe the traditional dietary laws. Are we to conclude from this that it might be Reform halacha to have a Christmas tree, while it is against Reform halacha to eat *kasher?* Or should we not be warned by this admittedly extreme example that no conclusions for the standardization of religious practice can be drawn from data furnished by a more or less de-Judaized generation? But even under ideal conditions, can we call that halacha which is practiced by the majority of the people? Does Judaism really equate *vox populi* with *vox Dei?*

Zacharias Frankel, in the last century, seemed to think so. Yet it would be safe to assert that, in this day and age, the leadership of Conservative Judaism holds to more exacting standards of Jewish practice than could be obtained from a general consensus of what the majority of Conservative Jews actually observe. One might suspect that the dietary laws would fare rather badly in the official platform of Conservative Judaism if their actual observance were taken as a criterion. The same would undoubtedly apply to the Sabbath. The Talmudic injunction, "Go and see what the people are doing!" [9] which is so often quoted in justification of such a statistical approach, is really irrelevant to the present state of affairs. In its original context it had references to certain minutiae of the law concerning which an individual rabbi lacked an authentic tradition, and concerning which he could trust the common people to have preserved the correct practice. It presupposes what we can no longer presuppose—that halacha as such is the norm of daily life which has penetrated all strata of society.

The endeavor to foster Jewish observance by a "sales appeal," in imitation of the marketing of cigarettes and soap ("Five hundred congregations from coast to coast can't be wrong!") is merely further proof of the fact that, judging only by the official statements of Reform doctrine, *there can be no halacha for Reform Judaism!* Where individual rabbis encourage "ceremonies," they do so either because they have Reconstructionist leanings and treasure "folkways," or because modern educational theories have opened their eyes to the necessity of audiovisual aids, or again, because they feel the need to lend a certain warmth and emotional appeal to an otherwise rather "cold" worship service. All these reasons and motivations are good for an *ad hoc* "ritualism."

But it will be conceded that we are dealing with "religious pageantry"—not with halacha.

The implications of this are far-reaching. It has to be borne in mind that—the drift of our discussion so far notwithstanding—halacha is not exclusively a matter of customs and ceremonies. What is often so blithely called "the moral law" is as much part of halacha in its traditional connotation as are, for example, the dietary laws. If there is no commanding God behind the one, on what grounds do we posit Him to be behind the other? And if God is said to reveal Himself in our conscience, but not in the codes of ritual law, then it would have to be proved that He actually reveals Himself more fully in the conscience of the Jew than in that of any other man. After all, one does not need Judaism solely for the preservation of the moral law. That law, as the rabbis maintain in their discussion of the Noahitic laws, antedates Judaism, and, as the deists tried to demonstrate, is by no means confined to peoples laying claim to revealed Scriptures. And what else is the meaning of the clause in the Columbus Platform that "Revelation is . . . confined to no one group and to no one age"?

It may well be that many Reform Jews view with favor this (backward) progress from Sinai to the elementary morality of the "Seven Laws of the Sons of Noah," whereas traditional Judaism knows of progress in the opposite direction. Paul, too, was fired by the thought of the pre-Sinaitic Patriarchs who were "saved" without the law, and, in this sense, the new dispensation he preached was a return to pristine simplicity. There is, therefore, no need for halacha in circles where Sinai is either deplored or rejected, and where Torah simply means respectability and good will.

But conceivably there may be Reform Jews whose concept of God does not exclude the likelihood of "revelation," and whose concept of history makes allowance for an actual "covenant" between God and their people. Such Reform Jews will not be satisfied with the vague formulations of the official platforms from which no bridges can lead into the realm of halacha. Reckoning with the possibility of both *mitzvah* and *metzavveh*, they will push their investigations further into the central core of Judaism, in order to find the solution to their "Problems of Reform Halacha."

III

Our discussion has now reached the point where halacha has been shown to be impossible unless it can be grounded in the very basis of religion—in the idea of God. What, then, do we mean by "God"? What, to enlarge the scope of the question, does Judaism mean by "God"? Is there a uniform God-concept among Jews of all ages? This last question can immediately be answered in the negative. Surely, the God-concept of Maimonides was not identical with some of the more anthropomorphic views held by many of his predecessors and contemporaries. Nor would the *Tatenyu* of a Hasidic *Zaddik* have too much in common with the neo-Kantian "guarantor of our ethics," as Hermann Cohen conceives of God. Yet all Jews have ever united in confessing at least this: that God is One! Perhaps it is this declaration of the Unity of God, and it alone, which permits us to speak at all of *the* Jewish idea of God.

But why stress the Unity? No doubt, the *Shema* can be shown to have originated at a time when the religion of Israel was first placed in contrast to polytheism. Later it was the battle-cry against Persian dualism, and still later it was Judaism's *raison d'être* in the face of Christian trinitarianism. Yet, is this really what the Jew has in mind when he recites the *Shema?* Is he indeed conscious at all times of the apologetics and polemics in which his religion must engage against competitors in the realm of the spirit? The Jewish philosophers, perhaps, but it is hard to conceive of the ordinary Jew in this role every morning and night, and at the last conscious moment of his life.

Perhaps we can approach the truth a little nearer if we understand the *Shema* to express the Jew's conviction that, though he experiences God in many different spheres and on many different levels, all his different and diverse experiences are nonetheless the manifestations of the same One God. And—this needs stressing— the Jew *does* deal with manifestations of the Divine on different levels. The famous passage in Exodus 6:2 ff. where *Elohim* reveals Himself to Moses as YHWH, stating at the same time that the Patriarchs had not known Him under this aspect, but only as *El Shadday*—this passage would indicate that the authors of the Bible were not unaware of the different levels on which God is experienced, or of the different aspects under which He is known.

A similar recognition was forced upon the medieval Jewish philosophers who were acquainted, on the one hand, with the Aristotelian-scholastic proofs for the existence of God, and, on the other, with the "revealed" God of the Scriptures. Yehudah Halevi is quite outspoken in the distinction he makes between the "God of Aristotle" and the "God of Abraham." For the Jewish thinker there can, of course, be only One God, and he will have to insist that the philosopher and the prophet speak about the same Deity, adding, however, that "revelation" can give us certitude where philosophical speculation may not.

But not all religionists have succeeded in making this ultimate identification. Characteristic of a certain type of Kabbalistic aberration is the God-concept propounded by the eighteenth-century Sabbatian heresiarch, Nehemiah Hiyyah Hayyun.[10] We are not here concerned with demonstrating how and why Hayyun was heretical.[11] It will suffice merely to mention the sharp distinction made by Hayyun between the Infinite (*En Sof*), on the one hand, and the "God of Israel," on the other. The *En Sof* is really, by definition, unknowable. He is the God of the Philosophers, the First Cause. The Bible is not concerned with Him at all, for the Bible speaks of a God who can be known, a God who created the world and revealed His Torah. He, *not* the First Cause, is the "God of Israel" of whom Judaism speaks.

We would miss the point of Hayyun's doctrine if, in addition to noting its formal heresy, we were to ignore in it the repercussions of the man's personal reactions to religious experience. It is for this reason that we have brought Hayyun into our discussion in the first place. In this context it is not necessary that we abide by the Aristotelian definition of the *En Sof* which Hayyun assumes. Let *En Sof*, as far as we are concerned, stand for the philosophical God-concept as such. Inasmuch as the Jew today describes himself as a "believing Jew," he would own up to some philosophical God-concept or other—be it naïve or sophisticated. Whether that God be described in pre-Kantian, Kantian, or post-Kantian terms, the concept will be used to make sense of, or account for, the universe. To serve this purpose, such a concept of God will have to be conceived in universal terms. It becomes difficult to associate this God with the destiny of one people in particular, and impossible to regard Him as the author of any specific "revelation." (Is the "Life Force" concerned with the putting on of *tefillin?*)

Where, then, "God" for the modern Jew is simply a philosophical concept ("God of Aristotle," *En Sof,* etc.)—this both Halevi and Hayyun have rightly seen—"revelation" is impossible. And to revert to our overall subject: where there is no revelation there can be no halacha. It may perhaps be said that, homiletical phrases notwithstanding, the official formulations of Reform Judaism have never *really* committed themselves to anything but the "God of the Philosophers." This may explain the difficulties in finding a basis for a Reform halacha.

It will, however, be conceded that Judaism, as a historical phenomenon, did not grow out of a philosophical God-concept. Halevi saw this very clearly when he pointed out that the first of the Ten Commandments does *not* say: "I am the Lord, thy God, who created heaven and earth." But it *does* say: "I am the Lord, thy God, who brought thee out of the land of Egypt, out of the house of bondage." In other words, the "God of Israel" is a God whose existence and nature were made manifest to Israel in certain historical situations of a more or less well-defined character.

The liberation from Egypt was one such event. The "passing through the Red Sea" was another—and so on throughout Jewish history. One of these historical situations was the "standing at Mount Sinai." It was there that Israel entered into a covenant relationship with God, taking it upon themselves to abide by a code containing both moral and so-called ritual laws. The God who had revealed Himself as the author of liberty in the Exodus revealed Himself as the author of law at Sinai. What is more, He manifested a special interest in the people of Israel, who were henceforth to describe themselves as the "chosen people."

Is all this legendary? Many describe it as such. But if so, then for the past two and a half millennia and more, Jews have been the victims of a very clever deception, perpetrated, as it were, *in coram publicam.* After all, Halevi's argument is not so easily refuted. When he tries to prove the authenticity of the Sinaitic revelation by calling attention to the fact that 600,000 Israelites actually witnessed it, we may, if we like, quibble about his statistics. But it still remains a *fact* that the people, as a whole, accepted certain obligations as part of their covenant commitment. Even if, for argument's sake, we dispense with the "miraculous" and conceive of the "covenant" in more mundane terms (such as are described in Nehemiah 10:33, where the people say of themselves: "We also lay upon ourselves obligations . . ."), we are still forced to admit that any such "acceptance of the Law," at Sinai and/or later, took place in response to a nationwide religious experience.

If the God-idea has been a dynamic factor in Jewish life and history, then it was precisely the idea of a God who led the ancestors out of Egypt, who revealed His law, and who watched over His people throughout their many wanderings. He was the "God of our fathers," whom the Jew invoked in his prayers. Is He merely a "reported God"—as some would now have it? Yes, but that does not rule out His reality! It was, after all, the "reported God" of historical experience who alone held out hopes of present salvation.[12]

But it was not only in the past that God manifested Himself. There is also the religious experience of the *present*. Judaism has a word for it: *Shekhinah,* "the indwelling presence of God." We may say that the personal religious experience of the individual— and not only that of the mystic—is a manifestation of *Shekhinah.*[13]

There are, then, at least three aspects to the Godhead. Regard them as completely distinct from one another, and you leave the confines of Judaism. Regard them as the different levels on which man can experience God, and you adhere to the Confession of Unity expressed in the *Shema.* This means, of course, that when you experience God on any one level, you must never completely leave out of account the various other levels on which God *can* be experienced.

Thus, the mystical experience of God vouchsafed to an Israel Baal Shem Tov may be peculiarly his very own. But a Baal Shem Tov would insist that the God he has encountered is none other than the God of Israel's history, since there is, after all, only One God. Again, the God who, as Saadia Gaon thinks, can be proved by logical reasoning is, for this philosopher, none other than the One who revealed Himself at Sinai. Or, to take an example from the opposite extreme, the *élan vital,* discovered by Bergson through his biological and philosophical researches, is recognized by him to be the very source of *mystical* experience whose existence is attested by a long line of religious mystics.

If, then, we insist that the characteristic Jewish contribution to

the idea of God is the belief in *unity*, we fail to do justice to this
concept if we deny the possibility of the various levels of authentic religious experience which this belief is meant to *unify*. In
other words, if "God" is only that which appears at the end of
my chain of logical reasoning, and not also the *Elohe Yisrael* and
the *Shekhinah*, the "reported God" and the God of religious experience, what meaning could there possibly be in stressing the
unity of God?

We may now return to our consideration of the problems of
Reform halacha. It has already been stated that we cannot very
well connect the "God of the Philosophers" with either revelation
or halacha. But then, as has been shown, the "God of the philosophers" by no means exhausts the divine as understood by Judaism.
The "God of the philosophers" is, after all, but *one* avenue
through which a Jew may receive intimations of the divine. And,
while the "God of the philosophers" may not reveal Torah, the
Elohe Yisrael does! If, however, it be argued that the *Elohe Yisrael* is only a "reported God" who has no immediate relevance to
the present-day Jew, Judaism would insist that an experience of
Shekhinah is within reach of all; [14] and, as we have noted, to the
Jew an experience of *Shekhinah* carries overtones of the other
aspects of God as well. Indeed, while an experience of *Shekhinah*
is possible even in unforeseen circumstances, man can consciously
make himself more receptive to it.[15]

It is obvious, however, that an experience of *Shekhinah* is a very
subjective state. We are moving in the realm of what William James
called "the varieties of religious experience." One would naturally
be very wary of regarding every subjective state of spiritual ela-
tion, any "vision" or feeling of being "reborn," as authentic manifestations of God! That is where the Jewish belief in the unity of
God comes in, with its insistence on the identity of *Shekhinah*
and *Elohe Yisrael*. The Jew's experience of the one serves as a
check on the validity of the experience of the other. Thus, if the
apprehension of God in a subjective religious experience is not
contradicted by what is known of the character of *Elohe Yisrael*,
it may be regarded as authentic. We have no reason to doubt, for
example, that the so-called false prophets of biblical days had
their religious experiences, their "visions" and "revelations." What
made their prophecy "false" in the eyes of the "true" prophets was
that the happy prognostications they offered were felt to be out

of keeping with the character of Israel's God who had revealed Himself in history.[16]

To sum up, the unity of God, as proclaimed in the *Shema,* means that there is only *one Reality*—though we may get to know about It by diverse routes: by philosophical speculation, by tradition, and by personal religious experience. No *one* approach, however, is sufficient. Neither philosophical speculation alone, nor yet a mere personal "experience," will reveal to us the full meaning of the idea of God in Judaism. The *Elohe Yisrael,* the concept of the God whom Israel encountered in history, and who, *in coram publicam,* revealed His Torah to Israel, is the *conditio sine qua non* of any continuity within Judaism.

This, of course, is the point at which the views of modern Jews will diverge. Do they believe that, throughout all these generations, Jews have been the victims of a tremendous delusion, since the "covenant" is, at best, a "pious fraud"? Or do they see in the course of Jewish history "the finger of God," testifying to something very vital and real (Halevi's *inyan elohi*), which lends weight to the conviction of previous generations that there *is* a covenant relationship between God and Israel? Admittedly, this is a matter of faith (critics might call it "credulity"). But to those who share that faith, a "revealed" law of God is by no means an absurdity, and a sound basis for halacha is given. Conversely, without such a theological foundation, it is hard to see how *any* suggestion to graft concepts like *mitzvah* and halacha onto the status quo of Reform Judaism can be taken seriously.

Whether American Reform Judaism is capable of undergoing such a revolution in theological thinking, whether it will be prepared to progress from the "Seven Laws of the Sons of Noah" to the foot of Sinai, is, of course, a question that many people will answer in the negative. It is one thing to pass expedient resolutions in favor of ceremonies. It is quite another to reinstate the God of Israel as the "Giver of Torah," when the very *raison d'être* of Reform, as a denomination, is represented as the emancipation from this belief.

Here is the crux of the whole problem. Recent statements by men claiming to speak in the name of Reform Judaism have clearly shown that the process of denial goes beyond the denial of revelation. Once revelation is denied, the denial of God's existence is now seen by some to be the next logical step. On the other

hand, Reform Jews who are unwilling to give up their faith in
God may find that, in the final analysis, their "God talk" is *religiously* meaningful only to the extent to which God can be said
to have *revealed* Himself to man. God and His Torah are interrelated. If one takes God seriously, one must take revelation seriously, and *vice versa*. It is only when God and revelation will
again be taken seriously by Reform Judaism that the "Problems
of Reform Halacha" can be properly faced.

NOTES

1. E. S. Brightman, *A Philosophy of Religion* (New York: Prentice-Hall,
Inc., 1940), p. 37 ff.
2. Cf. Ismar Elbogen, "Der Streit um die 'positiv-historische Reform,'" in
Festgabe fuer Claude G. Montefiore, Berlin, 1928, p. 26 ff.
3. Sifre Shofetim, Piska 146: *ahubhah la-abhoth senuah labanim*.
4. Moreh Nebhukhim, Part III, chap. 32.
5. Cf. R. Levi in *Leviticus Rabbah* 22:8.
6. Bk. VIII, Sefer ha-Abhodah, and Bk. IX, Sefer Korbanoth.
7. *Or Nogah, Nogah Hatzedek*, Dessau, 1818.
8. Cf. particularly the Reform position in England in the 1840's.
9. E.g. in b. Erubhin 14b.
10. Cf. his tract, *Oz L'Elohim*, Berlin 1713.
11. This has been done at length by David Nieto in *Esh Dath*, London,
1715; cf. the present writer's *The Theology of Haham David Nieto* (New
York: Bloch Publishing Co., 1954), pp. 114-18.
12. Cf., for example, the whole of Psalm 106, with its climax in verse 47,
and the *Anenu* prayer in the *Selihoth* liturgy.
13. Cf. the many illustrations in J. Abelson, *The Immanence of God in
Rabbinical Literature* (London: Macmillan, 1912).
14. Cf. Aboth 3:7.
15. Cf. B. Berakhoth 64a, where the man who, on leaving the synagogue,
repairs to the House of Study to occupy himself with Torah is said to be
zokheh umekabbel pene shekhinah; and the many parallels in rabbinic literature where different moral or "ritual" precepts are singled out as leading to
the same result.
16. Cf. Jeremiah 28:8.

THE CONCEPT OF ISRAEL

Bernard J. Bamberger

Theology differs from other forms of discourse in its frank admission that it starts out with a positive conviction. Scientific and historical research, as well as philosophic speculation in the classic sense, are supposed to be free from such initial bias, to examine a well-defined area by a controlled, impartial method, and to accept whatever results the inquiry may yield. Of course, the assumptions implicit in the selection and treatment of data are not always so self-evident and indisputable as they are taken to be; critical examination of such assumptions may reveal a considerable measure of subjectivity in philosophic and even scientific studies. But in the case of the theologian there is no need to ferret out unconscious subjectivity; he himself freely admits that he is seeking to clarify, explicate, and defend his beliefs. This approach is not incompatible with the highest standards of scholarly precision and critical logic. Rationalization is not discredited by being recognized as such; it is discredited only when it is shown to be irrational.

If a theologian speaks for a group within which there is a general consensus, he can, indeed, operate with a certain degree of objectivity, for the subjective decisions have already been made by the religious community as a whole. The theologian can then expound its sacred documents or its articles of faith with authority; his personal contribution will consist only in the elaboration of details or in the application of accepted principles to new situations.

Such a consensus does not presently exist within the Reform rabbinate. Instead we find a broad spectrum of belief, ranging from religiously tinged naturalism to several varieties of neo-orthodoxy. Between these extremes is a group that adheres more or less closely to the liberal theology evolved by earlier generations. It seems proper, before approaching the specific theological problem in question, to indicate my own general approach.

I therefore identify myself as one of the old-fashioned liberals. The members of this group have not, indeed, been untouched by changes in the outside world and in the world of thought. The vehement anti-nationalism of early Reform appears to me obsolete, its optimism highly premature. Moreover, some Reform theologians stressed generalities of a rather abstract and rationalistic kind, whereas I have tended to concern myself more with specific moral and religious experience in the life of the individual and in the life of the Jewish people. In the natural sciences a hypothesis is validated not merely by its plausibility or logical consistency, but fundamentally by experimental proof. In theology controlled experimental verification is not possible. Nevertheless, the theologian has the obligation to check his religious theorizing as far as possible against all the facts of life.

Such an open-minded experiential, if not experimental, approach is particularly needed in considering the concept of Israel; for on this theme some flatly dogmatic assertions have been made in recent years. On the one hand, Will Herberg unashamedly calls Israel "a *supernatural* community, called into being by God to serve his eternal purposes in history" [1] (italics his). On the other hand, Mordecai M. Kaplan rejects the idea of the election of Israel as intellectually untenable and morally objectionable. He will allow at most that Israel has a "vocation," as every man and every people may have its proper vocation.[2] We shall be well advised, then, to take a careful look at realities, with a minimum of presuppositions.

The realities are those of history. No informed and fair-minded student has, to my knowledge, discovered a parallel to the over-all history of the Jewish people. The efforts that have been made to fit Jewish experience into some preconceived historical pattern are forced and produce results that are plainly distorted. (I have always suspected that Mr. Toynbee's real grievance against the Jews is their ungentlemanly refusal to arrange their history in accordance with his scheme.) Jewish history is notable not simply for its length, but even more for its character: a people have survived without a homeland and without inclusive political institutions; they have survived despite repeated and determined attempts to bring about their physical destruction and their disintegration as a community; and, out of all proportion to their numbers, this people have contributed richly to human welfare and cultural progress. Moreover, the Jewish group have been deeply involved in many of the critical and decisive moments of world history—as victims or as active participants. Somehow the fate of the Jews has served as a measuring rod of human advance or retrogression. There is nothing comparable to this whole story.

That is why the old arguments as to whether the Jews are a race, nation, or church were bound to be futile. The usual categories simply do not fit. A people with a unique experience emerge as a unique people, if only in sociological terms. Thus, for example, one not born of Jewish parents can become a Jew by conversion to the Jewish religion. But the born Jew who adopts another faith, even in full sincerity, does not wholly cease to be a Jew. Such asymmetry may seem unreasonable, unfair even, but it is an empirical fact.

One who sets out with some theory of economic or historic determinism will apply his hypotheses to the facts of Jewish history as well as he can. If he is honest, he will admit that such explanations do not adequately account for the facts. He will perhaps declare that the lacunae are due to insufficient data and to our *as yet* incomplete mastery of method in the social sciences. That is, he will make a profession of faith that some day social scientists will be able to explain not only how the history of Israel came about, but why it had to come about as it did. Such faith seems to me naïve. I can understand that the development in ancient Israel from a pastoral to an agricultural economy, and then to an urban civilization, conditioned the teachings of the prophets. But many peoples passed through similar economic-social changes, and only Israel produced an Amos. I doubt that intensified research will explain why.

Among the data to be considered are the beliefs of the Jewish people concerning themselves. Such beliefs may or may not be rationally tenable; the vehemence and tenacity with which an opinion is held are no criterion of its correctness. Nevertheless, the belief itself is a datum of experience and therefore requires examination.

One may choose to dismiss the doctrine of the "Chosen People" as no more than an expression of corporate arrogance, and to classify it with the belief, held by such military peoples as the Assyrians and Romans, that they were chosen by their gods to conquer, rule, and exploit. Or the idea may be explained, a trifle less maliciously, as a compensatory device by which a small, downtrodden people bolstered its shaky self-confidence. As for the first view, there are, indeed, some brutal and bloody pages in our ancient texts; we would be happier if they did not exist. Yet such passages have had surprisingly little impact on Jewish theology or even on popular Jewish thought. There is nothing characteristically Jewish about these cruel utterances, but perhaps there *is* something significant in the fact that the programs of extermination were not consistently carried out! [3] More typically Jewish, almost without parallel, are the repeated statements in Deuteronomy that Israel was not selected for any merits of its own. [4] So, too, is the severity with which the prophets condemned the moral failures of their people, declaring that the special favor God had shown to Israel entailed a higher degree of responsibility to Him. [5]

More and more, likewise, it was noted that entering the covenant with God imposed heavy burdens. Yet Israel had accepted the commandments without first demanding an exposition of them: they were "a rash people who spoke up (in commitment) before they heard." [6] A similar irony pervades the Kaddish of Rabbi Levi Yizchok of Berdichev: "What do You want of Your people Israel? You are always at them: Command the children of Israel, charge them; enjoin them—and then You demand flawless performance!" [7]

The characteristic utterances on the subject of Israel's election describe it as a privilege, an undeserved privilege, but one that carries heavy obligations. The vast range of Jewish literature contains some crude expressions of chauvinism, but more often one finds in it that "love of Israel" exemplified by Rabbi Levi Yizchok

—the insistence that the Jews are doing pretty well with an overwhelmingly hard task. The sense of chosenness is not infrequently combined with a sense of tragic destiny. This is relieved somewhat by glowing hopes of messianic bliss, though one may suspect a note of wry humor in the apparently naïve accounts of roast leviathan and wine aged in the original grapes.[8]

In the classic Jewish literary expressions of Israel's chosenness, even in the liturgical formulations, there is a certain tension which is not difficult to understand. The individual Jew has usually been impelled by the same drive as other men, the desire to make a secure and happy life for himself and his family. Yet he has also been aware of historical forces and of a religious commitment which impose an exacting discipline and may on occasion demand limitless sacrifice. Men rarely want to be heroes or martyrs. But the records of Jewry contain not only words of complaint, of irony, even of resentment, but also and more frequently recognition of the grandeur and glory that go hand in hand with responsibility: "How goodly is our portion, how pleasant our lot, how beautiful our heritage!"[9]

We confront, then, a twofold reality: the objective uniqueness of Jewish historic experience, and the fact that Jews have understood this experience as stemming from a divine appointment. Considering these realities, I am filled with wonder and awe. And therefore I am wary of glib explanations. The nineteenth-century German Jewish philosopher Samuel Hirsch found in the survival of the Jewish people a sufficient proof that literal miracles can and do occur.[10] His view seems to me overly dogmatic. But, as I have already remarked, the sociological explanations of Jewish history, though frequently stimulating and, in regard to specific details, sometimes convincing, do not appear to account adequately for the total Jewish experience. Zangwill's epigram about the "choosing people" is ingenious but does not suffice. Of course, as Scripture and tradition testify, Israel gave its assent to the covenant, but the proposal came from God, not from man. This is affirmed in all the sources, and however critically or even skeptically we view these sources, it does not appear that the Jewish people envisioned their historic role in advance. This role emerged rather in a long series of events and circumstances. On occasion the people said "Yes!" to events and situations, but they did not create these.

I have alluded several times to the covenant, a concept to which recent writers on Jewish theology have given much attention. (It will be better to use the Hebrew term *b'rith*, since the rendering "covenant" is not altogether precise.) The word *b'rith* recurs constantly in the Hebrew Bible and students cannot but give it serious attention, but I am not sure that our own present situation is much clarified hereby. A covenant is an agreement entered into by two or more parties, in which their respective obligations and rights are specified. Such agreements are usually for a limited time, often with a provision for renewal. Ordinarily they can be terminated if both parties assent. If one party fails to live up to the terms of the agreement, he may be subject to certain penalties, or the covenant may thereby be abrogated.

Is such the meaning of *b'rith* in the Bible? Sometimes, no doubt. But the very first *b'rith* mentioned in Scripture (Gen. 9) is not a mutual undertaking; it is God's unilateral promise to the earth and its inhabitants that He will not send another flood. As for the *b'rith* between God and Israel, one wonders about the legal and moral propriety of an agreement by which men bind themselves and their descendants for all time (Deut. 29:13-14). Would such an agreement stand up in any court of law? And what about an arrangement whereby one party can determine that the other has breached the contract and thereupon take punitive action, while the other party can do no more than complain if he feels aggrieved?

If the word *b'rith* normally means a kind of contract, then apparently it applies to the relation between God and Israel only by way of analogy and, as so often happens with analogies, it does not exactly fit. Was the entrance of Israel into the *b'rith* altogether voluntary? There are many statements in the Bible and Talmud that the people eagerly accepted the Torah and its duties, but there is at least an undercurrent of feeling that they really had no choice. This, presumably, is the intent of the strange Talmudic statement that God held Mount Sinai over the heads of the Israelites and threatened to drop it on them if they did not accept His Torah.[11] It is certainly the implication of Ezekiel's blood-chilling words: "That which cometh into your mind shall not be at all, in that ye say: We will be as the nations, as the families of the countries, to serve wood and stone. As I live, saith the Lord GOD, surely with a mighty hand, and with an outstretched arm, and with fury poured out, will I be king over you" (Ezek. 20:32-33).

The intent of the entire chapter is not: You made a covenant with Me, and I insist on your living up to it. It is rather: I, God, planned a career for you, and I will compel you to carry it out, whether you will or no.—I am, of course, not citing Ezekiel as an irrefutable authority, but simply as a witness to what Jews have often felt or believed. Yet nowhere, it seems to me, has this strange prophet come closer to reality than here.

I find myself, then, unable to give a full rational explanation of the fact of Jewish chosenness. Yet the fact itself seems beyond dispute. A responsible scientist, confronted by a datum he cannot fully explain, does not deny its existence. Nor does he try to show that any partial or tentative explanation is correct and complete, distorting or disregarding evidence to the contrary. He lives as well as he can with a problem not yet solved.

The various explanations of Jewish experience—fundamentalist, existentialist, positivist—are all interesting and sometimes helpful. None of them, in my judgment, illuminates satisfactorily the complex mystery of Jewish existence. We should by all means continue to study and speculate, excluding no aspect of the subject and no method of research. If such efforts help illuminate even small areas of the subject, or disprove some unfounded theories, that will be a gain. But the critical mind is not incompatible with the humble spirit; perhaps the two are really inseparable.

In the meantime we have to live with the fact of our Jewish identity and with the datum of our chosenness. The practical aspects of the matter are less complicated, though they are not easy. For whatever may be the origins—divine or human—of Jewish experience and Jewish uniqueness, they appear to me to impose an ineluctable obligation upon the Jewish people and the individual Jew. One who has had experiences should profit by them. One who has been educated ought to use what he has learned. One who has enjoyed privileges must acknowledge an obligation, and one who has suffered should thereby be sensitive to other men's pain. The recipient of a heritage has the duty to employ it responsibly and to conserve, enhance, and transmit it.

As I see it, the Jewish community has the obligation to continue to exist. The individual Jew has the obligation to identify himself as a Jew, to contribute to Jewish group survival, and to learn, teach, and practice the religious and ethical values of Judaism. Commitment to the cause of freedom, justice, and peace is not binding upon us only because, historically, the forces of tyranny have been hostile to us and those of liberalism generally friendly. More important is the fact that these moral values are at the heart of Jewish experience. "You shall not oppress a stranger, for you know the feelings of the stranger, having yourselves been strangers in the land of Egypt" (Exod. 23:9). Our heritage and our experience mark out our mission.

This is, I hardly need say, not a matter of blood. Anyone who wants to join Judaism and the Jewish people is free to do so. He is like one who clambers aboard a moving vehicle, from which the present riders will reach out their hands to pull him aboard. But to jump off the vehicle, which has such considerable momentum, is risky; one can hardly do so without sustaining injury.

Finally, in affirming the chosenness of Israel, I am not denying that other peoples, nations, groups, and creeds have their vocations, their dignity, their worth. One who accepts a hard task, a heavy responsibility, an arduous office, can hardly be unaware that this is an honor and a distinction; to pretend that it is not would be both dishonest and silly. But he was not called to the job in order that he may congratulate himself. He is there to get on with the task.

NOTES

1. Will Herberg, *Judaism and Modern Man* (New York: Farrar Straus & Young, 1951), p. 271.

2. M. M. Kaplan, "Shall We Retain the Doctrine of Israel as the Chosen People?" in *The Reconstructionist*, XI (No. 1, February 23, 1945); and see the present author's critique, "Are the Jews a Chosen People?" (*ibid.* [No. 16, December 28, 1945]), and Dr. Kaplan's rejoinder, "The Chosen People Idea an Anachronism," in the subsequent issue of the periodical.

3. Judges 1:21-2:5.

4. Deuteronomy 7:7 ff., 9:4 ff.

5. Amos 3:2, Hosea 2:10 ff.

6. Sabbath 88a, Kethuboth 112a: *ama peziza d'kadmeto pumecho l'udnecho.*

7. I paraphrase the well-known Yiddish song.

8. See, e.g., Sanhedrin 99a, where some statements give the impression of being meant literally, and others are not so serious in tone.

9. From the *Shaharith* service.

10. S. Hirsch, *Die Religionsphilosophie der Juden* (Leipzig: 1842), pp. 551 f.

11. Sabbath 88a.

THE NATURE AND DESTINY OF ISRAEL
Joseph R. Narot

American Jewish teachers seem, with impressive unanimity, still inspired by faith in the existence of a partnership between the Master of the Universe and the people of Israel.[1] The question, however, of whether the point at which Israel's consciousness of this partnership awakened should be defined in natural or supernatural and in spontaneous or evolutionary terms is by no means unanimously answered. The problem, it would appear, is not with the truth of the Zohar's dictum that "God, Israel, and Torah are one" but rather with which element of this Jewish "trinity" we must begin.

Though it may ultimately be granted, by some at least, that "both these and these are the words of the living God,"[2] there is nevertheless a choice to be made between a fundamentally mystical and a fundamentally rational approach to understanding the character and destiny of the Jewish people. There is a choice to be made between faith and history as the appropriate medium not only for interpreting Israel's strivings and achieve-

ments in the past but also for delineating Jewish responsibility
in the future.

A reading in the *Commentary* Symposium of 1966 of what a
representative section of the contemporary American rabbinate
believes about God and Israel and about the election, covenant,
and mission reveals a widespread recognition of theological alternatives and an almost equally extensive readiness to begin
with historical perceptions rather than with dogmatic pronouncements. Such a reading suggests that we would do well to begin
with Israel, to trace but not to conclude—for the search for
God, like God Himself, is without end—Israel's quest for God
through Torah, and then continue toward the new yet authentic
Jewish theological vistas that are now required.

Regarding revelation, Jacob Agus (Conservative) writes, "the
word of God in the heart of man is not an auditory hallucination,
but a power, a deposit of energy, a momentary upsurge toward
a higher level of being." [3] Bernard Bamberger (Reform) declares, "I do not see how any revelation can come to man except
through man." [4] "Despite what the Torah claims for itself . . .
I believe it is a human document," [5] asserts Ira Eisenstein (Reconstructionist). "*How* God did actually contact man—patriarchs and prophets—and covenant with them . . . will continue
to be the subject of both conjecture and interpretation," [6]
Emanuel Rackman (Orthodox) admits.

It is precisely this conjecture and interpretation that can no
longer be a minor or peripheral aspect of our theological understanding of Jewish peoplehood but its major and central
concern. For the Jew of today will not find vital significance in
the doctrines of election, covenant, and mission until theological
conjecture and interpretation are directed toward ends which
his mind can relate to historic realities and rational possibilities.

The historic reality is that Israel existed and still exists, the
reasonable possibility is that Israel will continue to exist. We
may, however, no longer cling to any certitude that Israel will
exist necessarily and forever. The martyrdom of six million of
our people in Nazi Europe; the flight of tens of thousands more
to the Church in order to escape martyrdom; the continuing
spiritual destruction of three million Jews in Soviet Russia; the
realization that one atomic bomb could annihilate the State of

Israel; and the adoption on the part of Jews the world over, and particularly in America, of these grim and overriding facts as reasons for moving away from Judaism—all this has shattered the old theological foundations. To pretend that these foundations still stand, to refuse at this moment to concede that other demagogues could harness their hate to the same (if not improved) technological weapons of death and thus complete Hitler's "solution to the Jewish problem," and to fail in this hour of world history to perceive that we must rebuild our theology anew, means to lose whatever hope there may still be for maintaining the inner strength of Israel and keeping alive its message to mankind.

We are at a juncture in our people's history comparable to, but far exceeding them in magnitude and severity, the crises that confronted Israel during the Babylonian captivity in the sixth pre-Christian century and again some seven hundred years later when Rome destroyed the second Jewish commonwealth. On these two occasions new dimensions were added to the concepts of election, covenant, and mission in order to make them viable and meaningful to a people ravaged in body and battered in soul. Now, however, it is not only the body that has been bruised and the soul that has been tormented but also the mind that has finally rebelled. Jews in our time are no longer able or willing to find solace in answers devised for other ages.

Six hundred years before Christianity it was a new and comforting revelation for Jews to be told by Jeremiah [7] that they should settle peacefully wherever destiny had taken them, even far from Zion. This has no meaning for us. Nineteen hundred years ago it was helpful for Israel to be reassured by Rabbi Joseph, whom tradition pictures as having been granted a vision of the afterlife, that "those who are on top here are below there." [8] Such a promise that justice perverted in this life will be restored in the life of the world to come has no significance for the Jew of today. Throughout the dark and bloody centuries that followed the destruction of the Jewish state by the Romans and the rise of Christianity, there may have been multitudes of Jews who were consoled by the rabbinic faith that if Israel suffers and, searching its heart, finds no sins commensurate with that suffering, it should understand that it is the "chastisements of love" [9] that God has inflicted. Such theologically phrased masochism offers no consolation to the present-day generation of Jews.

Elie Wiesel speaks for many of today's Jews, particularly those who themselves lived through the horrors of Nazism. "Why should I bless God?" Wiesel asks. "Because He had had thousands of children burned in His pits? Because He kept six crematories working night and day, on Sundays and feast days? Because in His great might He had created Auschwitz, Birkenau, Buna, and so many factories of death? How could I say to Him: 'Blessed art Thou, Eternal, Master of the Universe, who chose us from among other races to be tortured day and night, to see our fathers, our mothers, our brothers, end in the crematory? Praised be Thy Holy Name, Thou who hast chosen us to be butchered on Thine altar?'. . . This day I had ceased to plead . . . I was the accuser, God the accused. My eyes were open and I was alone—terribly alone in a world without God." [10]

Contemporary Jews need a new and bold theology that will give sense to their remaining Jews, or they will founder in chaos and despair—which is precisely what they are in great part already doing.

The chaos and despair which the Jew of today feels because of his Jewishness are certainly not softened by the chaos and despair in the larger, non-Jewish world about him. Now more than ever before the Jew is in constant communication with that world, and the rebuilding of "the fence around the law" is neither desirable nor possible in the eyes of most Jews. Furthermore, the general theological underpinning of society at large is, if anything, even shakier than our own. "Modern man is the product of a world which has moved too quickly for him to assimilate," we have been told, "a lonely creature who wants so much to communicate, to have someone understand him, a rebel without a cause, a lover who finds no one to love. He is perplexed by the world, paralyzed with doubt, filled with fear, alienated from a God grown, it seems, silent." [11]

When the attempt is made to put even a small portion of all that has been said about man's alienation in our world between the covers of one book,[12] we have indeed a frightening testimonial to the fact that man's faith has been shattered and must be completely re-created if he is to be saved from his terrors.

No area of man's life, individual or collective, has escaped estrangement, isolation, rootlessness. In work and business; in culture and religion; in politics, science, morality, and family relationships; in capitalist and in communist economies—wherever we turn, authorities see man's aloneness as "the critical dilemma of our time." Never in any other epoch of their history have Jews been surrounded by so much spiritual upheaval and on such a global scale as they are today.

Egypt may have gloated prematurely on her clay monuments that "Israel is desolated, his seed is not," and Rome may have rushed too soon into imprinting on her coins the announcement that "Judea is taken." [13] These, however, were victories which gave the conquerors confidence and added to their sense of omnipotence. Today the larger world is permeated with a sense of defeat and impotence. In the past, when the Jewish minority was persecuted by the Christian majority, the persecution was said to be to the glory of Christianity's God. Now Christian theologians have announced that their God is dead,[14] and some among them have suggested that we should do away with the very word "God." [15]

Nor is it only God and His name that have been declared dead in the world in which the Jewish people today finds itself. Dying, too, if not already deceased, for many is the collective search for a new faith. Because man is alone, if and when he seeks belief, meaning, purpose, and goals at all, he seeks them alone. The need for organized religion appears dubious, even nonexistent for him. "We have all become doubting Thomases," Dr. Nathan Pusey, president of Harvard University, declared recently. There are many who are "torn with doubt as to whether theological education still made sense," he asserted. "No creedal formulations now seem possible because there can be no supernatural reference to undergird such a creed. . . . And if creeds go, what then becomes of the church?" he asked rhetorically.[16]

Rabbis have recently lamented the lack of responsiveness to the idea of *K'lal Yisrael*, the total community of Israel, among Jewish students and intellectuals. But merely to lament it is not to cure it. Our Passover Haggadah for centuries has called those who fail to see Jewish teaching and Jewish history as having any personal relevance to them "wicked sons." If this still be wickedness, it is of a kind very prevalent in our midst, for Jews today seek an understanding of values, morality, and God which responds to their personal needs as human beings and not to what Solomon Schechter used to call "catholic Israel." [17]

It is clear, therefore, that, if not in all of "catholic Israel," at least in a preponderant portion of it, several processes have supervened to change our understanding of the meaning of Jewish peoplehood. Our theology has been progressively humanized and the concepts of Israel's election, covenant, and mission have been individualized and universalized. Furthermore, what is of supreme importance, these developments were inherent in the original, classical teachings; they have, through overt and covert selection from among all other accents, by both official and unofficial pronouncement, been led to assume their present large dimensions. The contemporary understanding of them is the direct and inevitable consequence of four thousand years of Jewish travail and thought.

To examine these four thousand years of Jewish history theologically is to find, among all other elements, an almost rectilinear course leading from the God beyond man to the yearning for God in the heart of man, from a supernatural entity revealing itself mysteriously to human life to a profound, unending search by man for the meaning of his life. What must have been a startling proclamation in Jeremiah's day, as he envisioned radical changes in the relationship between God and Israel,[18] is taken for granted in our day. The prophet hoped for the time when the old covenant, imposed from without, would be replaced by another, written "in their inward parts," and when it would no longer be necessary for any man to teach God to another, for they should all know Him "in their heart." Revelation would then come to the Jew, as to all men, from within. The awareness of God would be a response on man's part to the universe, a response affirming faith in the presence of meaning, purpose, and direction in the processes of nature and history.

Such an emphasis on beginning with man rather than God in Jewish theology, the procedure which is common today, was continually promoted and expanded by rabbinic commentary on the Bible. Where the Book of Genesis defined God as the sole creator, the rabbis regarded man as a partner in creation.[19] Where Exodus proscribed the portrayal of God in any form or image, Maimonides forbade ascribing to Him any positive attributes whatsoever.[20] Where Micah declared that God requires of man only justice, mercy, and humility,[21] the Jerusalem Talmud was willing to believe that God would not be offended if man abandoned Him as long as he fulfilled the requirements of the Law.[22] And where the Pentateuch taught that man could never see God but has Him proclaim "I will make all My goodness pass before thee," [23] Kaufmann Kohler asserted that "We cannot really know what God is; we can only know what God is *to us.*" [24]

To describe this progression from God-centered to man-centered theology is to illumine our past and to brighten our future. We see from it that Israel reacted to life with a great longing to ennoble and sanctify it. Out of this desire it embarked on a quest for God. The Bible is the written record of a major portion of that quest. Other chapters followed—for is it not true that the "oral law," which came after the Bible, is held to be as sacred as the "written law," the Bible itself? This oral expansion and development will continue as long as Israel lives.

The epochal record of the Jewish people's search for God has included both peaks and valleys. Abraham at Moriah, Moses at Sinai, Amos at Beth-el, and the rabbis in their moments of inspiration represent the heights. The wonder of it all is not that there were valleys—primitive, crude, outdated chapters— between these peaks, but that the latter have uplifted the eyes and hearts not only of Israel but also of other peoples, and not merely in the past but up to the present hour. There is little doubt that they will remain eternal and deathless, for they embody insights to which every sensitive human being can respond as he seeks the meaning of life.

This has been Israel's destiny: to pioneer and persist in the quest for meaning in terms of moral values. The Egyptians made their mark in the building of great monuments. The Greeks developed philosophy and discovered the grace of form. The Romans achieved military power and created legal and political organizations. In the East the peoples sought escape from the suffering involved in desire. Israel alone urged mankind to make desire meaningful by endowing it with the breath of ethical aspiration.

Yet we cannot now claim this task for ourselves alone. Others, Christians and non-Christians—all whom Pope John XXIII once addressed in an encyclical as "men of good will"—now share the search for moral meaning. Mordecai Kaplan may be correct in declaring that "the Jewish religion is the most authentic religion in the world because it is indigenous to the . . . Jewish people . . . whereas Christianity is an 'adopted' religion." [25] Nevertheless, in present reality, many peoples and individuals besides Jews are seeking improvement in the conditions of life for all men, and both we and they would reject any claim to supernatural uniqueness.

If, then, the idea of the election of Israel has any continuing validity or relevance, how are we to understand it? The idea, I believe, must be seen as reflecting the reality of Judaism's unique and irreplaceable insights. In brief, election means the chosenness not of the Jew but of Judaism and refers to the historic influence which Judaism has had on the Jew and, consequently, on the world's opinion of the Jew as an adherent of this faith.

Judaism, as Abba Hillel Silver reminded us, had the courage to differ from other religions in many of its teachings. [26] Its very concept of God, even in its most traditional form, contained factors which permit us now to modify our theology and remain within an authentic Jewish context: the insistence that we cannot know God directly but only through His works; the doctrine that moral commitment and action are the final goal of our belief in Him and our worship of Him; the idea that faith in Him must ultimately be shared by all mankind. These and other definitions have distinguished Judaism.

Just as Judaism developed its unique faith stressing the oneness and spiritual character of God, so it parted company with other world outlooks in insisting that God is a reality effective in life. There is an ultimate ground to life and being. There is a cosmic source and destiny for creation. There is an essential sacredness and goodness inherent in man's existence. Moreover, Judaism said—and, in so saying, moved away from other religious philosophies—this goodness and sacredness are to be fulfilled in men's lives here and now, on earth and in this life. Most compelling is Silver's conclusion that rabbinic Judaism finally adopted the eschatological notion of the life of the world to come only reluctantly and after much prodding by forces from within and without.[27]

There is little doubt that these distinctive emphases have affected the life and thought of the Jewish people to this day. We may, as religious Jews, deplore the philanthropic Jew, the humanist Jew, the secular Jew, or the social-justice Jew on the ground that these have reduced their Jewish loyalty to but one aspect of the tradition to the exclusion of all others. We must recognize, however, that they are nevertheless heirs to all the different emphases which have characterized Judaism as a religion.

Significantly, if somewhat belatedly, these emphases are being recognized in positive ways by the larger religious world. The Protestant theologian, Harvey Cox, has urged his coreligionists to return to the Hebrew Bible's three central ideas: that not nature but the God of nature is to be worshiped; that freedom, as exemplified by the Exodus, is the *sine qua non* of human existence; and that, because man can and does devise idols, the truth of his faith and values must continually be reexamined.[28]

The Roman Catholic scholar, Father Edward Flannery, addressing an international conference on Jewish-Christian relations in London in the summer of 1966, observed that "From the rigid monotheism of Judaism a Christian can gain a greater sense of the majesty of God. From Judaism comes a concept of worldliness which is better developed than in Christianity, an insistence on the goodness of the natural order which should be a counterforce against the Puritanism that has often beset the church, and a sense of social justice which can be the blight of the selfish individualism that has often marked much of modern Catholic life." [29]

This increasing awareness of Judaism's particular relevance to all the world, it must be noted, has come not in spite of but because of the historic process through which its teachings were humanized, universalized, and moralized. Judaism has not suffered nor has the vigor of its message been diminished because, for example, the belief in the life-after-death was minimized and faith in the personal Messiah all but eliminated among many Jews in modern times. On the contrary, the diminution of stress within Judaism on abodes beyond this world, the resurrection of the dead, and the promise of divine retribution following man's earthly career, and the simultaneous purification of the human longing for immortality by centering attention on the soul and its this-worldly obligations, has cleared the air of vague belief and distracting fears. Similarly, the widespread rejection by many Jews in the modern era of the idea that the Jewish people or any people should wait on one individual to bring the Kingdom of God and the determination instead to assign to all men, races, and nations a part in the fulfilment of the messianic expectation and responsibility have certainly sharpened our focus on the universal problem of achieving a just and peaceful world order.

What has happened, then, is that in the eyes of both Jew and non-Jew Judaism has come to occupy a peculiar and crucial place, and that for both Jew and non-Jew the Jewish people have assumed the image of the eternal rebel against injustice. To this day in Western thought, at least, no one is more clearly the symbol of the human struggle for right and of man as the tragic victim of wrong than the Jew. In both these senses Judaism is the chosen faith and the Jew the chosen people, and their mission is to speak out ceaselessly, struggle relentlessly, and, if need be, suffer greatly in defense of freedom, truth, justice, and peace. Not all Jews will share this conviction and not all non-Jews will admit it. Enough in both camps, however, do share and admit it to prove its validity.

To the long and dreary chapter of race prejudice in the United States there will be many footnotes. The one, it seems to me, that belongs in the present consideration of the chosenness of Judaism and Jews is the story of the White Citizens' Councils in the Deep South. When these groups of bigoted white supremacists were organized, a prominent Jew in one community wished to identify himself with their cause. Quite understandably, he was scorned by many other Jews. That, however, is not the main point. The fact is that the white men who organized the society refused to accept him because, as they said, it was not conceivable to them that a Jew could be a good member of their council! There was something wrong, they implicitly recognized, with his wish to be associated with them.

The chosenness of the Jew is vividly highlighted on still another level in the mind of the contemporary Jew and non-Jew alike in Bernard Malamud's recent novel *The Fixer*.[30] It is instructive to note that when Malamud set out to write a story of man as the universal symbol of the war between justice and injustice, he chose as his protagonist a Jew. In his imaginative and fictionalized account of the real Jew Mendel Beiliss, accused by the Czarist regime of ritual murder, the author meant to convey the suffering that comes to all men—the Negro in America, Sacco and Vanzetti, as well as Beiliss and Captain Dreyfus.[31] Malamud, of course, knows Jewish history and its relatedness to all of human history. What is far more important, however, is that the non-Jewish reviewers of his novel knew at once what Malamud had in mind and saw in *The Fixer* the symbol of Everyman. Granville Hicks perceives that Yakov Bok, the central character of the novel, "has recognized his historic role and, though he laments its being forced upon him, he accepts it. 'We're all in history,' he thinks, 'that's sure, but some are more than others, Jews more than some.'"[32]

"Does this symbolic universal Jew, lacerated by man's psychosis to persecute, convince us of his growing passion for freedom and justice even while suffering hell on earth? Yes, ever and again," declares Webster Schott.[33] And Jonathan Baumbach asserts that "he [Malamud] dreams the dream of our failed heroism and conceives us as better men for having risked defeat. It is an optimistic vision, and one hopes—on the other side are more pogroms, more genocide, more Vietnams—that we can live up to it. It takes either courage or madness to write about the dignity of the individual in the United States in the year of our Lord 1966."[34]

The courage and madness are certainly not shared by all Jews. Some are timid and "realistically" sane. Some Jews would run from the challenge. Some are hostile or apathetic to it. There are Jews who frankly say that they are tired of being different. But, then, was it not always so? Did not some of the Children of Israel, when they had left Egypt, resist marching toward Sinai and the covenant? Judging from prophetic denunciations of ancient Israel and Judah, we know that many ignored the teachings of ethical monotheism and flirted with idolatry, immorality, and pagan callousness. Is it not true that ever since Israel's origin its leaders have often had to cajole and rebuke its recalcitrant sons and daughters?

Nevertheless, there are many Jews in our generation who would be true to the election, covenant, and mission, if these were given a contemporary significance shorn of the supernatural and grounded in historic experience. For such Jews the meaning of Israel lies in our people's millennial quest for the word of God and in the unique way in which this quest unfolded. A passion for justice, freedom, and peace has led the Jewish people to assume an unmistakable identity of its own, regardless of where and when it has lived, what garb it has worn, and what language it has spoken. At one and the same time we Jews have sought to keep alive and enhance this identity and asked others to share our ideals, ideals which have never been limited by either time or geographic boundaries. In our vision man is the center of creation, this world is the scene of it, ethical commitment is the heart of it, and a better life for the whole human race is the goal of it.

Is it possible that the people of Israel can receive new strength of identity and more significant continuity in this context? This is not only possible but has, indeed, already occurred. *Mitzvah* as external divine commandment has been transformed by historic insight into *mitzvah* as inner-directed act of reverence. In the words of Irving Greenberg, "this has been the holy community, forced into being Jews, elected by God first and then by history; and then, sometimes, when history no longer elected them . . . elected by their sentiments and emotions." [35]

To our "sentiments and emotions" we must surely add our reasoning powers, our awareness of the specific philosophic and ideational perceptions which have always been basic to Judaism. Among the perceptions which still have relevance not only for Israel and our understanding of Israel's election, covenant, and mission but for all the nations as well are Judaism's view of the place of man in the universal scheme of things, its deprecation of dogma and corresponding allowance for skepticism, its greater stress on this life than on any life to come, its conviction that man is a free and responsible moral agent and the corollary that society is likewise responsible for communal morality, its devotion to study and knowledge and its readiness to admit into its purview the best findings of every age, its aversion to superstition and idolatry, and its unflagging belief in human progress.

Earlier in this discussion reference was made to contemporary theologians in both Protestantism and Catholicism who have urged Christianity to return to basic Hebraic teachings concerning God, man, and the universe. It is not only the clergy but the laity as well that seem to share this view. An interesting example is an address recently delivered by Emmanuel G. Mesthene, Executive Director of the Harvard University Program on Technology and Society, before the World Council of Churches. "I think," said Dr. Mesthene, "that to see a sense of failure as a condition of religious experience is a historical relic, dating from the time an indifferent Nature and a hostile world so overwhelmed men that they gave up thought for consolation. . . . It surely does no glory to God to rest his power on the impotence of Man. . . . What is Man's work, and what is God's? Man's work is to be wise and good. It is God's work to reveal himself to Man as wisdom and as goodness. . . . God and Man are partners in the work of the world, in other words, which means at least that Man must do his part. But his part is precisely what Man has not done for more than 2,000 years." [36]

Surely these words describe what has been Israel's message from ancient times to the present hour. This is the message for the proclamation of which Israel always regarded itself, and may still regard itself, as chosen. The covenant means a partnership between Man's work and God's work, a partnership which has inspired our people through the centuries. The actualization of that partnership is still Israel's mission, realizable only in history and dependent now as always on the extent to which and the intensity with which all men will share it with Israel.

When such words as those quoted above are proclaimed in our world and in our time, we may believe that the vision of Isaiah is being realized more profoundly than we and perhaps even the prophet himself imagined: "And it shall come to pass in the end of days, that the mountain of the Lord's house shall be established at the top of the mountains, and shall be exalted above the hills; and all nations shall flow unto it. And many peoples shall go and say, Come ye, and let us go up to the mountain of the Lord, to the house of the God of Jacob." [37]

NOTES

1. See the Symposium "The State of Jewish Belief," in *Commentary*, August, 1966, pp. 73-160.
2. Erubin 13b.
3. *Commentary*, August, 1966, p. 73.
4. *Ibid.*, p. 77.
5. *Ibid.*, p. 85.
6. *Ibid.*, p. 128.
7. Jeremiah 29.
8. Pesachim 5a.
9. Berachot 5a.
10. Wiesel, *Night* (New York: Hill & Wang, 1960), p. 73.
11. Anthony Padavona, *The Estranged God* (New York: Sheed & Ward, 1966), p. 16.
12. Eric and Mary Josephson, eds., *Man Alone* (New York: Dell Publications, 1962).
13. Solomon Grayzel, *A History of the Jews* (Philadelphia: Jewish Publication Society, 1947), p. 174.
14. T. Altizer and W. Hamilton, *The Death of God* (Indianapolis: Bobbs-Merrill, 1966).
15. John Robinson, *Honest to God* (Philadelphia: Westminster Press, 1963), p. 47.
16. *New York Times*, September 28, 1965.
17. *Studies in Judaism*, Third Series (Philadelphia: Jewish Publication Society, 1924), p. 10.
18. Jeremiah 31:31-34.
19. Shabbat 10a.
20. *Guide for the Perplexed* (New York: Dutton, 1928), p. 68.
21. Micah 6:8.
22. Hagigah 76 C.
23. Exodus 33:19.
24. *Jewish Theology* (New York: Macmillan, 1928), p. 135.
25. *Commentary*, August, 1966, p. 109.
26. Abba Hillel Silver, *Where Judaism Differed* (New York: Macmillan, 1956).
27. *Ibid.*, p. 265.
28. Harvey Cox, *The Secular City* (New York: Macmillan, 1966).
29. *Dialogue Newsletter*, National Catholic Welfare Conference, Volume I, No. 23, August 17, 1966.
30. Malamud, *The Fixer* (New York: Farrar, Straus & Giroux, 1966).
31. Granville Hicks, "One Man to Stand for Six Million," in *Saturday Review*, September 10, 1966, p. 390.
32. *The Fixer*, p. 38.
33. *Life*, September 16, 1966, p. 14.
34. *Commonweal*, October 28, 1966, p. 99.
35. *Proceedings of the American Jewish Committee 1966 Annual Meeting*, p. 127.
36. *Saturday Review*, November 19, 1966, pp. 29 ff.
37. Isaiah 2:2-3.

A LOVER'S QUARREL WITH

THE MISSION OF ISRAEL

Daniel Jeremy Silver

The idea of the mission of Israel, which occupies so large a place in the theology of the nineteenth-century founders of Reform Judaism, has been treated as an update of classic Jewish themes and as an argument for the significance of Jewish survival. I believe it to be first and fundamentally a tone poem, exalting a Jewish life suddenly full of possibilities.

"The most significant thing about the frontier is that it lies at the hither edge of free land." [1] The words are Frederick Turner's and they are from his classic interpretation of the impact of the frontier on American institutions and attitudes. In the nineteenth century, Jews too stood at a frontier. The Jew was in Europe but not of Europe. He waited at the hither edge of freedom. Beyond lay citizenship and the broad places of European civilization. The Jewish frontier existed in time, not in space. Often the Jew

---

This paper was published in somewhat different form in the *Journal* of the Central Conference of American Rabbis, June 1967.

had to travel no farther than a city's university or bourse or polling place. But the frontier's impact on those who crossed over was as radical as if they had been pioneers setting out from St. Louis in a covered wagon. Ahead lay a new life.

The frontiersman was outward bound. He had to leave family and home behind. Few men can simply pull up their roots. Most men need the reassurance of the familiar. So they carry their value world with them. Churches were quickly raised in the new settlements. The song the pioneer sang linked him to his religious and American past and to the cherished hopes of mankind.

> Have the elder races halted?
> Do they droop and end their lesson, wearied over there beyond the seas?
> We take up the task eternal, and the burden and the lesson, Pioneers! O pioneers! [2]

The frontiersman was contemptuous of the stay-at-home and yet, psychologically, he carried the old home with him. He needed to link his destiny to the task eternal. The Jewish pioneer was contemptuous of those who clung to the parochial world he had left, but he too needed to take his old faith with him and to link his destiny with the task eternal. Manifest destiny transposed into Jewish terms became the mission of Israel. Combine restlessness with nostalgia, the thrust of opportunity with the thirst for belonging, a confusing new world with secure childhood memories, and you have the themes of the poetry of mission. The Jew who went out into the nineteenth century convinced himself that he was not deserting his family or faith but simply responding to a rare opportunity to carry out the ancient mandates.

> Keep us, O Lord, according to Thy will, for Thou hast again taken hold of us and hast again put the torch of Thy light into our hands. [3]

The frontier was a place of religious revival. The preacher was never far behind the outrider. In the new land men wanted the old-time religion; reassurance, but not cathedrals nor pomp and circumstance; encouragement, but without theology and learning. The preacher with a sense of responsibility offered the reassurance and a deeper and older wisdom. Men asked for cool water and he gave them cool water and the warmth of old wine.

The mission of Israel began as a simple song—the dream of home and childhood holiday and a paean to sweeping opportunity and incredible freedom. The Reform rabbi who was never far behind the outriders played on this restlessness and nostalgia in his preaching. "You want to carry out the task eternal. Understand it. Be worthy of it!" He turned a vague optimism into a personal challenge—that is, if he were wise and willing.

The frontier analogy can be pressed too far. Its basic virtue is that it permits us to recognize the mission idea as an emotional response to freedom—as a mood, a song, a hope.

The mission is rhetoric rather than a careful statement of Jewish principles. The mission is excitement rather than a carefully drawn justification of Jewish survival. The mission is a mood and not a message for the ages. Why must this be said? Because the frontier is closed. The Jew has crossed over. The buoyancy of those early days no longer lightens men's hearts. Yet such is the force of habit that preachers and writers in Reform Judaism today still evoke the mission—not, of course, as a natural expression of our times, but as a presumedly valid explanation of Jewish purpose and as a presumedly sufficient definition of Jewish doctrine. Unfortunately, the concept of mission is embarrassing as an explanation of Jewish survival and inadequate and inaccurate as a definition of Jewish doctrine.

In its classic form the mission is a ringing Jewish manifesto: so, for instance, Isaac Mayer Wise declared in 1849:

> The mission of Israel was and still is to promulgate the sacred truths to all nations on earth; to diffuse the bright light that first shown on Sinai's sanctified summit all over the world.[4]

Such declarations are usually defended as contemporary restatement of familiar themes. Kaufmann Kohler claimed that "The idea of Israel's mission . . . forms the very soul and the life force of the Jewish people in its history and literature."[5] Samuel Schulman labeled the mission theme a "doctrine" and baldly asserted that "to deny the mission of Israel is to deny the claims and ideals of the Jew."[6] If the mission theme lies at the core of the Jewish tradition, it ought to be located there. But it cannot be located there, certainly not in a fully defined form. The mission conceit is not so much a clarification of familiar doctrine as an improvisation built on stray themes and fugitive citations.

The biblical and rabbinic tradition believes that the Jewish people have a central role in God's providential plan, but the tradition never loses sight of the fact that the plan is God's. God is in need of man, to be sure, but "except the Lord build the house they labor in vain that build it." [7] God is in need of man but not dependent on man. Judaism preferred the middle ground between the "either" of human helplessness and the "or" of human self-assertion.

A striking novelty of the mission idea is its unconscious homocentricism. Mystery is bled out of history. The context of most mission pronouncements is secular and its legitimacy rests on an evolutionary philosophy of history. Israel as the lamplighter lights the lamps of progress, and these lamps burn ever more brilliantly. Man is not only God's partner in creation but the working partner of the firm.

To illustrate the secular emphasis I would place in juxtaposition two definitions of the role of Israel in the Diaspora. The first is, again, by Isaac Mayer Wise:

> We look upon the destruction of the second Jewish commonwealth not as a punishment for the sinfulness of Israel but as the result of the divine purposes revealed to Abraham, which, as has become ever clearer in the world's history, consist in the dispersion of the Jew to all parts of the earth, for the realization of its high priestly mission, to lead the nations to the true knowledge and worship of God. [8]

Hasdai Crescas, the fourteenth-century philosopher, places the same idea in its more familiar religious context:

> It is through our being exiled and scattered among the nations that His name is proclaimed among all men and the message of the prophets is articulated . . . When the truth is revealed in time, all the nations will come to serve Him, shoulder to shoulder. [9]

Israel was always aware of a special role in God's history. Humility and piety kept the people from defining that role. Thus the familiar rabbinic adage *ein baal ha-nes makkir b'niso*, "the agent of the miracle is unaware that the miracle is being performed through him." [10]

The language of mission is assertive. It is implied that Israel can draw up the specifications of his task and it is boldly suggested that he can fulfill that role. This language borrows more from a confident secular liberalism than from that faith which bowed to God's inscrutable will and that patience which insisted: "Yours not to fulfill the task, but neither are you free to desist from it." [11]

The mission takes the reins of history from God's hands and shifts the focus of responsibility from Israel to the world. The thrust of its ideas is centripetal. Earlier ideas of election, covenant, and commandment emphasized the sanctification of Zion or of the people of Israel; the brunt of the mission rests on the individual as a "do-gooder" in his community. Before the modern idea of the mission was developed by nineteenth-century Reform, Judaism had insisted that if the Kingdom of God were to be realized on earth, it must first be realized in one place, somewhere, before it can be everywhere: "Out of Zion shall go forth the law." [12] Israel's primary obligation was to become a sanctified people: "A kingdom of priests and a holy nation." [13] *Kishet atzmecha v'achar kach kishet acherim,* "First purify thyself and then adorn others," is the way the Talmud puts it.[14] The mission literature nods perfunctorily toward "Israel's priestly function" but the emphasis is on the social crusader rather than on the sanctification of the community. Among the "missionaires," "particularism" is a word loaded with negative connotation.

The mission literature routinely requires religious teaching along with the mandates of civic responsibility. "We should lead all mankind to advance in morality, humility, love of man, and true worship of God." The unique virtue of Judaism is trumpeted.

> It is the messianic task of Israel to make the pure knowledge of God and the pure law of morality of Judaism the common possession and blessing of all the peoples of the earth.[15]

I know of no other period in which preaching seems to come closer to the claim that Judaism is the true and only way. "The religion of the future will be Judaism in its pure denationalized form." [16] A second glance reveals that whatever this religion of the future is, it is not Torah. *In situ* "the pure knowledge of God" suggests a gentle deism rather than the God who revealed Himself at Sinai, and "the pure law of morality of Judaism" suggests the tenets of nineteenth-century melioristic social reform rather than the apodictic *mitzvot* of the Torah or the revolutionary demands of the prophets. Samuel Holdheim pointedly continues, "We do not expect of the nations that, by accepting these teachings, they would give up their historic characteristics in order to accept those of our people." [17] For the first three-fourths of a century of its life in Reform Judaism the mission idea was deemed inimical to proselytism, despite the patent congruence in language and hope and despite the traditional encouragement of such activity. *Lo higlah ha-kadosh baruch hu et Yisrael b'umot elah k'dei she'yityasfu aleihem.*[18] In 1919 Kaufmann Kohler, in his defense of the mission, brought these two ideas back into juxtaposition. What he failed to say was that the rabbinic context of proselytism is Torah. The *ger zedek* was not simply a generous agnostic philanthropist but one who would worship the God of Israel and observe the *mitzvot*.

Those who preached the mission sought to validate their improvisation by citing biblical credentials—especially, and almost exclusively, certain texts from Deutero-Isaiah:

> Behold, My servant, whom I uphold;
> Mine elect, in whom My soul delighteth;
> I have put My spirit upon him,
> He shall make the right to go forth to the nations . . .
> I the Lord have called thee in righteousness,
> And have taken hold of thy hand,
> And kept thee, and set thee for a covenant of the people,
> For a light of the nations.[19]

Several reservations must be entered. Deutero-Isaiah's image of the people of Israel as a light of the nations is idiosyncratic. One searches the rest of the Bible vainly for similar imagery. It is absent from the Torah, where the paradigm for Israel's responsibility is God's summons to Abraham: "Get thee out of thy country, and from thy kindred, and from thy father's house, and unto the land that I will show thee. And I will make of thee a great nation, and I will bless thee, and make thy name great; and be thou a blessing." [20] Neither the way nor the goal is made clear, only God's promise and the moral obligation.

Deutero-Isaiah developed the image of the Jew as "a light unto the nations" within the context of a "covenant of the people." He neither normalized nor glorified the exile, but looked forward to a return to Zion. Once returned to Zion, a purified Israel would witness to the purity of God's faith. The emphasis was on inner group discipline, not on a centripetal and external mission to the larger world.

The "missionaires" chose not to heed Deutero-Isaiah's specific warning not to draw out the terms of God's program:

> For My thoughts are not your thoughts
> Nor are your ways My ways, saith the Lord.
> For as the heavens are higher than the earth,
> So are My ways higher than your ways,
> And My thoughts than your thoughts.[21]

Indeed, they directly violated his spirit when they reduced mission metaphor to specifics. The very text in Deutero-Isaiah which alludes to Israel's divinely ordered role includes a specific injunction against prating about that role.

> Behold, My servant whom I uphold
> Mine elect, in whom My soul delighteth.
> I have put My spirit upon him,
> He shall make the right to go forth to the nations.
> *He will not cry out or lift up his voice*
> *Nor cause his voice to be heard in the street.*[22]

The classic commentaries all understand these lines as an injunction against a self-proclaimed mission. Rashi comments on this verse: "Let him not raise his voice nor busy himself to instruct or prophesy about the nations, for they on their own shall come to learn from him." [23] Ibn Ezra wrote in a similar vein: "Nor cause his voice to be heard in the streets—in order that people should flock unto him." [24]

When Kohler discusses the rabbinic period in his long defense of the mission, he is reduced to emphasizing the openness of normative Judaism to proselytes. The issue is not the non-parochialism of Judaism (that is another matter entirely), but the narrower question: did the Jews recognize the obligation of a specific outward-bound mission to mankind? Our answer must be that Jews never doubted their usefulness to God but that they rarely dared to explain God's ways to other men or to themselves.

Deutero-Isaiah looked to an ingathering of the exiles. Those in Reform Judaism who have claimed his mantle have often warred against the concept of ingathering, and, for the most part, have spent little energy in elaborating what must have been of great concern to Deutero-Isaiah, the specific disciplines of holiness which would purify Israel.

Samuel Holdheim chose to deal with the mission in a letter which had as its counterpoint a denigration of particularism, that is, of all that established the religious uniqueness of Judaism.

> Since the continuance of Judaism is no more actively threat-
> ened from without, particularism in our religion is no longer
> necessary. No need to wait till the ideal brotherly union has
> taken root outside our ranks. He who first discovers a truth
> must be the first to lay it upon the altar of humanity, the first
> to prove its power by the force of living examples. As Jews it
> is our duty to outstrip other faiths in the realization of those
> ideals that are to prevail in the messianic kingdom. As ours we
> claim the mission to bring that kingdom to pass. Far higher
> than the particularism of Judaism is the universalism of the
> prophets, which appeals to all mankind. As surely as we
> recognize its beginnings in the destruction of our former na-
> tionality, so surely is it our duty to promote the building up
> of the future kingdom where all men shall be as brothers.[25]

For some of the reformers, mission was a club with which to beat the very "covenant of the people" which was so precious to Deutero-Isaiah. Paradoxically, the mantle of the very prophet who had rejoiced that "together they sing for joy; for eye to eye they see the return of the Lord to Zion" was claimed by Hold-heim when he ordered *Tisha b'Ab* removed from the liturgical calendar of his congregation because "the destruction of Jerusa-lem was really the beginning of Israel's larger mission to the world and had therefore resulted in good." [26] Deutero-Isaiah's hope of a Torah-radiant Israel clustered around Mount Zion was again and again attacked in the name of the prophet's own con-victions. Kohler defined Zion not as a place but "as the symbol of united humanity, of the realization of mankind's highest ideals at the end of time," [27] that is, he denied Zion. H. G. Enelow drew out the full bill of particulars implicit in the mission idea:

Do not ask my people to become Zionists and go and confine their best energies within that little beloved land beyond the Mediterranean blues. God bless Zion—Israel's cradle and the prophet's home and the patriarchs' great tombs. God bless those that seek the peace of Jerusalem and even today would enhance its glorious beauty. Who will not rejoice to send loving gifts and ornaments to the silver-haired mother of ours— the mother of religion and divine progress? But will ye say that my people has toiled and loved these many years, that it has struggled its way through the world, that it has lived the strenuous and heroic life, that it has taken part in the trade, the arts, the letters, the science, the politics of all nations, that it has gone through all flames and passed through all waters and bled on all battlefields, in order now to go back to Palestine, and form a secluded spiritual sect, or a tenth-rate political state? Ah, no! [28]

The Deutero-Isaiah text does not fit into the context of the mission idea. The mission language suggests an evolutionary philosophy of history, humanism, and a diffusion of activity and responsibility which is unique. Why then does one still hear echoes of mission rhetoric? Many graced it with their deep and proud faith without examining its implications. The mission conceit offered an effective frame for many telling sermon comparisons between the shallow idolatries of secular man and the warm and wise light which shines from the ancient annals. Many saw the mission as no more than a statement of urgency and high responsibility. But whatever its rhetorical value in the past, honesty now compels us to recognize that this whole complex of ideas is a stumbling block to the Jew who would seriously confront his faith in an age which has known Auschwitz and Israel and the closing of the frontier.

To abandon the idea of mission does not require us to deny that Israel has a unique relationship to God and a providential role to play in God's plan, or to argue that Israel ought to cut back its active involvement in social reform. For hundreds of years before the 1840's, Jews accepted covenant, election, and social responsibility without even being aware of the idea of mission. It is still possible for them to do so today.

Its protagonists defended the mission idea as an accurate re-

statement of the central values of Jewish tradition. We have seen
that it is not. The mission idea was also defended as an effective
and useful justification of Jewish survival. This claim needs to be
examined. I believe that such high-flown talk is neither effective
nor compelling but, rather, an obstacle for many who seek to
understand why they should continue the uncertain journey
which has been, and for the foreseeable future will be, the Jews'
destiny.

N'gad sh'ma avad sh'me, "A name made great is a name destroyed." [29] As rhetoric, it is the *chutzpah,* the arrogance, implicit
in the mission conceit, which is its gravest fault. Men smile
tolerantly when they hear claims that thirteen million Jews can
effectively lead "all mankind to advance in morality, humility,
love of man, and true worship of God." Who are we to claim
the mission to bring the Kingdom to pass? Modern thought is
unsentimental. It is well aware that every self-identifying culture
assumed or assumes the priority, if not the sacred character, of
its particular destiny. It asks what is there in the way of life
of a suburban American Jew or of an Israeli farmer-soldier that
can claim a unique standard of holiness? Have the patient
Quaker confraternities of service, or the brave apostles of passive
resistance, or the saints, teachers, and healers in every land and
every community no share in God's providential plan? Did not
Deutero-Isaiah know that Cyrus had a God-appointed role to
play?

The more thoughtful "missionaires" realized that the rhetoric
of mission was not really congruent with the reality of congregations of shopkeepers and salesmen. So Kohler declared:

> To help in the redemption of the world by righteousness is
> his [the Jew's] messianic mission. Nor is it sufficient to claim
> the title of priority for these principles of social justice. He
> must substantiate his mission by its practice in so large a
> measure so as to become from a mere materialistic pursuer of
> wealth, which he has so often been declared to be, the very
> banner bearer of idealism, to command the world's admiration
> and emulation.[30]

The mission's high-flown idealism was a useful standard for
Yom Kippur sermons but embarrassing theology. More often
than not, unyielding reality forced the "missionaires" to fall back

not on specific examples of saintliness in the life of the Jew but on those very claims of primacy in time against which Kohler had warned. Simply by being contemporary exponents of the mission, some hold, the Jew serves the world, reminding it of God and Sinai. Our mere physical presence somehow triggers the superego of Western man.

No, Jews will not vanish. For even if we do not choose to be Jews, the world needs Jews—and Jewish values. If there were no Jews, the world would have to create us. Jacques Maritain, distinguished Roman Catholic philosopher, described Judaism as ". . . like an activating leaven injected into the mass, it gives the world no peace, it bars slumber, it teaches the world to be discontented and restless as long as the world has not God; it stimulates the movement of history." Jews without Judaism are nothing; Jews, living out their Judaism, are a leaven of civilization, and must survive for the sake of the world.[31]

Such is the intricate love-hate relationship between Judaism and her daughter that Jews and Judaism still play a role within the religious conscience of Christendom. But does this symbolic role have any force among the legions of atheists and humanists or in the vast, thronging non-Christian world of Asia and Africa? We must also wonder whether today's Jews will continue to accept Judaism for no better reason than that some non-Jews require the presence of Jews as a reminder of their Old Testament patrimony?

A meaningful philosophy of Jewish existence must validate Jewish existence in personal terms: "What will it mean in my life if I identify myself with Judaism? Will I be wiser, more stable, more aware of the possibilities of my being?" We cannot survive as puppets in a theological shadow play nor as pensioners of bygone dreams. The happy piety that the survival of Judaism is quintessential to the world encourages a loyal few, but only a loyal few. We are a statistically-minded generation: thirteen million people out of a world population of over two billion hardly encourages dreams of supreme importance. We are a self-analytic generation and we know that we do not qualify as the *Lamed Vavniks* [32] of mankind. There can be a world without Jews, and we cannot be confident that such a world would

be any more damned than our world may be despite our
presence.

Israel's primary responsibility has always been to cultivate
dignity and justice within Israel. The far mystery, the cosmic
usefulness of that achievement, we leave to God. "The miracle
is not always recognized by him who experiences it." The messianic vision has it that in the end of days the many will flock
to the mountain of the Lord. They will come to Zion because
Zion has kept the faith and represents the faith. To keep the
faith and to represent the faith is the first responsibility of the
faithful. In that sense Israel's example is important. What is not
found in our tradition is the image of Don Quixote setting out
to overthrow all the evil of the world with a broken lance and a
swaybacked horse. Our fathers insisted that he who saves but
a single life is accounted as if he saved the whole world.

Those who would discuss the survival of Israel should keep
in mind the oft-told tale of the rabbi who set out with high
hopes to save the world until repeated disappointments taught
him that this task was beyond his capacity. Then he had hopes
of kindling the fire of faith throughout his congregation. Despite
all his work, many remained unresponsive and indifferent. Then
he sought to raise his family in certain decency, but even here
he stumbled; each home has its profligate. Finally, at the end of
a long and industrious life, he realized that religious responsibility rests on the energetic cultivation of one's own soul. The
hope that one's labor will bear fruit encourages us to do more,
but it is a hope that only God can validate. What an achievement it would be if we could truly forge Israel as a kingdom of
priests and as a holy nation! Perhaps the holiness of that nation
would encourage or shame others to be more energetic and more
disciplined. We certainly hope so. The point is that we do not
know. God's ways are not our ways.

The validity of Jewish survival can be established in terms of
the growth and the sensitivity and the maturity which Judaism
makes possible for those who opt for the Jewish way of life.
There is, or can be, a formative tension between traditional
ideas and institutions and the Jew who searches for understanding and seeks an inspiring vision. For Israel to be a witness of
God to the world there must be a uniqueness and a distinctive-
ness to our religious culture. Simply to exist as a carbon copy of

surrounding cultures is neither a commendable nor defensible accomplishment.[33]

Abraham Joshua Heschel has stated the particular dilemma which faces anyone who would justify Jewish loyalty to the modern Jew:

> The doors of Western culture are open before him, and whenever he wishes to enter, he finds a welcome place. Why should he not assimilate? The worthwhileness of belonging to the Jewish people must not be taken for granted. Why should he not detach himself from the Jewish community and join another community? Can we in all sincerity say to the Jew: "he who separates himself from Judaism commits spiritual suicide?" [34]

The alternative to Judaism is no longer the boorish and sodden peasant culture of Eastern Europe. The list of Nobel laureates is heavy with scholars born of Jewish parents who, in their adult lives, made no effort to identify themselves with the Jewish people and their cultural or religious institutions.

Mission sermons dilated on the universal vision but neglected the Jewish people and their unique way of life. The mission emphasized a reformist crusade but not the reforming pieties. Yet it is these pieties which alone provide an environment in which the Jew can grow not only in knowledge but in understanding, not only in independence of spirit but in social responsibility, not only in awareness but in holiness. In a confused, materialistic age there are all too few stable spiritual environments. Our age, for all its scientific progress, has not been radically successful in providing an environment in which children can grow up into balanced, wholesome, and sensitive people. Men have been taught to compete, to subordinate their interests to the state, to mistake possession for happiness, to accept the blasphemy of war, to dull their instinct for sympathy. Educational decision has been governed largely by economic and political ideologies. The home has been reduced to an economic unit, and parents place on others many of the responsibilities of training and guidance. The education of the whole man has been neglected for the education of the technician, the soldier, the faithful comrade, the patriot. Judaism, *per contra*, over the centuries has developed a way of life which insists and emphasizes

that the soul of each child is precious and that man justifies and
fulfills himself not as a servant of the machine or of the state but
of God. Our classic texts are biographical and humane rather
than scientific and political. Our classic achievements are a
sensitive home, a truth-seeking school, and a synagogue searching for God. Our religion is a sanctified way of life, a culture
which sets as its goal the disciplined man, fully informed, spiritually independent, but socially conscious and morally bound to
the Commandments of God. Such a culture, if it is seriously
pursued, justifies its existence.

Around every people, each in his way and each in his place,
there is something hidden. But around this people there is
more of the mystery rising out of eternal mystery. When the
poets and the prophets, the teachers and the thinkers who
arose from the people's midst came to think about their people—each in his time and in his way—they contemplated the
unending worlds, the harmony of the spheres, the "heavens
which declare the glory of God." Then they spoke to this
people of its ways and its hope, of the commandments which
it must follow in order to encounter peace. Only one whose
soul has opened to the great mystery which dwells in all,
whether he stands within or sees from without, will be able
to understand the reason why this people is to exist and why
it does exist.

Every people can be chosen for a history, for a share in the
history of humanity. Each is a question which God has asked,
and each people must answer. But more history has been assigned to this people than to any other people. God's question
speaks stronger here.[35]

There is unique benefit in being Jewish. It is a unique opportunity to be a Jew, to participate in this particular unfolding of
truth and life. Our fathers lingered on the people's response to
the invitation of God at Sinai: *na'aseh* precedes *nishma*. Once
there is the original sense of corporate identity, the unique corporate responsibility of the people flows inevitably; out of its
lifelong task of admiration and emulation comes the unfolding
of that which is unique to it. As it reaches for the truth, it draws
truth to itself. A history as long and successful as that of the

Jew is, in its own way, the proof of the virtue of its particularity and validates its claim to our continued partnership in it.

NOTES

1. Frederick J. Turner, *The Frontier in American History* (New York: Henry Holt & Co., 1948), p. 3.

2. Walt Whitman, "Pioneers! O Pioneers!"

3. Samuel Holdheim, *Gebetbuch* (Berlin: 1848), I, 191 (translated by W. Gunther Plaut, *The Rise of Reform Judaism* [New York: World Union for Progressive Judaism, 1963], I, 140).

4. Isaac M. Wise, "The Occident, 1849" (quoted in D. Wilansky, *Sinai to Cincinnati* [New York: Renaissance, 1937], p. 29).

5. Kaufmann Kohler, "The Mission of Israel and Its Application to Modern Times," *CCAR Yearbook*, XXIX (1919), 265.

6. Samuel Shulman, "Comments on the Mission of Israel . . ." *Ibid.*, p. 289.

7. Psalms 127:1.

8. Quoted in James R. Heller, *Isaac M. Wise* (New York: Union of American Hebrew Congregations, 1965), p. 536.

9. Hasdai Crescas, *Or Adonai*, 2:4:3 (quoted in Jacob B. Agus, *The Evolution of Jewish Thought* [New York: Abelard–Schuman, 1959], p. 218).

10. T. B. Nid. 31a.

11. M. Pirke Abot 2:21.

12. Isaiah 2:3.

13. Exodus 19:6.

14. T. B. B. M. 107b.

15. Samuel Holdheim, *Neue Sammlung Jüdischer Predigten* (Berlin: 1862), I, 156 (quoted in Plaut, *op. cit.*, p. 141).

16. Wise, in Heller, *op. cit.*, p. 536.

17. Holdheim, *loc. cit.*

18. T. B. Pes 87b.

19. Isaiah 42:1-6.

20. Genesis 12:1-2.

21. Isaiah 55:8-9.

22. Isaiah 42:1-2.

23. Rashi to Isaiah 42:2.

24. Ibn Ezra to Isaiah 42:2.

25. Samuel Holdheim, "Reply to Herzfeld" (quoted in "Samuel Holdheim, the Jewish Reformer" by I. H. Ritter, *Jewish Quarterly Review*, Old Series, I, 211).

26. Samuel Holdheim, sermon quoted in David Philipson, *The Reform Movement in Judaism* (New York: Macmillan, 1907), p. 353, Note I.

27. Kohler, *op. cit.*, pp. 286-87.

28. Hyman G. Enelow, *Selected Works*, (ed. F. A. Levy, 1935), I, 134.

29. M. Pirke Abot 1:13.

30. Kohler, *op. cit.*, p. 283.

31. Maurice N. Eisendrath, *Can Faith Survive?* (New York: McGraw-Hill, 1964), p. 22.

32. In East European Jewish folklore, the *Lamed Vavniks* are those thirty-six hidden saints in every generation through whose piety alone the world continues to exist. The legend is based on a passage in the Talmud.

33. Cf. Numbers Rabbah 20:22: *Kol makom she'ne'emar ha-am lashon gnai hu, kol makom she'ne'emar Yisrael lashon shevach hu.*

34. Abraham J. Heschel, "The Problem of the Individual," in *Proceedings of the Jerusalem Ideological Conference* (Jerusalem: World Zionist Organization, 1959), p. 347.

35. Leo Baeck, *This People Israel* (New York: Union of American Hebrew Congregations, 1964), pp. 401-02.

THE ELECTION, THE COVENANT,
AND THE MISSION OF ISRAEL

Samuel E. Karff

I

During the late Bronze Age a group of Hebrew slaves united under the leadership of Moses and escaped from Egyptian bondage. In the wilderness of Sinai this "mixed multitude" learned the meaning of its liberation. Fate became faith and the people Israel was born.

> The Lord called to him from a mountain, saying, Thus shall ye say to the House of Jacob and declare to the children of Israel, "You have seen what I did to the Egyptians, how I bore you on eagles' wings and brought you to Me. Now then if you will obey Me faithfully and keep My covenant, you shall be My treasured possession among all the peoples. Indeed all the earth is Mine, but you shall be to Me a kingdom of priests and a holy nation." [1]

To be a son of the covenant is to remember that mixed multitude's liberation from Egypt as "that which the Lord did for me." It is to share the experience and accept the obligations of that people whom Yahveh, the Nameless One, redeemed and consecrated to His service.

When he asks "What mean *ye* by this service?" the wicked son of the Passover Haggadah is guilty of faithlessness to the covenant. He fails to identify with his people's sacred history. He denies the actuality or, at least, the personal relevance of Israel's escape from bondage and God's redemptive act.

The modern world has created a fifth son. He accepts the enduring relevance of his ancestor's bondage and liberation but is unable to celebrate those events as "that which the Lord did for me." He may feel himself addressed in some special way by the injunction, "you shall not oppress the stranger" and may nod approvingly at the words, "for ye were strangers in the land of Egypt." He shares his people's fate and some of the values forged on the anvil of its common destiny, but he cannot respond to that sacred alchemy by which fate became faith and values became Torah. He acknowledges a covenant with his people, but it is a covenant in which God is at best a silent partner.

For this secular son of Israel Egypt's Pharaoh may be paradigmatic—an ominous portent of Nebuchadnezzar, Antiochus, Titus, Torquemada, Hitler, Stalin. He does not deny that Auschwitz addresses him, a Jew, with special significance. Indeed to be a Jew is to be refused the privilege of forgetting that Egypt may not be too far behind. To be a Jew is to be a member of a particularly vulnerable minority in an imperfect world.

Let two contemporary Jewish writers speak for this fifth son. "Whatever the distance that separates me from a certain part of Jewry in the world," writes Albert Memmi, "I know that we are living a similar experience. What touches them, what affects them, may one day touch and affect me. They must suffer the same apprehension I do, the same expectation, the same ordeals." [2]

Albert Memmi writes out of his experience as an Algerian refugee. Bernard Malamud's vision has been tempered by the placid breeze of a free society. He remains nonetheless Memmi's covenant kinsman. In a fictionalized account of the Mendel

Beiliss case, Malamud describes a Jew who learns that he cannot easily escape the "burdens of history." Unable to acknowledge a covenant with God, this Jew makes a "covenant with himself" and accepts "responsibility for those who are similarly entangled" until the day dawns when the Jew will be the truly liberated son of a universal brotherhood.[3]

Is the modern Jew's endurance simply the by-product of the gentile emancipation's broken promises? Is Jewish self-consciousness merely, as Sartre contends, our defensive response to a world which insists that we are Jews?

Monford Harris has convincingly argued that the Zionist movement, even in its most secular form, was impelled by a Jewish will to survive, an inchoate recognition that the Jews qua Jews ought not disappear from the earth.[4] The American Jewish parent who exhorts his marriageable son: "We are not religious, but one thing I expect from you . . ." offers a Diaspora equivalent of this will to endure. To be sure, the world does remind us that we are Jews, but we find in this reminder the confirmation, not the source, of that ill-defined feeling that our Jewish vocation—whatever it may be—has not ended.

According to our sacred history, the Jew's endurance is the by-product of two forces. The first of these is a God whose love and providential purpose will not release this people. He may punish but will not forsake them. For His name's sake, this people must remain His distinct, if not always steadfast, witness until the end of days.[5] The second factor is Israel's faithfulness to its vocation. God's experience with the people is not an uninterrupted series of dismal disappointments. Israel has frequently proved ready to suffer and even die for the covenant. Quoting Psalm 44, the rabbinic sages affirm anew, "because of Thee we are slain the whole day long, we are counted as sheep for the slaughter."[6] And Judah Halevi's Rabbi reminds the Khazar monarch, "think of the thoughtful men among us who could escape this degradation by a word spoken lightly . . . but they do not do so out of allegiance to their faith."[7]

Surely the contemporary American son of the covenant does not suffer for his faith, but he does have the option of escaping through calculated assimilation the still vulnerable status that his Jewishness entails. That many a "nonreligious" Jew eschews

this option is not merely a response to lingering gentile exclusiv-
ism but the acknowledgment of a claim which he believes ought
not to be betrayed.

Yet if the fifth son is to recover the depth of his covenant consciousness, he must regain the posture of Jacob-Israel and truly
wrestle with his sacred history. He must explore and seek to
understand that call-response through which Israel was born.

Jewish theology is the Jew's interpretation of his history.
Whether its monotheistic faith came to it decisively during the
period of the Exodus or gradually ripened in the prophetic era,
a living people emerged which dwelt in an ideological realm far
removed from its neighbors. A people was born which acknowl-
edged the sovereignty of a single, universal, imageless, creative,
and moral power, unencumbered by mythological counterparts—
the sole Ruler of fate, nature, and history. This God demanded
exclusive loyalty from His worshippers, and His will was intended to govern every sphere of their lives.

How did Yahveh, the Nameless One, become the God of
Israel? How and why was a particular relation (covenant) established between Yahveh and this people? The biblical historian's
answer is unequivocal. God took the initiative by revealing Himself to this people as its Redeemer and Lawgiver. God's love
was then, at least officially, reciprocated by Israel. The people
accepted the sovereignty of the Lord and pledged to serve Him.
Thus the covenant was born.

Why this particular people? The traditional answer given in
rabbinic literature embodies two diverse strands. The one accen-
tuates the mystery of divine love:

> We would not know whether God chose Israel for His
> treasure or whether Israel chose the Holy One, Blessed be He.
> The answer is taught in the following: "And the Lord, your
> God, chose you." And whence do we know that the Holy
> One, Blessed be He, chose Jacob? Because it is said, "not
> like these is the portion of Jacob, for He is the creator of all
> things and Israel is the tribe of His inheritance . . ." (Jere-
> miah 10:16).[8]

The other, seeking a rational ground for the particular destiny of the Jews, explains that God revealed Himself to other peoples as well but Israel alone accepted the demand and promise of the covenant.[9] Only after the people responded "we shall do and we shall hearken" did God refer to Israel as "my people." [10] Rabbi Jose b. Simon has God remind Israel, "Were it not for your acceptance of my Torah, I would not recognize you or regard you any more than the other nations." [11]

Later covenant theologians also sought to rationalize God's love for Israel. Judah Halevi posited a biogenetic endowment which empowered this people to receive God's revelation.[12] And, much later, Kaufmann Kohler was to speak of "hereditary virtues and tendencies of mind and spirit which equip Israel for his calling." [13] But to speak of biogenetic or hereditary endowments is not to dissipate the mystery. Why was Israel so endowed? Ultimately he who seeks to explain the birth of this unique people must invoke such terms as "ripe historical conditions," "chance," "creative genius"—terms no more compelling or explanatory than the claim of revelation and the mystery of divine grace.

III

Jews of today may feel a duty to survive without understanding the meaning of that duty. How did our forebears interpret the significance of their liaison with God? The people of Israel was born by the recognition of God's role in its history and God's claim (the Commandments of the Torah) upon it. This covenant community actually became a missionary people when monolatry ripened into the full blown monotheism of a Second Isaiah; then Israel's faithfulness to Yahveh became a vehicle for His ultimate dominion over all the children of men.[14] The earlier phase of Israel's existence is represented in the declaration, "ye shall be unto me a kingdom of priests and a holy nation"; [15] the final phase embraces the promise, "in thee and thy seed shall all the nations of the earth be blessed." [16] But the rabbis knew no historical development: from its very *birth* Israel was a "light unto the nations," and Abraham was the first Jewish missionary.[17]

Whereas the gentile, according to rabbinic teaching, may fulfill his pre-messianic destiny by observing the Noahide laws, the

Jew's greater burden of commandments is commensurate with his special divine vocation.[18] By fulfilling the Torah he bears witness to God and hastens the coming of the Kingdom.

By his observance or nonobservance of the *mitzvot*, the Jew either sanctifies or profanes God's Name in the world.[19] When an Israelite observes the Sabbath he bears witness to God as Creator of the world.[20] Indeed, his recitation of the Sabbath prayer renders him, as it were, "a partner with God in the creation." [21] Of the Chanukah *Menorah* the Talmud asks rhetorically, "Does He then require its light? Surely during the entire forty years that the Israelites travelled in the wilderness, they travelled only by His light." To which the following conclusion is given: the light of the *Menorah*, the publication of the miracle, is testimony to mankind that God's presence rests in the midst of Israel.[22]

The transcendent significance of Israel's faithfulness to the covenant is rehearsed in many statements, the boldest of which is attributed to Simeon b. Yochai: "Scripture declares, 'ye are my witnesses and I am God.' This means, so long as you testify to me I am God. If you cease to testify to me, I am no longer God." [23]

Significantly, Israel's vocation was not dependent on an active and successful proselytizing campaign. After Rome's alliance with the Church prohibited Jewish missionary work, Jews still believed that by their very endurance as the *mitzvah*-observing people they were in some direct way hastening the day of redemption.

Jewish existence was, however, not solely the instrument of providence. By covenant faithfulness the individual Jew also attained personal fulfillment. What life has greater meaning than that of the man who believes he is needed by, and has the power to serve or betray, the Source of his being? The Pharisees accentuated this personal dimension of Jewish existence. They elaborated what Ellis Rivkin has called a "*mitzvah* system of salvation," whereby the individual Jew believed that his personal destiny in this world and in the world to come was contingent upon his covenant faithfulness. Under the Pharisaic aegis, Rosh Hashonah was transformed from a ceremony celebrating the enthronement of Yahveh to a day of personal judgment in the presence of the Creator and Ruler of the world.[24]

The motif of personal fulfillment receives its crispest formulation in Rav's rhetorical question, "for what difference does it make to God whether one slaughters [an animal] from the back of the neck or the front of the neck? Hence, the commandments were not given save to purify God's creatures." [25] The Jew, claims Rav, has received a precious path to self-humanization through which he may attain blessing in this world and in the world to come. To the question, "Why should I be a Jew?", the rabbis thus offered a twofold answer: *covenant existence is both the means to my personal fulfillment as a man who was born a Jew and the way I may share my people's unique vocation in the world.*

Later theologians, reflecting on the covenant, have accentuated one or the other of these dual motifs. In his *Guide for the Perplexed*, Maimonides explains that man's "possession of the highest intellectual faculties, the possession of such notions which lead to true metaphysical opinions as regards God . . . gives him immortality, and on its account he is called man." [26] And how does the Jew attain this goal? Maimonides' Commentary on the Mishnah portrays God as declaring: "If you will heed my commandments, I will assist you in their performance, so that you may attain perfection in them . . . the persons who strive to do the commandments will be healthy and secure until they have attained that degree of knowledge through which they will merit the life of the world to come." [27] Even the messianic age itself, Maimonides claims, is but a tranquil state of earthly existence such as would enable the Jew (man) to cultivate his highest intellectual faculties.[28]

If Maimonides conceived the covenant, with its commandments, as a unique and splendid instrument for man's self-realization, Judah Halevi gave priority to Israel's divine vocation in the world. Israel is a prophet people, the bearer of God's truth until the time of the world's redemption. Israel's credentials are certified by its willingness to die for the faith, its steadfast loyalty despite suffering, its very survival, and its unbroken tradition of transmitting the Torah from generation to generation.[29] This people is punished and purified through suffering, but the Torah remains the vehicle for the discharge of its exalted task. Thereby Israel is able to "cleave to the divine quality in prophecy and states of mind that are close to it." [30] Israel, says Halevi, is the

"heart of mankind"; as this organ is afflicted by the diseases of
the body, so too the health of the heart radiates blessing to the
entire body.[31] He speaks also of Israel as a seed "which falls to
the ground and apparently is transformed into earth, water and
dung without leaving a trace," but in reality this seed "transforms
earth and water into its own substance . . . [until] the tree (all
mankind) bears fruit like that from which it had been produced." [32]

The distinction between Maimonides and Halevi must not be
pressed excessively. Whereas one is especially gripped by the
self-fulfilling dimension of Jewish existence and the other by the
mission of a living, suffering, and witnessing people, Maimonides
surely affirmed that the Jews were also custodians of a unique
truth and Halevi regarded the Torah as an avenue to personal
salvation as well. But what for them was a matter of emphasis
has become in modern times almost a matter of separation.

It may be argued that Jewish liberalism, in its early phase,
defined the covenant primarily, if not exclusively, as the vehicle
of the world's redemption. To Hermann Cohen, the Jew was the
sole bearer of a truth essential for "the religious progress of mankind." Its elements included the unity and uniqueness of God,
man's direct confrontation with his Creator, the freedom and
moral responsibility of the individual, and the messianic hope.[33]
Cohen's concept of the Jew as a servant of a religious idea became, for Kohler, a people's obligation to a personal God Who
consecrated it as "the bearer of the most lofty truth of religion
among mankind." [34] Kohler affirmed that past periods of oppression and enforced isolation had caused many a Jew to "lose sight
of his sublime mission for the world at large," a mission best
expressed in the *Neilah* service of David Einhorn's *High Holyday
Prayerbook:* "Endow us, our Guardian, with strength and patience
for our holy mission and grant that all the children of Thy people may recognize the goal of our changeful career—one humanity on earth even as there is but one God in heaven." [35] At
times, it seems, Jewish religious liberalism was so preoccupied
with what the Jew could offer the world that it virtually ignored
what living within the covenant could offer the Jew.

This emphasis of classical Reform theology was totally reversed
by Mordecai Kaplan's Reconstructionism. "Jewish religion," writes
Kaplan, "is that aspect of Judaism which identifies as holy or
divine whatever in the cosmos impels and enables the Jewish

people, individually and collectively, to make the most of life ethically and spiritually." [36] Whereas Kohler saw Jewish survival as an instrument for the fulfillment of a divine mission among the peoples of the earth, Kaplan has viewed Judaism as an instrument for the survival and self-realization of the Jew.

To be sure, Kohler would not have denied that Judaism humanizes its adherents, and Kaplan, in his later writings, has been drawn to speak of a Jewish vocation in the world. In his book *The Purpose and Meaning of Jewish Existence,* Kaplan contends that "none of the historical religions other than that of the Jewish people is capable of undergoing the reconstruction which is essential to rendering [it] relevant to the urgent needs of contemporary mankind." [37] Thus he who once disdained Reform's concept of a mission for Israel has himself lately assigned a transcendent and unique role to the modern Jew.[38] Whereas Kohler viewed Israel as the bearer of ethical monotheism in its most exalted form, Kaplan's Jew is potentially a unique teacher of the role a desupernaturalized religion ought to play in the life of man. Nevertheless, Kohler saw Israel chiefly as the bearer of God's word, while Kaplan continues to view Judaism primarily as an instrument for the self-realization of the Jewish people.

IV

One who believes that the Jews have a unique and essential role in the history of redemption must still ask: how shall this task be fulfilled? In the pre-emancipation era all Jews would have agreed that the "yoke of commandments" was the way to fulfill the mission of a holy people. However, with the breakdown of the Torah's binding power and the growing self-image of the Jew as a more active shaper of his own destiny (and that of the world about him), the strategy of covenant fulfillment has been reappraised. Let us consider three distinctive answers that have been offered in the modern world.

Negating the Exile, Liberal Judaism in its classical form saw the Jew as a creative catalyst for messianic redemption within the land of his domicile. Like Hermann Cohen before him, Leo Baeck regarded the Jew as the potential vanguard of the spirit of ethical monotheism which would, in time, become the cornerstone of a just and benevolent society. In his classic volume, *The*

Essence of Judaism, Baeck enjoined: "The good that one practices
is the best witness of God that one can give . . . the standard
of action thus becomes the following test: will it bear witness
for Judaism?" [39] The American Reformers found a soil uniquely
hospitable to this witness. In response to the query "why be a
Jew?" Emil G. Hirsch once replied:

> Our distinction results simply from the keenest sense of
> responsibility and the consciousness that whether other men
> may or may not choose to be slow to do the right, we must
> ever be quick and exemplify the higher life in the eyes of the
> world. As individuals or by our social institutions, by our
> public morality, by our deeds and in the secrecy of our closet
> even, we must so live that indeed through us God's name be
> sanctified and the families of the earth be blessed through our
> influence for the good, noble and true. [40]

The Jew, said Hirsch, must fulfill his divine vocation as "sentinel
and soldier of righteousness."

At first, one would hardly regard Emil G. Hirsch and Martin
Buber as theological kinsmen. Yet each affirmed that it was the
Jew's task to serve as God's exemplar. Commenting on Isaiah's
messianic vision, Buber declared: "Nations can be led to peace
only by a people which has made peace a reality within itself.
The realization of the spirit has a magnetic effect on mankind
which despairs of the spirit." [41] The "spirit of Israel," Buber
maintained, is Israel's understanding that man must initiate the
creation of a "true community" and its acceptance of the mandate to lead the way: "There is one nation which once upon a
time heard this charge so loudly and clearly that the charge
penetrated to the very depth of its soul." [42]

Buber thus shared the vision of the classical Reformers: Israel
is commissioned to demonstrate, by word and deed, the goal
which God has set for all men. But whereas the Reformers saw
the Diaspora Jew as an effective witness for prophetic truth,
Buber regarded the rebirth of the Jewish community in Palestine, and particularly the creation of the kibbutz, as the most
fertile soil for the cultivation of the Jewish spirit in the contemporary world. In the Diaspora the Jew all too often merely
proclaimed his faith in the Messiah without taking seriously the
"preparation of the world in readiness for the Kingdom." [43] In

the modern Diaspora the "American of Jewish faith" is apt to neglect or even betray his task through lack of any true communal existence. Israel—and here Buber agrees with Ben Gurion—offers the Jew a unique possibility to fulfill his sacred vocation.

> For only an entire nation which comprehends peoples of all kinds can demonstrate a life of unity and peace, of righteousness and justice to the human race as a sort of example and beginning . . . a true history can only commence with a certain definite and true nation . . . the people of Israel was charged to lead the way toward this realization.[44]

To the question of the content of the Jew's divine vocation, Rosenzweig offered still a third answer that is at variance with the more promethean activism of Hermann Cohen, Emil G. Hirsch, and Martin Buber. The Jew, said Rosenzweig, is at once a stranger in the world and at home with God. By his biological endurance and his continuing response to the commanding presence of the God of Abraham, by bearing children, and by observing the precepts of Torah, the Jew simultaneously anticipates the world's redemption and declares that the Messiah has not yet come.[45] Rosenzweig eschewed the role of the Jewish activist. The Jew is already "with God," the God from whom the world remains estranged. His exile is a sign of the world's alienation. In the pre-messianic age, the children of the covenant have no responsibility for God's world save to endure as a faithful community. The Jew need seek no converts, establish no model communities, involve himself in no social movements, to advance God's kingdom. Thus, Rosenzweig could write without fear of misunderstanding: "Insofar as it has reached the goal which it anticipates in hope (for all mankind) . . . its soul . . . grows numb to the concerns, the doing and the struggle of the world." [46]

Two fundamentally distinct modes of Jewish witness have thus been suggested. Hirsch, Buber, Cohen, Baeck, all affirmed that what the Jewish people must offer God is *active engagement in the task of transforming the world in His behalf,* whether as proclaimers of truth, "sentinels of righteousness" in the Diaspora, or builders of a true nation in the land of Israel. For Rosenzweig what the Jewish people offers God is simply its *presence* in the world, a presence which in and of itself proclaims God's sovereignty, casts judgment on all of man's penultimate solutions, and patiently waits for the messianic redemption.

The difference between Rosenzweig and Buber is essentially the distinction between what Sheldon Blank has called the "passive" and "active" mission in biblical prophecy.[47] The "passive mission" is the prophetic claim that God's impending restoration of Israel's glory and Israel's grateful acknowledgment of His grace and power will sanctify God's name and hasten the day of His universal kingdom. *God's* acts are here regarded as the crucial factor. Israel serves Him by receiving and publicly acknowledging *His* benefactions. "I even I am the Lord, and beside Me there is no savior. I have declared and I have saved . . . . Therefore ye are My witnesses saith the Lord, and I am God."[48] The "active mission," also embodied in Deutero-Isaiah, commissions this people to speak God's word and to share God's work. "I, the Lord, have called thee in righteousness, and have taken hold of thy hand, and kept thee, and set thee for a covenant of the people, for a light of the nations, to open the blind eyes, to bring out the prisoners from the dungeon and them that sit in darkness out of the prison-house."[49] Rosenzweig offers a modern equivalent of Deutero-Isaiah's concept of the passive mission. Israel's very endurance is a vindication of God's sovereignty, "wordless evidence which gives the lie to the worldly and all-too-worldly sham eternity of the historical moments of the nations."[50] Buber's vision, on the other hand, is more akin to the active mission of a prophetic people whom God has charged to pave the way and begin the work of redemption.

V

"The teachers of Judaism," wrote Abba Hillel Silver, "almost instinctively rejected a formula of either-or in assaying religious values. They avoided all sharp antinomies, all irreconcilables which lead to a spiritual impasse."[51] Let this wisdom guide us as we seek to find the contemporary meaning of the covenant. To the question, why be a Jew? let us answer with the best of normative Judaism: *covenant existence is equally and unequivocally the road to personal fulfillment for a man who is born a Jew*

*and his way of sharing the vocation of a people consecrated to
God.*

Each man is the offspring of particular parents. Each man in-
herits a particular history. When a man or people respond to
an event with the words, "this is what the Lord did for me,"
history becomes revelation. Each man turns to his own "inner
history" for the meaning of his individual life. Here, in part,
is what continues to separate Christian and Jew. The Christian
remembers Bethlehem and Calvary, the Jew remembers Egypt
and Sinai.

That sign of God's love which one has found in the Incarnation, the other has received in his liberation from bondage and
the gift of the Torah. That standard for piety which the devout
Christian finds in the life of Jesus, the Jew obtains from the
teachings of Torah. That forgiving grace which one derives from
a sacrificial death, the other receives from the God who says,
"Am I not like a father unto you, O house of Israel?" That confidence in God's death-transcending, value-conserving power
which the Christian affirms through the resurrection, the Jew
derives from his covenant relation to Him who is the Author of
death and the Renewer of life. That redemptive hope which one
finds through him who came and will return, the other finds in
him who has been promised and is yet to come. Those categories
of meaning which the Christian has found in Father, Son, and
Holy Spirit, the Jew has discovered in God, Torah, and Israel.

As a Jew, I need not deny that the mystery of divine love and
grace is present in the sacred history of my Christian neighbor,
and I disavow the implication—admittedly present in some of
my forefather's utterances—that God loves me more than him who
dwells outside my covenant. I believe in the mystery of election
but reject the concept of special love. Nor must I deny that
Christian and Jew each has a role in the work of redemption.
But even as the sacred history through which the Christian finds
personal salvation is not mine, the truth to which he bears witness subtly and at times not so subtly diverges from my own.
Each of us anticipates the coming of God's Kingdom; until then
we must wait for the decisive arbitration of our conflicting claims.

The Christian gospel is derived from God's revelation in Jesus
Christ, the mission of Israel is grounded in the covenant of Sinai.

The key to an understanding of my unique Jewish vocation may be found in *the very structure of the covenant itself, for God's relation to Israel is the paradigm of His covenant with all men.* He whom we have known in our history lifts all men to the dignity of sharing in the work of redemption: "The human world is meant to become a single body through the action of men themselves. We men are challenged to perfect our own portion of the universe." [52]

Man's dignity derives in part from his divinely appointed task, from his power to transform the world in accordance with a divine design. This truth is embodied in the conditional dimension of the covenant. Man is commanded and is accountable. His acts are laden with profound consequences. Through Israel, the Nameless One reveals man to himself as a partner of God. But if one dimension of the covenant affirms man's power, another no less dramatically confirms his finitude. The covenant was born when God's power and unmerited love liberated a band of helpless slaves. The people is called upon to judge itself in terms of a transcendent source of value—a standard given to and not created by man. The people bears witness to a kingdom which God alone must bring to pass.

Israel's life with God uniquely reveals a creative tension in all men's relation to the Source of Being. *We live our lives astride accountability and grace, justice and love, forever poised between an affirmation of our significant power and an acknowledgment of our dependence on divine gifts.*

The Jew is called to proclaim a twofold truth for all men: we mortals stand before God "creaturely and creative." Man both receives life and holds it in custody. He accepts Torah and performs significant deeds. He must wait for the Messiah even as he prepares the way for his coming.

For a covenant-affirming Jew the contemporary theological ferment is a two-edged sword. He will respond to the spirit of the "secular city" with one hand that beckons and another hand that repels. When its prophets call on man to accept a significant measure of responsibility for the work of the world, the Jew will give his gladsome approval. When, however, the "new theology" seeks to deny the transcendent power of a God who creates worlds, redeems the oppressed, and reveals value, the authentic Jew will suspect a new idolatry. The covenant does not call man to glorify God by celebrating his own nothingness, but neither does it permit man to create himself in the divine image.

Twentieth-century man's staggering power lends unprecedented urgency to the prophetic demand for man's acceptance of his human responsibility. An Isaiah reincarnate would hardly counsel reliance on divine love to prevent the nuclear apocalypse. Our prophetic legacy also impels us to see the plague of racial turmoil as warning and judgment upon all who refuse to "let My people go." Man remains, however, God's partner, not His cosmic successor. Man is summoned to share the work of redemption and suffer the consequences of default, but covenant man will deny that he is himself the Redeemer.

The greatest of commandments is the prohibition of idolatry. To serve the Nameless One is to disarm the numberless claimants to His throne. No cult, ideology, social order, or person deserves our uncritical devotion. Indeed, even our *images* of God and Torah are themselves subject to continuing reappraisal. Man's continuing openness to transcendence is his greatest safeguard against worshipping himself or the work of his hands. Such openness is also his deepest ground for hope.

VI

The very structure of the covenant confirms the Jew in a mission at once "active" and "passive." That dimension of his faith which affirms his partnership with the divine summons him to share with all men in the work of the kingdom.

It has been frequently said that we Jews are the "barometer of history." Our fate appears to be inextricably bound up with a nation's response to the issues of justice. When a society in which we dwell fails to build with the plumb line of justice, we who merely *share* in these failures are *singled out* as the most vulnerable victim of the crumbling social order. Is this perhaps the eerie meaning of Amos' prophecy: "You only have I known of all the families of the earth; therefore, I will punish you for all your iniquities"?

When the Jew is tempted to identify with the oppressor or turn a deaf ear to man's cry for freedom, the great weight of covenant responsibility is soon suspended over his head. The Jewish bigot soon discovers that he must ultimately choose between a George Lincoln Rockwell, the neo-Nazi who hated the Jew no less than he did the Negro, and a Martin Luther King.

That individual Jews may betray their heritage, or that many a non-Jew surpasses a son of the covenant as witness for justice, does not compromise, much less invalidate, the primary obligation of a people who first heard the words of the prophets and remain charter witnesses to the divine demand for *tzedek*. That demand addresses the Jew both in the Diaspora and in the land of Israel. If in America we stand especially accountable for the quality and intensity of our involvement in "social action," in Israel we are summoned to build a Jewish state which submits to the judgment of its prophetic legacy. By *tzedek* the prophets meant more than doing justly, but surely nothing less.

What of our "passive" mission? We are history's most illustrious survivors. This in itself lends a unique dimension to our covenant faithfulness. To deny that redemption is here and yet attest that "my Redeemer liveth" is a witness fraught with special significance when borne by history's most time-tested survivor in a world that proclaims "God is dead."

By our Sabbath observance we continue to affirm that life is a purposeful gift, not an accident. The Seder testifies that the tyrants of history do not speak the last word, for man is not alone in his eternal quest for freedom. Our annual observance of the Feast of Revelation and our weekly reading of the Torah confirm that true values are ultimately man's discovery, not his creation. The Jew who "in spite of everything" joyfully brings his children into the covenant of Abraham thereby denies that life is nothing more than a sick joke or a dirty trick, even as the Jew who kindles the *menorah* and pridefully admits that he is a cultural outsider in the Christmas season most poignantly proclaims that the day to which Israel first pointed has not yet arrived.

By all these "ritual" acts which bind him to the covenant of his fathers, the Jew becomes a member of Rosenzweig's "eternal people," affirming that God—the Creator, the Giver of Torah, the Redeemer of the oppressed—is not dead, though His Kingdom has yet to be established upon the earth. By his life as a Jew the son of the covenant "binds creation to redemption while redemption is still to come." [53]

The most formidable task of our time, however, is to develop a

generation for whom Jewish history can become once again revelation, a generation able to remember the Exodus as "that which
the Lord did for me." Technologically *nouveau riche,* modern
man finds it difficult to see beyond his possessions and powers; he
feels no compulsion to confess that he is the receiver of divine
gifts. Those forces which have corroded modern man's response
to transcendence have surely afflicted the Jew with even greater
intensity. (After all, is this not what Halevi meant by the price
of being "the heart of mankind"?)

The staggering enormity of demonic evil in our time has compounded man's incapacity to hear by God's failure to speak. The
"hiddenness of God" is responsible for the fifth son among us
who affirms Jewish fate without faith. His predicament should
engage, not the self-righteous scorn, but the empathy of even
the most theologically committed Jew. Anyone who takes seriously God's silence at Auschwitz may be forgiven the occasional
thought that perhaps Moses was the only hero of the Exodus
after all. Yet surely the goal of an authentic covenant existence is
a reunion of fate and faith, of history and revelation. The authentic Jew is Yisroel, the one who contends with God but does
not deny Him, who argues while he prays, who doubts as he
serves, and whose very demands of his Creator betray a primordial trust yearning for confirmation.

Covenant theology speaks of a God Who would much prefer
to be honestly challenged than ignored. If in this age of God's
eclipse, the Jew remains Yisroel, dare we not hope that in time
fate will acknowledge faith and history, revelation? Then the
pre-messianic vulnerability of the Jew will be traced once again
to Sinai, and his duty to survive will be experienced as an answer
to a claim which is at once an inescapable burden and a precious
heritage. That heritage will need no longer be transmitted, that
burden no longer assumed only "on that day when the Lord
shall be One and His name One."

NOTES

1. Exodus 19:3-6.
2. Albert Memmi, *Portrait of a Jew* (New York: Orion Press, 1962), p. 275.
3. Bernard Malamud, *The Fixer* (New York: Farrar, Straus & Giroux, 1966).
4. Monford Harris, in Arnold J. Wolf (ed.), *Rediscovering Judaism* (Chicago: Quadrangle Books, 1965).
5. Ezekiel 36:20-24; Sifre 35b, 112a.
6. Sifre 73a; Canticles Rabbah 1:15; T. B. Gittin 57b.
7. Kuzari, Book IV:23.
8. Sifre 134b; cf. Deuteronomy Rabbah 5:6.
9. Mekilta Bahodesh, Lauterbach Edition, II, 234 ff.
10. Tanhuma B. Vaera 9a.
11. Exodus Rabbah 47:4.
12. Kuzari, Book I:95.
13. Kaufmann Kohler, *Jewish Theology* (New York: Macmillan, 1928), p. 328.
14. Isaiah 42:6; cf. Exodus 20:3.
15. Exodus 19:6.
16. Genesis 12:3.
17. T. B. Sotah 10b; Genesis Rabbah 43:8; cf. Sifre 134b.
18. T. B. Sanhedrin 56a.
19. Mekilta Shirata, II, 28f.
20. *Ibid.*, Shabbata, III, 200.
21. T. B. Shabbat 119b.
22. *Ibid.*, 22b.
23. Sifre 144a.
24. T. B. Rosh Hashonah 16a.
25. Genesis Rabbah 44:1.
26. *Guide for the Perplexed*, Book III, chap. 54.
27. Maimonides, Commentary to Tenth Chapter of Sanhedrin.
28. *Ibid.*
29. Kuzari, Book II:30-44.
30. *Ibid.*, I:109.
31. *Ibid.*, II:44.
32. *Ibid.*, IV:23.
33. Hermann Cohen, Lecture to World Congress for Religious Progress (1910), cited in S. Bergman, *Faith and Reason* (Washington, D.C.: B'nai B'rith Hillel Foundation, 1961), p. 33.
34. Kohler, *op. cit.*, p. 323.
35. *Ibid.*, pp. 339 ff.
36. Mordecai M. Kaplan, *The Purpose and Meaning of Jewish Existence* (Philadelphia: Jewish Publication Society, 1964), p. 55.
37. *Ibid.*, p. 310.
38. Compare above with Kaplan, *Judaism as a Civilization* (New York: Reconstructionist Press, 1957), chap. 10.

39. Leo Baeck, *The Essence of Judaism* (translated by Victor Grubeh-wieser and Leonard Pearl [New York: Schocken Books, 1948]), p. 271.

40. Emil G. Hirsch, "Why Am I a Jew?" in *My Religion* (New York: Macmillan, 1925), p. 30.

41. Martin Buber, "Plato and Isaiah," in *Israel and the World* (New York: Schocken Books, 1948), pp. 110 f.

42. Martin Buber, "The Spirit of Israel and the World of Today," *op. cit.*, p. 186.

43. *Ibid.*, p. 188.

44. *Ibid.*, p. 187.

45. Selections from "The Star of Redemption" in Rosenzweig, *Franz Rosenzweig: His Life and Thought* (ed. by Nahum Glatzer [New York: Farrar, Straus & Young, 1953], pp. 292 f.

46. *Ibid.*, p. 339.

47. Sheldon H. Blank, *Prophetic Faith in Isaiah* (New York: Harper, 1958), pp. 143-60.

48. Isaiah 43:11 f.

49. Isaiah 42:6 f.

50. Rosenzweig, *op. cit.*, p. 340.

51. A. H. Silver, *Where Judaism Differed* (New York: Macmillan, 1957), p. 108.

52. Martin Buber, "The Spirit of Israel and the World Today," *op. cit.*, p. 186.

53. Rosenzweig, *op. cit.*, p. 340.

REFORM JEWISH THEOLOGY TODAY

Bernard Martin

I

The renaissance in Christian theology which began with the publication of Karl Barth's *Römerbrief* in 1919 and is still not exhausted (though in America, at least, its demise may be heralded by the recent so-called "death-of-God" movement) has undoubtedly been one of the major events not only in the religious life of the twentieth century but also in its general intellectual history. As a result of the work of such theologians as Barth, Emil Brunner, and Rudolf Bultmann in Germany, Jacques Maritain and Gabriel Marcel in France, William Temple, Alan Richardson, and Austin Farrer in England, Reinhold Niebuhr, H. Richard Niebuhr, and Paul Tillich [1] in America, and Nicholas Berdyaev and Serge Bulgakov in Russia,[2] Christian theology in the last half-century has come to be recognized as a great spiritual and intellectual achievement that has something of importance to say regarding the fundamental questions about human existence that sensitive and intelligent persons both inside and outside the church are asking.

The revival of creative theological thinking in Christianity has still not been paralleled in Judaism. To be sure, we have our great trilogy of German-Jewish theologians—Hermann Cohen, Franz Rosenzweig, and Martin Buber—whose contributions to Jewish religious thought have been massive and highly significant. And there have been a number of lesser figures in England, America, and Israel whose sustained efforts to explicate the meaning of Judaism in contemporary terms deserve respectful attention. Nevertheless, it must regretfully be admitted that neither in scope nor in depth do the achievements of twentieth-century Jewish theological thought approximate those of Christianity.

A number of reasons are generally cited in explanation of this phenomenon. Some are cogent and relevant, others are not. The one perhaps most often proffered is that the Nazi Holocaust, as well as the other great cataclysms of the twentieth century that struck such fearful blows at the Jewish people and rendered its very survival precarious, necessitated the dedication of Jewish energies to the tasks of rescue and rehabilitation to such a degree as to preclude the expenditure, in any significant measure, of intellectual and spiritual effort on such a relative "frivolity" as theological reflection. This explanation of the matter is hardly convincing. As Will Herberg pointed out years ago: "Insecurity and disaster are nothing new in the history of Israel, but never in the past did they paralyze the sources of spiritual creativity. On the contrary, every great achievement in Jewish religious thought came into being in response to crisis." [3]

Nor does the explanation that Judaism is essentially a "non-theological" religion, that it is more a way of life than of belief, that in it the legal precepts of halacha have traditionally taken precedence over the theological fancies of *aggadah*, contain a substantially greater degree of cogency. That one's manner of living has generally been regarded in Judaism as more relevant religiously than the content of one's theological beliefs and that halacha has traditionally been given priority over *aggadah* cannot be doubted. Furthermore, Judaism has been distinctively "existential" in spirit, as Martin Buber long ago recognized when he wrote: "In the religious life of Judaism, primary importance is not given to dogma, but to the remembrance and expectation of a concrete situation: the meeting of God with men. Dogma can only arise where detachment is the prevailing attitude to the concrete, lived moment—a state of detachment which easily becomes misunderstood in dogmatics as being superior to the lived moment itself." [4] Nevertheless, the supposed anti-theological attitude of Jewish tradition is largely a myth. Whatever reality it has is mainly of twentieth-century provenance. If theology be understood as something other than the writing of a *summa* in the manner of Thomas Aquinas—and of course it must be so understood—it has always occupied a supremely important place in Jewish religious life. Herberg put it well when he wrote:

> From the Scriptural writers and Prophets to Rosenzweig and Buber, Jewish thinking has been a continuing effort to interpret problems and events in terms of the divine-human encounter and the working-out of God's providence. The renunciation of theology in modern times is not so much a continuation of Jewish tradition as a more or less definite break with it, although it must be said that there are aspects of the tradition itself that have made this break possible.[5]

Perhaps the most adequate explanation of the relative neglect of theology so obviously manifest in twentieth-century Judaism is the mood of secularism and—scandalously enough for a religion that has long prided itself on the supreme importance of cultivation of the mind—of anti-intellectualism that has come to dominate large segments of Jewry in recent decades. In certain quarters Jewish existence has come to be defined in exclusively secular and ethnic terms, and the creative tension in the tradition itself between the ethnic and the religious has been ignored. Elsewhere it has been raucously proclaimed that Judaism is primarily concerned with "the good life" (what this means is rarely defined with any precision) and that for "the good life" theological speculation is an irrelevance. In still other circles Jewish nationalism or Jewish culture or Jewish philanthropy has usurped the primacy in Jewish life, dispossessing Jewish religon of the place it once occupied.

Numerous signs are emerging, however, that this situation is beginning to change, especially in America. An increasingly larger number of Jewish thinkers are beginning to occupy themselves seriously with problems of Jewish religious life. Where once, not too long ago, programs on social justice and the sociological issues involved in the survival of the Jewish people were given the central place in rabbinical conventions, that place is now often given to sessions on Jewish theology. Where a little more than a decade ago not a single significant journal primarily devoted to discussion of Jewish theological questions was published in America, several now appear and are becoming increasingly sophisticated and mature; among the best are the quarterly *Judaism*, sponsored by the American Jewish Congress, *Tradition*, issued under Orthodox auspices, *Conservative Judaism*, published by the Conservative Rabbinical Assembly, and the *Journal of the Central Conference of American Rabbis*, sponsored by the Reform rabbinate. In addition, a number of important and creative books on Jewish theology have been published in the United States in the last twenty years. The present volume, it is hoped, will prove a worthwhile contribution to this growing body of literature.

II

But—some will, in all good faith, persistently demand—is Jewish theology really so terribly important? Is it genuinely indispensable to the survival of Judaism in the contemporary world? My own answer to these questions is an unequivocal Yes.

First of all, there is, particularly on the part of the more intellectually alert and informed young people in the Jewish community, a growing dissatisfaction with a merely "practical" Judaism and a tendency to reject as ultimately irrelevant to their lives and deepest interests the ersatz faiths mentioned above that seem to have displaced Jewish religion in many circles, such as the cults of Jewish nationalism, culture, and philanthropy. These young people acknowledge the value of Zionism and the State of Israel, the importance of Jewish literary and artistic creativity, the necessity of Jewish social service institutions and Jewish participation in the cause of social justice. But these are not enough for them. They ask also whether Judaism has not any deep insights that may give meaning to their apparently meaningless existence, any healing truths that may knit up their broken and fragmented lives.

Furthermore, the threat to Jewish loyalties presented by Chris-

tianity with its massive and profound theological systems is not
to be minimized. The fact that Jewish students flocked by the
hundreds to the lectures given by the late Paul Tillich at Harvard
and the University of Chicago—and that some responded warmly
not only to his doctrine of God but to his Christology—cannot be
dismissed as insignificant. Christianity, as a heretical form of
Judaism (many Christians, I suppose, would return the compli-
ment and describe Judaism as a Christian heresy), has always
presented a troubling and pointed challenge to the Jew; it does
so even more vigorously and effectively now, in the light of the
great theological revival that Christendom has seen in the last
half-century. Though theology has never been so intensively and
extensively cultivated in Judaism as in Christianity, the strongest
efforts must be made to narrow the gap. If the task is not pursued
with the utmost vigor we shall, I fear, not only suffer the loss of
many of the most spiritually sensitive of our young people but
also find that many who remain within the Jewish community
are Jews in name only, adherents of a Judaism that hardly
touches the deepest levels of their personal existence.

From what I have said it follows that the kind of theology we
require is an apologetic theology—in the non-pejorative sense of
that term. Eugene Borowitz complains that "in general, liberal
Jewish theology this past century has been apologetic theology"
and then goes on to say, "Apologetics is an important practical
task, not only for the Jew who does not believe but also for all
those men of good will who seek its truth. . . . But apologetics
cannot be our primary intellectual task today. Before we devise
a theology for the outsider, we must clarify what those inside the
circle of faith share." [6] It is true that we must explicate what
Judaism teaches and what those inside the circle of faith believe,
but we must not at the same time overlook the "outsiders"—for
their number within the Jewish community is legion.

In the Protestant tradition Paul Tillich eschewed the purely
kerygmatc approach to theology (such as Karl Barth has often,
though not exclusively, followed). Instead—and it was in this
that a large part of his greatness lay—he favored, as I have
pointed out elsewhere, "an apologetic or answering approach,
which recognizes the necessity that theology speak pertinently
to the contemporary human situation—understood as the philosophical, scientific and artistic, the economic, political and ethi-

cal forms in which men of today express their interpretation of human existence." [7] I remain convinced that this is the road Jewish theology must follow if it is to be relevant to present needs. A theology that is little more than the collection and arrangement, under appropriate headings, of scriptural and rabbinic passages, with some halfhearted attempts at modernizing interpretation, cannot hope to speak pertinently to the Jew of today. Kaufmann Kohler's classic *Jewish Theology*, which is largely such a work, cannot be read with any sense of great intellectual excitement or religious relevance in the 1960's.

Perhaps Reform Judaism requires theological work more than do the other Jewish "denominations" currently on the American scene. Of the classic trilogy of Judaism—God, Torah, and Israel —which, according to the Zohar, are one, Orthodoxy in modern times has laid primary emphasis on observance of Torah, Conservatism has placed its major stress on the people Israel and its culture or civilization, and Reform has been chiefly concerned with God and His moral will. To be sure, the elimination of any of these three, or the overemphasis of one at the expense of the others, must result in a distortion of Judaism. Nevertheless, Reform, which has not, until recently, concentrated on Torah observance or the ethnic and civilizational elements of Judaism, has a special need to give an account of its position in theological terms. It must explicate what it means not only by God, but by Torah and Israel as well. The essays in this volume are individual attempts to present such an explication, and what their authors have attempted to do must be done by others with different perspectives, over and over again.

The great exponents of nineteenth-century *Wissenschaft des Judentums*—Leopold Zunz, Moritz Steinschneider, Marcus Jost, Heinrich Graetz, J. L. Rapoport, and the others—have put us in their debt with their magnificent contributions to the exploration of Jewish history and literature. But these scholars were generally quite unconcerned with Jewish theology. Only the Reform leaders—Abraham Geiger, Samuel Holdheim, David Einhorn, Samuel Hirsch, and several more—had a substantive interest in theological issues, and their response was largely to reinterpret Judaism in terms of prevailing philosophical movements, particularly German idealism as represented by Kant and Hegel. It is a response that will not meet the needs of our time.

But we must follow their example and wrestle with the philosophies and ideologies of our time—not to explain Judaism in their
terms (Borowitz is right about that), but to show that Jewish
tradition has a wisdom that can hold its own with theirs and,
indeed, transcends it in profundity and relevance to life.

It is not likely that any one theological system will come to
dominate Reform Jewish life or, for that matter, the life of the
other "denominations." The materials of the tradition with which
the theologian has to work are the same for all, but each brings
to them his own unique outlook, temperament, and mode of en-
countering reality. The result in our time must be a multiplicity
of Jewish theologies to which different Jews will respond in different ways. But that is nothing new in the history of Judaism.
The Hebrew Bible, despite its overarching unity, is a composite
of several different theologies, and so is the Jewish Prayer Book.

III

The major theme of our theology must clearly be God. Arnold
Wolf is, of course, right when he reminds us that "God is, whatever else, a Mystery. And Judaism must be, whatever else, humble
before Him who spoke and theology came to be." [8] And he
properly warns us against putting "too much stock in sincerity
and not enough in patience, too much emphasis on our being
right and not enough on God's being superior to our idea of
God." [9] Nevertheless, inadequate as our finite, human concepts
must forever remain to the comprehension of the ultimate reality
we call God, we cannot avoid them. Nor should we try. It is
senseless to say that the man of true faith does not need to know
what he means when he speaks of God. Of course, he cannot
know everything about God, but if he does not or cannot make
clear to himself what he does know or believe, then it is doubtful
that he knows or believes anything. Theology is a hopeless enterprise if it presumes to exhaust the nature of the God who is
ultimate reality, but, undertaken with proper humility, it is
unavoidable and deeply necessary.

Jewish theology in our time must explicate the various means
by which man can arrive at some knowledge of God. Jakob
Petuchowski writes that "the unity of God, as proclaimed in the
Shema, means that there is only *one Reality,* though we may get

to know about It by diverse routes: by philosophical speculation, by tradition, and by personal religious experience." [10] We need to make clear what we mean by these various routes and what their respective strengths and weaknesses are.

The route which would approach God through philosophical speculation or scientific inquiry requires closer scrutiny by Jewish theologians than it has received before. Perhaps the dominant movement in Jewish theology in America in the twentieth century has been the naturalist or rationalist movement, represented by Mordecai Kaplan and many other thinkers. This movement has operated with a number of unexamined presuppositions. Undoubtedly the most basic of these is that religious faith must not conflict with empirical fact. But the relationship of the realm of faith to the realm of fact has not been explored with any clarity or precision. Furthermore, the nature of scientific inquiry has not always been adequately appreciated by naturalist or rationalist theologians, many of whom blithely ignore the fact that some of the foremost scientists of today deny categorically that science gives any final and absolute knowledge concerning the reality even of the natural phenomena with which it concerns itelf and tend, instead, to regard their scientific formulas and laws more as symbols or constructs that make it possible for us to use and control nature than as cognitive statements that give us information about its real character.

It is also essential that we make clear what we mean when we speak of Jewish tradition as an approach to Jewish theology. As I have had occasion to point out in another context, "The tradition, in its millennial vastness, obviously contains numerous and diverse theologies and theological affirmations that are, in many respects, contradictory and inconsistent with each other. Some choice, some decision on the part of the theologian as to what is ultimate and primary in the tradition and what is derivative and secondary is required." [11]

We must also clarify what we understand by personal religious experience. Is such experience in every case self-validating? What of contradictory experiences? What criteria for choice and decision between these are possible and feasible? Questions such as these must be asked and answered.

The question must also be considered how the diverse approaches relate to each other. It is not enough to say that "no one approach . . . is sufficient. Neither philosophical speculation alone, nor yet a mere personal experience, will reveal to us the full meaning of the idea of God in Judaism." [12] That is true, but we must investigate the respective boundaries of philosophical speculation, personal religious experience, and tradition, and come to understand their mutual interrelationships.

Petuchowski insists that "if one takes God seriously, he has to take revelation seriously and *vice versa*." [13] But precisely what does revelation mean? How are we to understand the statement that God reveals himself to man? What is the part played by man in receiving divine revelation? All these questions require further theological exploration in a Jewish context.

David Polish maintains that "the God who disclosed himself with no witnesses at Creation, disclosed himself to Israel at Sinai. The God who gives us the universe is the God who gives us His law." [14] The question of the divine nature of the law is a major problem; more will be said of it below in the discussion of Torah and halacha. Here I would only suggest that we need to clarify what we mean when we speak of God as Lawgiver. Roland Gittelsohn has insisted that the naturalist conception of God makes room for the traditional view of God as Lawgiver since "the earliest adumbrations of our moral values" are traceable to "the very physical structures and functions of nature." [15] Deeper investigation, I believe, is required before we can decide whether it is possible to derive moral value from physical fact, or whether the moral demands with which the living God of the Bible confronts man can, in any meaningful way, be identified with the principles of order, cooperation, individualization, and freedom which naturalist thinkers like Gittelsohn tend to see manifested in the thrust of the evolutionary process.

Jewish tradition has spoken of God as creator, and in the mainstream of the tradition it is *creatio ex nihilo* and creation as an act of the past that has been proclaimed. David Polish contends that the traditional envisagement of God as creator must be maintained: "Whatever that role may be, if God is not to be identified with *maaseh b'reshit* then integrity will demand that we declare Him irrelevant, or certainly less than God. . . . To abstract God from creation is to reduce Him to an idol created by our own cleverness and theological acuity and nothing more." [16] But the question must be explored whether we need not, indeed, whether we must not, as Polish himself implies when he speaks of continuous creation, radically reinterpret our understanding of God as creator. Is there not much wisdom to be found in the tradition of Kabbalah which held that creation is a nontemporal, eternal act, and especially in the teaching of the nineteenth-century founder of *Habad* Hasidism, Shneour Zalman of Liadi? We ought to ponder deeply the teaching of Shneour Zalman, according to whom, as Abraham Joshua Heschel writes,

> The work of God who created heaven and earth is not to be thought of as being analogous to the work of man. Once a craftsman has made a vessel, it no longer depends on him for its existence. "Fools imagine that heaven and earth are likewise made . . . but they fail to see the vast difference between the work of man, which consists of making one thing out of another already existing, and the work of the creator who creates being out of nothing." The miracle of coming into being out of nothing is only possible through the continual action of God. His power is constantly present within all His Creations, and were He to remove Himself for a moment they would revert to their natural state, which is nothingness. However, because that Divine power or light is concealed, it appears to us as if they exist by themselves. In a true sense, therefore, the world that we know is nothing compared with the Power of God that contains it. Things appear to us to be existing by themselves only as long as we are unable to perceive the Divine.[17]

As an answer to the problem of "surd evil" in the world, which for many is the chief obstacle to faith in God, a number of Jewish thinkers in recent years have adopted the doctrine of finite divinity. The chief advocate of this view in America has, of course, been the Christian personalist philosopher, Edgar S. Brightman. Brightman himself did not speak, as is commonly supposed, of a finite God but of a God "whose will is finite." The divine will, which is eternally active and entirely good, is limited, in Brightman's view, by a factor which he called "the given." The latter is a complex consisting of a number of elements—the uncreated laws of reason, i.e., logical and mathematical relations, and uncreated, nonrational consciousness, e.g., evil desires, pain, suffering, and every other source of surd evil. Within the experience of God, according to Brightman, this given is eternal, but it is not a product either of God's will or of His creative activity.

The attractiveness of the doctrine of the finite divine will is obvious, but it bristles with difficulties, from both the vantage point of intellectual validity and religious relevance. Brightman's idea is, of course, only a contemporary version of the ancient teaching that there is an eternal, uncreated "matter" upon which the divine will works and which both facilitates and frustrates the divine creativity. To say that God's will is finite means, according to Brightman, that on occasion it will be frustrated, but since God's goodness is infinite, no defeat of His will is final. But no victory is final either. As Professor John E. Smith, interpreting Brightman's doctrine, has said:

> No defeat is final for God, and yet God is always subject to the given. That no defeat is "final" can mean no more than that there is an infinite future and an endless process. The very nature of the given makes it clear that nothing that happens in the cosmic process can alter the given in a fundamental way. That no defeat is final is to say that *every* defeat is, in a sense, final, unless there is a basic drift in both the divine consciousness and the cosmic process towards conquest of the given itself.[18]

Jewish theology, I would suggest, is ill advised in seeking to solve the problem of evil by recourse to a God whose will is finite. It is too easy and obvious a solution, and the ultimate metaphysical dualism that it involves is, in my judgment, entirely inconsistent not only with biblical monotheism but with philosophical reason.

To my mind, the contemporary theistic philosophy that seems most congruent with both biblical faith and reason is that presented by Charles Hartshorne, who has elaborated, with impressive logical power and acumen, some seminal ideas about God originally put forth by Alfred North Whitehead. Hartshorne is not only a deeply religious man but a logician of the first rank. In his philosophical theology, set forth in such books as *Man's Vision of God, The Divine Relativity,* and *The Logic of Perfection,* and in the introduction to *Philosophers Speak of God,* he has employed the techniques of strict reasoning and modal logic to present a doctrine of God which seems to me to do more justice to the God of biblical faith than any other which has appeared on the contemporary philosophical landscape.

Like Paul Tillich, Hartshorne has attacked classical absolutistic theism, represented in the Christian philosophic tradition by Augustine, Anselm, Aquinas, Descartes, Leibnitz, and Kant, and in the Jewish tradition by Philo, Maimonides, and most of the medieval Jewish philosophers. But while Tillich rejected classical theism because it turned God into a being besides other beings, Hartshorne takes issue with it for emphasizing the static perfection of God and consequently neglecting in God the factor of becoming, i.e., creativity, the ongoing realization of value, and the novelty implicit in future time.

Hartshorne reworks the classic ontological argument to arrive at a dipolar doctrine of God which he calls *panentheism*. In this doctrine God is the perfect or supreme exemplification of categories which have traditionally been taken to be polar and antithetical. As he himself has put it:

God is neither being as contrasted to becoming, nor becoming as contrasted to being, but categorically supreme becoming in which there is a factor of categorically supreme being, as contrasted to inferior becoming, in which there is inferior being. . . . The divine becoming is more ultimate than the divine being only in the simple sense of being more inclusive, of being concrete, while the other is abstract. . . . We worship supreme-being-in-supreme-becoming, supreme-cause-in-supreme-effect; that is, we worship the supreme, not any polar category. If it be said that, after all, supreme-inferior is a polarity, we reply that even here we worship the supreme-as-containing-the-inferior and deriving enrichment from this containing. Even inferior being-becoming is not degraded in this doctrine but glorified by the recognition of its contribution to God Himself. Nothing is debased to the status of irrelevance, whereas in the monopolar procedure all becoming and all effects are mere impertinences, since being just as being is held to have all value. God should least of all require the kind of praise that makes the better seem still better by saying that the inferior is even less than inferior, is nothing, merely evil, or wholly negligible. But that is the kind of praise he has generally received! We thus read our lack of imagination, or of generosity, or simply of love, into God Himself.[19]

It should be emphasized that Hartshorne's life's work has been an attempt to express the biblical idea of God in metaphysical terms and to show that an adequate metaphysics brings us finally to the God of biblical faith, that divine personality and love are ultimately required by the cosmic scheme itself. The ideas of pure actuality, immutability, passivity, and causeless cause that have been used to describe the divine nature in philosophical theologies of the past are, he has argued, inadequate to the divine nature. God is the supremely absolute but He is also the supremely relative, and as such He has a supreme sensitivity to the finite, contingent creatures and events of the world.

Hartshorne has dealt brilliantly with many of the traditional problems of theistic philosophy. Typical is his treatment of the idea of *creatio ex nihilo*.

> Whereas, it is commonly said, ordinary creative activity presupposes "matter," divine creation does not. Admittedly, ordinary cases of creative power lack, in principle, something reserved for the categorically supreme case. But, still, "out of nothing" is a dubious way of formulating this categorically privileged way of creating. Does God create an adult out of nothing or out of a child? The creative functioning of deity involved in the production of Beethoven's music certainly did not treat as nothing the free self-decisions of Beethoven's predecessors in composition. Only in connection with an absolute first moment of time has even divine creation no antecedent data or conditions.[20]

To those who have wondered whether reason demands that God be regarded not as personal but merely as a process, power, or principle, Hartshorne has provided a cogent answer in the negative. For him God can only be the Supreme Person. Indeed, from the logic of perfection it follows that God and only God is literally and fully a person in the "eminent" sense, and that all human persons are, by contrast, persons in a derivative sense, only through diminution and negation.

Hartshorne's panentheism provides rich resources for the Jewish theologian struggling to give a rational account of the God of biblical and Hebraic faith. I believe it needs to be explored far more deeply than has yet been done by any Jewish theologian.

IV

Jewish theology in our time must also again confront the problem of man. Max Scheler's words of forty years ago are even more true today than when he wrote them: "In no other period of human knowledge has man ever become more problematic to himself than in our own day. We have a scientific, a philosophical and a theological anthropology that know nothing of each other. Therefore we no longer possess any clear and consistent idea of man. The ever-growing multiplicity of the particular sciences that are engaged in the study of man has much more confused and obscured than elucidated our concept of man." [21] Perhaps theology can no longer give us a unified and compelling image of man, but it must not abdicate its responsibility and forego the attempt.

Christian theology of the twentieth century has rediscovered the reality of human sin and evil which nineteenth-century theological liberalism tended to ignore or even deny. Its indictment of liberalism is that the latter, as Herberg aptly summarizes,

> has systematically striven to break the tension that is the spring of spiritual energy by affirming the continuity of God with man instead of the "otherness" of God; by preaching an unwarranted confidence in the powers of human reason despite its clear limitations and corruptions; by insisting on the "innate" goodness of man and the essential unreality of sin and evil; by looking for the gradual realization of the Kingdom of Heaven in the course of social progress. Liberal theology is accused of having merely sanctified the relative standards of secular bourgeois society and having served as a sounding board for its prejudices. [22]

Jewish theologians of the twentieth century, especially in view of the horrible catastrophes undergone by the Jewish people at the hands of hordes of bestial and demonic men, could not—all of them—ignore the testimony of their own Bible and Talmud, as well as daily experience, and continue to maintain, as so many of them did in the nineteenth century, that Judaism proclaims the basic goodness of man, and that this is one of its fundamental *differentia* from Christianity.

Some, however, have refused to abandon their optimism. Thus Levi Olan, by his own admission an unreconstructed liberal, writes: "Judaism is more than is described under the rubric of modern liberalism, but the basic characteristics of belief in progress, the perfectability of the world and of man, and the virtue of reason are very much a part of its religious structure." [23] Olan deplores the fading of the liberal vision and insists that this fading is the result of ignoring certain scientific "facts" and "discoveries" which give grounds for the reinstatement of liberalism to religious and intellectual respectability. The meaning of these alleged "facts" and "discoveries" will have to be investigated in a far more stringent way before Olan's optimistic inferences can be accepted. But where Olan, it seems to me, is particularly vulnerable to objection is in his suggestion, if I understand him correctly, that Jewish tradition itself has been unambiguously committed to "belief in progress, the perfectability of the world and of man, and the virtue of reason." If many statements are to be found in the classical sources of Judaism—the Bible, the Talmud, and the Midrashim—affirming such belief, probably an equal number could be cited which point out man's tendency to regress through evildoing to lower stages of life, his perennial failure to improve himself and his world, and the inadequacies of reason as well as the distortions to which it is susceptible. It will not do, I think, to pit one set of passages against the other. To decide this issue, recourse must be taken to history and personal experience. The result of such recourse will be, I suspect, to show us that we cannot go far beyond, in Arnold Wolf's pungent phrase, "loving our crooked neighbor with our crooked hearts, and our far-off God with our libidinously contaminated apperceptive mass." [24]

Olan, writing in 1962, declares that contemporary culture represents man "generally, as a hopeless creature, unqualified in mind and heart for the arrogant role of creation that he has assigned to himself." [25] Whether or not this is an accurate assessment of the mood that prevailed half a dozen years ago, it is probably not that today. To be sure, there are still many voices to remind us of man's stubborn and seemingly ineradicable tendency to evil—and these voices are heard in literature, drama, sociology, psychology, and philosophy, as well as in theology—but the general mood, despite all the dismal events that testify to the fact that *homo homini lupus est,* is one of growing confidence in man's rationality and goodness. The proponents of "the secular city" in theology, and the "death-of-God" theologians as well, share this mood.[26] Perhaps the ripe wisdom of both Judaism and Christianity, with their sense of tragic realism about man, will have to repeat their warning about the dangers of overconfidence in him.

The status of human purposes and values also requires theological investigation. In the naturalist vein Olan writes, "Biology, psychology, and the social sciences can guide him [man] toward a comprehension of his purposes and values." [27] Perhaps they can, though most of their practitioners would probably reject the task as no concern of theirs. But religion generally, and Judaism particularly, have always been greatly concerned with man's goals and ideals and have seen these as essentially related to God. Olan, who represents an outlook that is widely shared in contemporary liberal Judaism, seems to be reflecting the view of Martin Heidegger, as popularized by Jean-Paul Sartre, when he says: "Today man is unfettered and charged with the responsibility of selecting goals among alternatives and to manipulate objects and behavior toward his selected ends. In the older view the purpose lay in the object, or in fate, or in God; the modern view puts the responsibility of selecting the goal upon man." [28] Does this statement mean to deny that God is the transcendent source of values? Or that there are any universally valid ethical purposes and imperatives? Perhaps. But if so, it is a radical departure indeed from traditional Judaism, and both its presuppositions and consequences require careful analysis. The terrible burden placed upon man when it is said, "Charged with the responsibility of selecting purposes and devising means, he [man] can no longer blame anyone but himself, if he fails to achieve a better life," [29] must be considered, and not just his supposed liberation.

In general, Olan, together with many other liberal theologians, does not take the anxiety of freedom—what Kierkegaard called the "dizziness of freedom," and what all of the existential philosophy deriving from his thought has seen as a crushing weight (significantly, Marjorie Grene entitled her fine study of existentialism *Dreadful Freedom* [30])—with any real seriousness. Olan celebrates human freedom: "man is today free to dream dreams for the future he has never dreamed before. The universe has room for his highest imagination, and he has the capacity to choose his direction and invent the means of reaching nearer to his destination." [31] "The universe," he maintains, "is wide open in time and possibilities." [32] How very different is his vision of man and the universe from that of the great artists and scientists, of whose insights Arnold Wolf reminds us: "Think of Shakespeare's *Tempest* with its sense that everything we are, everything the world is, passes and is gone; think also of Freud's penultimate essay called *Analysis, Terminable and Interminable*, in which he says that the process of healing is an infinite process and, therefore, man is condemned to permanent illness—this from a great physician and, I think, a great scientist, who understood that everything man is and has and knows are, in the most specific and literal sense, doomed." [33]

Olan, while aware of the limitations and dangers of human rationality, nevertheless affirms it: "Reason may lead us to error, and it often does, but anything else as a substitute guide is certain to bring confusion compounded into chaos." [34] Wolf, on the other hand, declares that "it is not certain that more atrocities have been committed in the name of unreason than in the name of reason . . . there is no escape from the problem of evil, neither with reason nor with unreason." [35]

The final issue between the visions of the world and man seen by Olan and Wolf is the source of human hope. For Olan hope is there, implicit in the "facts," in the structure of the universe. For Wolf hope "is a theological category. Hope can never be extrapolated from the facts. News is always bad news. Hope intervenes. It does not emerge." [36]

Jewish theology in our day will have to consider these polar visions, and others that swing between them, and decide which is most adequate both to the classical tradition of Judaism and human experience.

V

No doubt the fundamental practical problem—it is also, of course, a deeply theoretical one—confronting Reform Judaism is the problem of halacha, understood generally in this context as Jewish observance. W. Gunther Plaut points to the fact that the gulf between Reform and the more traditional branches of Judaism has been progressively widening because Reform has lost interest in halacha. Reform Jews and traditional Jews no longer speak the same language. And he is doubtless right when he says of the Reform movement that if it "does not now turn decisively away from its post-classical, radical phase, then indeed its critics will probably be right: it will have no future." [37]

Why has halacha been virtually abandoned by most Reform Jews? Jakob Petuchowski supplies some answers. He calls our attention to the fact that halacha has been undermined for many Reform Jews by a whole series of developments, including *die Wissenschaft des Judentums,* the Higher Criticism of the Bible, modern research in anthropology and comparative religion, and the general doctrine of evolutionism. Biblical criticism has perhaps been in fact more destructive than the others of the fidelity of Reform Jews to traditional halacha. Petuchowski, however, cogently demonstrates that even if the premises of biblical criticism are accepted *in toto,* "we can draw from them the logical conclusion that the Jew in the past was mistaken in his view about the authorship of the Pentateuch. What does *not* follow logically from the findings of the Higher Criticism is the widespread notion that, because Moses did not write the Torah, it can no longer be the authoritative rule of Jewish life." [38] One can hardly argue with his conclusion: "While the modern disciplines may radically alter our picture of early Jewish history, they cannot be considered competent to determine whether or not a given tradition is part of divine revelation—a commandment (*mitzvah*) which is binding (halacha) on all generations of Israel. This is a theological, rather than an archaeological or historical, problem and must be dealt with on a different level altogether." [39]

Petuchowski correctly points out that both the Pittsburgh Platform of 1885 and the Columbus Platform of 1937, the two major programmatic theological documents in the history of American Reform Judaism, were thoroughly ambiguous on the theological question of revelation, and more specifically, the revelatory character of the Bible. When the Bible was described in the Pittsburgh Platform as "the record of the consecration of the Jewish people to its mission as the priest of God" and as "the most potent instrument of religious and moral instruction," the description satisfied both those Reformers who regarded the Bible as the revealed word of God and those who regarded it as a completely human document. Again, the Columbus Platform does not, as Petuchowski shows, "rule out that view of God which cannot conceive of Him as actually revealing Himself in the form of direct commandments." [40] To be sure, it urges upon Reform Jews ceremonial and ritual observance, but it makes no attempt "to link the 'customs, symbols and ceremonies possessing inspirational value' with the concept of revelation and with the idea of a God who commands." [41]

Petuchowski is among the contemporary Jewish theologians who seek to take revelation seriously and have discovered in Franz Rosenzweig a mentor in their quest. David Polish is another. Speaking of moral law, Polish clearly reflects Rosenzweigian doctrine when he says: "I do not believe that this law or that is God-given, but I do believe that submission to the principle of moral law impels men to hunt endlessly for the most effective ways by which they can comply with it. What is given is 'I am the Lord.' What is derived is 'You shall not murder.'" [42] In a similar vein, Petuchowski has also spoken of love as "the *only* content of Revelation." [43] The remainder of the Torah, its specific laws and commandments, is regarded by him as human appropriation and interpretation.

Harold Schulweis has put the issue forcefully and clearly:

All the younger theologians who have capitalized Revelation may be asked the same question: Where does Revelation end and human appropriation begin? It is a question particularly pertinent to them because in actual fact they neither hold an Orthodox interpretation of Revelation nor do they attempt a radical break with its claims. They admit biblical criticism, are prepared to reject miracles and myths in their literal sense and acknowledge that "every single word any

prophet ever spoke is shot through with human interpretation," but will then strangely conclude that "had there been
no event of divine revelation there would have been no human
interpretation" (Emil Fackenheim). How this or that law in
the Torah developed is left to biblical scholarship; for the new
theologian it is enough to maintain that, behind the literary
history of the Pentateuch, there was "the impact of the Love
of God, the momentum of a Revelation which, in a profound
sense, enables us to this day to offer our praise unto Him who
is the 'Giver of the Torah'" (Petuchowski). A distinction between revelation and interpretation is abstractly stated only
to be collapsed into indiscernibility in the existential situation.
We are left to be content with the faith THAT something
must have happened without knowing WHAT happened. So,
too, in the matter of *Halakhah*, there is a call for commitment
but no objective criteria for acceptance or rejection of specific laws. Both Revelation and Law are revered, but they remain *forms* of belief without content, criteria or concreteness.[44]

In contrast to Petuchowski who insists on the indispensability
of restoring faith in revelation, Plaut takes a realistic view of
the situation actually obtaining within contemporary Reform
Judaism and concludes that "neither God nor Torah can be considered as universally commanding sources for Reform halacha."[45] He urges that the new theological foundations required
for a Liberal recapturing of halacha "must be fairly broad. They
must include Israel and deal with the God of Israel, the question
of Jewish survival and Jewish purpose, and relate all of these to
the possibility and need of worship."[46] The classic trilogy of
God, Torah, and Israel which has been the foundation of Judaism
for so many centuries must now, he declares, be supplanted by
"a spectrum that ranges from Israel to man to self, a spectrum
in which the light of God may or may not be perceived by the
individual, but where all who count themselves as part of this
fellowship agree that, through Israel, individual as well as human
uniqueness is validated in a special way and that whatever
Judaism has to say must speak to and of and through this
uniqueness."[47]

Plaut seems to be offering to the faithless and godless Jew a
possibility of relating himself somehow to the halachic tradition

of Judaism. But whether his prescription will have the desired effect appears debatable. He contends that *"the Reform Jew must again be made to feel that what he does is at least in part what he ought to do.* The 'ought' is the *mitzvah."* [48] But how is the Reform Jew to be made to feel this if, as Plaut suggests, the belief in God is absent among half the members of Reform congregations? From where will this sense of commanding obligation come? What "ought" can there be without an authoritative source of command? Is not Petuchowski closer to the truth when he declares that it is not possible to have a commandment without a commander? And is not Petuchowski also right in pointing out that statistical descriptions of actual Reform practice will not provide any basis for *halacha* and when he tells us that Judaism does not, despite the formidable authority of Zacharias Frankel and the Positive Historical School, equate *vox populi* with *vox dei?*

The problem of halacha, of course, includes far more than the traditional ritual or ceremonial law of Judaism. As Petuchowski reminds us: "What is often so blithely called 'the moral law' is as much a part of halacha in its traditional connotation as are, for example, the dietary laws. If there is no commanding God behind the one, on what grounds do we posit Him to be behind the other?" [49] Many theologians, of course, do not see God behind the moral law or else see Him as the source of moral imperatives only in a metaphorical sense. The kind of thinking that is particularly prevalent among naturalist theologians, many of whom tend to draw unjustified analogies between natural laws and moral principles, is exemplified by David Polish when he writes, "The laws of nature are revealed when man discovers them. Man unearths them. God reveals them. The twilight zone between discovery and revelation is dusky and obscure. The moral law is not so clear cut or so absolute. Yet, it too is not merely an invention but a discovery, however tentative, of what the creative act had flung into the world when life began." [50]

The tendency to draw analogies between physical laws or laws of nature and ethical imperatives is one that contains a host of problems. Closer investigation will be required before it can be determined whether or not moral imperatives or ethical principles can legitimately be regarded as implicit in nature or in creation. Experience to date seems to show that the attempt to derive ethical principles from nature is a highly dubious undertaking. In connection with the repeated attempts that have been made in recent decades to derive value from fact, Will Herberg has pointedly called our attention to the fact that "not so long ago the 'social Darwinists' tried to justify imperialism and capitalism on the ground that these were in line with the 'struggle for existence' and biologic evolution. At about the same time, Kropotkin turned the argument around and built up a case for libertarian socialism from the tendencies to 'mutual aid' that he found in nature. In both cases the argument proved nothing. The course of biologic evolution may conceivably show us how life has developed hitherto but it cannot possibly prove that any line of human action is right or wrong, good or evil." [51] To assert, then, as Polish does, that "the moral law is implicit in creation itself" or that "it is a derivative, like man himself, of the creative process" [52] is not altogether convincing.

In short, Reform Judaism will have to consider the question whether, once the belief in a revealing God is taken away, there is any basis for either moral or ritual halacha.

VI

Monford Harris has maintained that "the life of the Jewish people is . . . the central interest for a Jewish theology." [53] Other exponents of Judaism prefer to give the central place to God or Torah, but there is no question that Israel and its life constitute a primary theme of Jewish theology and that no such theology which does not wrestle seriously with the nature of Israel and its existence can be at all adequate.

The attempts, so characteristic of nineteenth- and early twentieth-century thought, to explain Jewish existence in general categories, such as race, nation, religion, or culture, have been largely abandoned. To be sure, there are still some who seek to define Israel in such reductionist terms, but they are a diminishing number. By and large, it has come to be recognized that Israel represents a unique phenomenon that cannot be analogized to any other. The "scandal of particularity" is no longer a *bête noire* for most serious thinkers who have applied themselves to the attempt to throw some light on the mystery of Jewish existence. Nor do the general sociological explanations, so popular a few decades ago, still carry much conviction. Bernard Bamberger soberly concludes that "sociological explanations of Jewish history, though frequently stimulating and, in regard to specific details, sometimes convincing, do not appear to account adequately for the total Jewish experience." [54] And he adds that "Zangwill's epigram about the 'choosing people' is ingenious but does not suffice." [55] So, also, Samuel Karff: "ultimately he who seeks to explain the birth of this unique people [Israel] must invoke such terms as 'ripe historical conditions,' 'chance,' 'creative genius'—terms no more compelling or explanatory than the claim of revelation and the mystery of divine grace." [56]

Bamberger insists that to understand Israel we must consider the realities of its history and its actual existence rather than abstractions. We must also, of course, take account of Israel's own self-understanding of its place and destiny in the world. If we look at the classic biblical and rabbinic statements concerning Israel's election, we find that they describe it "as a privilege, an undeserved privilege, but one that carries heavy obligations." [57] We discover also that "the sense of chosenness is not infrequently combined with a sense of tragic destiny." [58] There are some chauvinistic expressions, to be sure, but they are rather minor, in both frequency and significance.

Unwilling to accept *in toto* any of the theoretical explanations of Jewish existence that have been offered—whether fundamentalist, existentialist, or positivist—and insisting that none is really adequate to the mystery of Jewish existence, Bamberger nevertheless holds that the practical implications of the matter are clear. We must continue to speculate about the nature of Israel, but "in the meantime we have to live with the fact of our Jewish identity and with the datum of our chosenness." [59] Whether Jewish experience and Jewish uniqueness are of human or divine origin, they "impose an ineluctable obligation upon the Jewish people and the individual Jew. . . . The individual Jew has the obligation to identify himself as a Jew, to contribute to Jewish group survival, and to learn, teach, and practice the religious and ethical values of Judaism." [60]

As has already been noted above, most contemporary interpreters of Judaism have abandoned the use of abstractions and universal ideas in dealing with the problem of Jewish existence.

Joseph Narot, however, reflects the older liberal and humanist spirit when he writes: "Our theology has been progressively humanized and the concepts of Israel's election, covenant, and mission have been individualized and universalized." [61]

Indeed, Narot rejects the belief in the chosenness of the Jewish people. One of the reasons for his repudiation of the traditional doctrine is that "in present reality, many peoples and individuals besides Jews are seeking improvement in the conditions of life for all men, and both we and they would reject any claim to supernatural uniqueness." [62] It seems questionable whether "seeking improvement in the conditions of life for all men" is the hallmark of the election and the covenant, as these have been understood in the classical teaching of Judaism. Nor is it at all clear that a unique mission for the Jewish people must be understood, or has been understood, as excluding other missions for other peoples. Daniel J. Silver also questions the validity of a special mission for Israel on the basis of this interpretation. But it is debatable whether this is a justified interpretation of the tradition.

Both Narot and Silver tend to regard the idea of Israel's election and the corollary idea of its unique mission as manifestations of *chutzpah*. There is no doubt that these have been put forth by some in the history of Judaism in a spirit of arrogance, but Bamberger is certainly right when he points to the sense of tragic destiny and heavy burden that has generally been associated with the belief in the choice of Israel and its covenant with God.

Narot wishes to retain the word "chosenness" but to give it a radically different meaning than it has had in the classic tradition. Chosenness, he writes, "means the chosenness not of the Jew but of Judaism, and refers to the historic influence which Judaism has had on the Jew and consequently on the world's opinion of the Jew as an adherent of his faith." [63] Narot regards the Jew as "the eternal rebel against injustice." [64] He sees in his rebellion and in the sufferings that this has brought upon him the marks of his chosenness. "To this day in Western thought at least no one is more clearly a symbol of the human struggle for right and of man as the tragic victim of wrong than the Jew. In both these senses Judaism is the chosen faith and the Jews the chosen people, and their mission is to speak out ceaselessly, struggle relentlessly, and if need be, suffer greatly in defense of freedom, truth, justice, and peace." [65]

This is not at all an ignoble view of the mission and destiny of Judaism and the Jewish people, but what one misses in it is the sense of messianic optimism associated with the classical doctrines, the sense that through the power of God Israel will succeed in its appointed task and the Kingdom of Heaven become an earthly reality.

In a sense, at least, Silver is somewhat more radical than Narot. He wishes to deny that the idea of the *mission* of Israel, to which his essay in the present volume is restricted, is either "an update of classic Jewish themes" or "an argument for the significance of Jewish survival." [66] The mission for him is rhetoric, suitable for the nineteenth century, with its frontier mood of buoyancy and hope, when the German Jewish Reformers and their American successors stressed it, but no longer vital or relevant.

Silver denies the validity of the mission of Israel on a number of grounds. He objects that it puts man or Israel in the place of God at the center of the divine plan and, in doing so, is faithless to the classical tradition. The tradition itself, however, makes it fairly clear that it does regard Israel as occupying a central role in God's providential purpose for the world. It may be true that the mission idea as formulated by the founders of Reform Judaism over-emphasized Israel at the expense of God, a God whom many of them tended to reduce to the Kantian role of guarantor of morality, but this hardly justifies rejecting the idea altogether.

In maintaining that the nineteenth-century reformers nodded only perfunctorily toward Israel's priestly function and emphasized the social crusader aspects of the mission rather than the sanctification of the Jewish community, Silver, I think, is quite right. But again a temporary historical distortion of an authentic religious idea does not warrant its rejection. Silver also pointedly remarks that "for the first three-fourths of a century of its life in Reform Judaism, the mission idea was deemed inimical to proselytism, despite the patent congruence in language and hope, and despite the traditional encouragement of such activity." [67] Again, one may charge the early Reformers with failing to see the implications of a belief they professed, or possibly even with insincerity and a measure of hypocrisy, but this hardly invalidates the belief itself.

Silver, I think, makes too much of the fact that Deutero-Isaiah's image of the people of Israel as a "light unto the nations" is idiosyncratic in the Hebrew Bible. An idea need not be repeated constantly in order to be of supreme significance; the sheer number of times or places in which it figures is no proof of its importance. The fact, however, is that the idea of Israel's divine election and call, its being summoned to serve as a blessing to the nations of the earth, does find fairly prominent expression in the Bible, and it did become the motive power of a vast Jewish missionary movement in the Hellenistic world.

Where Silver makes a very telling point is in his contention that "Deutero-Isaiah developed the image of the Jew as 'a light unto the nations' within the context of 'a covenant of the people.' He neither normalized or glorified the exile, but looked forward to a return to Zion." [68] The nineteenth-century Reformers, with their anti-nationalism and rather artificial universalism, were certainly misreading Deutero-Isaiah and the great tradition which followed him.

The idea of Jacques Maritain that Judaism is to be "like an activating leaven injected into the mass" of the world in order to teach the world "to be discontented and restless as long as the world has not God" is rejected by Silver, who writes that "we cannot survive as puppets in a theological shadow play nor as pensioners of bygone dreams. The happy piety that the survival of Judaism is quintessential to the world encourages a loyal few, but only a loyal few. We are a statistically minded generation: thirteen million people out of a world population of over two billion hardly encourages dreams of supreme importance. We are a self-analytic generation and we know that we do not qualify as the *Lamed Vavniks* of mankind." [69]

For myself I must confess that I do not find Silver convincing here. I do not know of any way of disproving the faith that the survival of Judaism is necessary to the world, and there seems to me a good deal of historical evidence supporting this faith. Whether it encourages many or few is a question which cannot be answered on any basis of factual evidence. The fact that we are only thirteen million out of over two billion people in the

world need hardly make us feel insignificant; we have always
been a numerically insignificant minority in the world, but our
impact on its life has been far beyond what might have been
expected from our numbers. I quite agree that we Jews generally
do not qualify for the role of the *Lamed Vavniks* of mankind,
but I have a feeling that at least a few of the thirty-six are Jews.

The fact, however, is that Silver does not wish to deny that
"Israel has a unique relationship to God and a providential role
to play in God's plan." [70] Nor does he desire that the Jewish
people should reduce their activity in the cause of social reform.
But what, it may be asked of him, is this, if not the substance of
the mission idea as understood by most of the exponents of Reform Judaism? Again when Silver writes, "what an achievement
it would be if we could truly forge Israel as a kingdom of priests
and as a holy nation," [71] is he not, in effect, admitting the heart
of the mission idea? Silver is quite right when he criticizes the
nineteenth-century exponents of the mission doctrine for emphasizing "a reformist crusade, but not the reforming pieties" [72] and
when he insists that "it is these pieties which alone provide an
environment in which the Jew can grow not only in knowledge
but in understanding, not only in independence but in responsibility, not only in awareness but in holiness." [73] His point here is
very similar to that made repeatedly by the nineteenth-century
neo-Orthodox leader, Samson Raphael Hirsch, and his argument,
if I understand him correctly, is more for a return to meaningful
traditional observance than for an abandonment of the mission
idea.

It is interesting to note that Jacques Maritain's view of the
function of the Jew in the world which is strongly rejected by
Silver is warmly espoused by Samuel Karff in the present volume.
Maritain, of course, is not the originator of this view; it has a
long history. Probably its major twentieth-century exponent was
Franz Rosenzweig, and it has been vigorously urged in recent
years in America by Will Herberg and Arthur Cohen. Karff aptly
summarizes Rosenzweig's view when he says that for him "what
the Jewish people offers God is simply its *presence* in the world,
a presence which in and of itself proclaims God's sovereignty,
casts judgment on all of man's penultimate solutions, and patiently waits for the messianic redemption." [74]

Furthermore, Rosenzweig, in elaborating his doctrine of the

relationship of the synagogue and the church, had accepted the cathedral image of the synagogue, "which is immortal but stands with broken staff and bound eyes" and must renounce all work in this world, and had come to see the church as the militant agent of God, "with unbreakable staff and eyes open to the world," [75] converting the pagan nations of the earth. Judaism, for him, was "the eternal life," Christianity "the eternal way." The Jew was not to engage in the struggle to change the world but simply criticize all ideologies since these are necessarily idolatrous and self-defeating. In the liturgy of the synagogue and in observance of the sacred round of the Jewish year, Israel could live in a trans-temporal and trans-historical realm of holiness.

Karff affirms the "passive" mission of Israel envisioned by Rosenzweig when he writes: "To deny that redemption is here and yet attest that 'my Redeemer liveth' is a witness fraught with special significance when borne by history's most time-tested survivor in a world that proclaims 'God is dead.'" [76] But, against Rosenzweig, Karff also insists that the covenant between God and Israel necessarily involves the Jew in an active mission as well. He speaks of "the primary obligation of a people who first heard the words of the prophets and remained charter witnesses to the divine demand for *tzedek*." [77] That demand is addressed to both the Jew of the Diaspora and of Israel and means, in his understanding, that "if in America we stand especially accountable for the quality and intensity of our involvement in 'social action,' in Israel we are summoned to build a Jewish state which submits to the judgment of its prophetic legacy." [78]

A major objection raised by Silver and implicitly also by Narot to the classical idea of the mission of Israel is answered by Karff when he says, "That individual Jews may betray their heritage and that many a non-Jew surpasses a son of the covenant as witness for justice does not compromise, much less invalidate" the Jew's primary obligation to work for justice.[79] But he also agrees with an important point made by Silver when he writes: "At times, it seems, Jewish religious liberalism was so preoccupied with what the Jew could offer the world that it virtually ignored what living within the covenant could offer the Jew." [80]

Rosenzweig has obviously had a decisive influence on Karff's views. This becomes especially clear when he says that he need not "deny that Christian and Jew each has a role in the work of redemption. . . . Each of us anticipates the coming of God's Kingdom. Until then we must wait for the decisive arbitration of our conflicting claims." [81]

Karff does not minimize the difficulty the contemporary Jew has, in the face of Auschwitz and all the other horrors of the twentieth century, in believing in the covenant and the God of the covenant. But he insists that "the authentic Jew is Yisroel, the one who contends with God but does not deny Him, who argues while he prays, who doubts as he serves, and whose very demands of his creator betray a primordial trust yearning for confirmation." [82] Martin Buber, too, recognized that we live in a time of God's silence and asked the agonizing question how a life with God is still possible in a time in which there is an Auschwitz. His answer was that the cry of Job—the Job of the Bible and the Job of the gas chambers—must become our cry, and that rather than "stand overcome before the hidden face of God as the tragic hero of the Greeks before faceless fate," [83] we must contend with God and struggle with the world from which He seems absent.

It is interesting to note that Rosenzweig's doctrine of the Jewish people as a supernatural, meta-historical community—a doctrine shared, as noted above, by Will Herberg and Arthur Cohen —led all three of them to a negative attitude toward Zionism and the reestablishment of Jewish national life in Israel. Rosenzweig's staunch opposition to the Zionist movement in Germany in the 1920's is well known. Herberg rejected the Zionist attempt to normalize Jewish life because, as he put it, such efforts "run counter to the divine purpose in the creation and election of Israel." [84] And Arthur Cohen characterizes "the national restoration of Zion, the political rejuvenation of Israel, the punishing of the persecutors of the Jews, the miraculous return of the Jews to the Holy Land" as merely "Jewishness— the whole array of atavisms and sentimentalities which a secure minority can now afford." [85] Against such detractions of Zionism and the state of Israel, Karff properly reminds us that Martin Buber "regarded the rebirth of the Jewish community in Palestine, and particularly the creation of the kibbutz, as the most fertile soil for the cultivation of the Jewish spirit in the contemporary world." [86] And he himself insists, as we have already indicated, on a prophetic mission for the Jews of the State of Israel.

Reference has been made above to Rosenzweig's doctrine of the relationship between Judaism and Christianity. Theological investigation of the meaning of Israel in our time ought, I believe, to deal with this problem and seek to define how Israel stands in relation to that offspring which claims to be "the true Israel." Rosenzweig's own conception of Judaism and Christianity as equally true and organically linked, complementary aspects of God's one revealed truth, his view of Judaism as "the eternal life" and of Christianity as "the eternal way," his statement that no one comes to the Father except through the Son, save the Jew who is already with the Father—all these have not found general acceptance. They are strongly reflected in the work of Cohen and Herberg, as well as in the thought of Hans Joachim Schoeps.[87] One also finds them, strangely enough, in two Conservative rabbis, Hershel Matt and Seymour Siegel.[88] Most Jewish theologians, however—even those who will not claim exclusive truth for Judaism over Christianity—have come to recognize that Rosenzweig's formulations leave much to be desired. Furthermore, this "Judeo-Christian nonintervention pact," as it has been called, which "is prepared to hand the rest of the world over to Christian missionary activity,"[89] so long as the church does not seek to convert the Jew, has not worked out as Rosenzweig apparently intended. His doctrine that not one of the nations of the world comes to the Father except through Christ must certainly suggest to a Christian the essential superiority of the church over the synagogue and a significant defect in Judaism. And it has in fact been turned against Rosenzweig—who clearly meant it to be a rationale for the peaceful coexistence of Judaism and Christianity—as a justification of missionary activity toward Jews.[90] Something other than Rosenzweig's formulation is obviously required.

VII

One thing must never be forgotten by the Jewish theologian, and that is that theology and the religious life, though interrelated, are far from identical. This is particularly true in Judaism.

Arnold Wolf writes: "The *Shema* warns us not to expect intellectually to comprehend Him whom we are bidden to love with all our mind and self and power. The *Shema* is, accordingly, a proem to commitment. Theology in Judaism is always and only introductory." [91] I should prefer to say that it is subsidiary, but I am in total agreement with Wolf when he suggests that the religious life, the life of love, obedience, and trust, is what is essential and primary in Judaism.

It has been contended, and a strong case could be made in support of the contention, that the writing of theologies is a sin against God, that is, the God of the Bible. Wolf exemplifies this contention when he writes, "Theology inevitably involves us in blasphemy. Because we cannot say enough, our saying is a betrayal of God." [92] Theology, I repeat, may be an expression of sin and blasphemy if it presumes to exhaust the reality of God or even to prove God by reasoning. Nevertheless, theology does have an indispensable purpose insofar as it may help us clarify our beliefs, see their implications, and above all, destroy our false and inadequate images of God. What must never be overlooked, however, is that to arrive at a true, existential relationship with God, much more than theology is required. Lev Shestov made the point with his customary polemical vigor when he wrote: "The chief thing is to think that, even if all men without exception were convinced that God does not exist, this would not mean anything, and that if one could prove as clearly as two times two makes four that God does not exist, this also would not mean anything," and when, to the complaint that it is not possible to ask one to take a position which negates a universal conviction of men and flies in the face of ordinary logic, he replied, "Obviously! But God always demands of us the impossible. . . . It is only when man wishes the impossible that he remembers God. To obtain that which is possible he turns to those like himself." [93]

The Jewish theologian might also do well to ponder carefully the idea, propounded in recent years by a number of distinguished Christian theologians, that neither Judaism nor Christianity can properly be called a religion. The thought probably derives from Dietrich Bonhoeffer, but Joseph Sittler states it as explicitly as anyone else when he writes:

Religion is always a way by which man operates upon a malleable Ultimate in order to affirm, realize, give meaning to himself, save himself. Both Judaism and Christianity deny this anthropocentrism and affirm an utter theocentrism. . . . Neither is a religion. The terms *covenant* and *election* in Judaism and the terms *called* and *grace* in Christianity point to an entirely non-religious structure of the God-man relationship—and no single feature in the multitudinous data of that structure, either in word or in the central symbols of the cultus, is clearly exposed under the categories of religion.[94]

Judaism and Christianity certainly have significant affinities, and, as I have suggested above, one of the major tasks of Jewish theology in our time must be to define their relationship to one another. Nevertheless, Judaism must not be taken as merely the dialectical counterpart or antagonist of Christianity, as has been the case in the thought of some recent writers on Jewish theology. The uniqueness of Judaism is not, as Harold Schulweis has warned, to be found "in dogmas formulated *contra* Christianity." [95] Nor should the fact that some of the central doctrines of Judaism transcend what Paul Tillich called "ordinary" or "controlling" reason lead the Jewish theologian to regard Judaism and Christianity as equally anti-rational and paradoxical. Will Herberg exemplifies this tendency when he writes "The meeting of the divine with the earthly, the incursion of the eternal into time, the encounter of the infinite God with the finiteness of man in the theophany of Sinai seems to me just as irreconcilable with reason, just as paradoxical, just as 'absurd' as the Incarnation" and concludes that "Judaism is in a position no different from Christianity." [96] Against such thinking, Schulweis issues a deeply justified *caveat* when he says: "Judaism must certainly not be nationalism without religion, but neither must it become Christianity without Christ. We must resist the temptations to model ourselves in the Christian mirror. We must resist the social 'advantage' of dichotomizing ourselves into natural and supernatural Jews, secular and religious Jews, just as we have resisted the Christian dualisms of law and spirit, ritual and ethics, flesh and soul." [97]

The Jewish theologian has his own tasks and his own problems. While he may learn much from philosophers and theologians committed to other faiths, his own goal must never be lost sight of: to explicate the uniqueness of Jewish faith and Jewish experience in terms that are appropriate to it. In furthering this goal, his work will be richly compensated.

NOTES

1. Tillich, of course, began his theological work in Germany, but most of it was carried on from the time of his arrival in America in 1934 to his death here in 1965.

2. These two Russian émigrés wrote much of their work abroad where they lived after the Bolshevik Revolution.

3. Herberg, "Has Judaism Still Power to Speak?" *Commentary*, May, 1949, p. 455.

4. Buber, *Israel and the World* (New York: Schocken Books, 1948), p. 14.

5. Herberg, *loc. cit.*

6. Above, p. 15.

7. Martin, "Paul Tillich and Judaism," *Judaism*, XV (No. 2, Spring, 1966), 183-84.

8. Above, p. 44.

9. *Ibid.*

10. Above, p. 121.

11. Martin, "Comments on 'No Retreat From Reason,'" *Yearbook* of the Central Conference of American Rabbis, LXXIV (1964), 209.

12. Petuchowski, above, p. 121.

13. Above, p. 122.

14. Above, p. 58.

15. Gittelsohn, "No Retreat From Reason," *Yearbook* of the Central Conference of American Rabbis, LXXIV (1964), 197.

16. Above, p. 52.

17. Heschel, *Man's Quest for God* (New York: Charles Scribner's Sons, 1954), p. 73.

18. Smith, "Philosophy of Religion," in Paul Ramsey (ed.), *Religion* (Englewood Cliffs, N.J.: Prentice-Hall, 1965), p. 394.

19. Charles Hartshorne and William L. Reese, *Philosophers Speak of God* (Chicago: University of Chicago Press, 1953), p. 24.

20. *Ibid.*, p. 23.

21. Scheler, *Die Stellung des Menschen im Kosmos* (Darmstadt: 1928), pp. 13ff.

22. Herberg, *op. cit.*, p. 449.

23. Above, p. 24.

24. Above, p. 45.

25. Above, p. 30.

26. See especially Harvey Cox, *The Secular City* (New York: Macmillan, 1965), and Thomas J. J. Altizer, *The Gospel of Christian Atheism* (Philadelphia: Westminster Press, 1966).

27. Above, p. 34.
28. Above, p. 35.
29. Above, p. 36.
30. Published by the University of Chicago Press, 1948.
31. Above, p. 36.
32. Above, p. 28.
33. Above, p. 46.
34. Above, p. 35.
35. Above, p. 47.
36. *Ibid.*
37. Above, p. 90.
38. Above, p. 108.
39. Above, p. 110.
40. Above, p. 113.
41. *Ibid.*
42. Above, p. 59.
43. Petuchowski, *Ever Since Sinai* (New York: Scribe Publications, 1961), p. 72. Italics his.
44. Schulweis, "A Religion Like All Other Religions," in Ira Eisenstein (ed.), *Varieties of Jewish Belief* (New York: Reconstructionist Press, 1966), p. 235.
45. Above, p. 97.
46. *Ibid.*
47. *Ibid.*
48. Above, p. 100.
49. Above, p. 115.
50. Above, p. 60.
51. Herberg, *Judaism and Modern Man* (Philadelphia: Jewish Publication Society, 1951), p. 89.
52. Above, p. 58.
53. Harris, "Israel: The Uniqueness of Jewish History," in Arnold J. Wolf (ed.), *Rediscovering Judaism* (Chicago: Quadrangle Books, 1965).
54. Above, p. 127.
55. *Ibid.*
56. Above, p. 165.
57. Above, p. 126.
58. Above, p. 127.
59. Above, p. 129.
60. *Ibid.*
61. Above, p. 136.
62. Above, p. 138.
63. *Ibid.*
64. Above, p. 140.
65. *Ibid.*
66. Above, p. 145.
67. Above, p. 150.
68. Above, p. 151.
69. Above, p. 155.
70. Above, p. 153.
71. Above, p. 156.
72. Above, p. 157.
73. *Ibid.*
74. Above, pp. 171-72.

75. Glatzer, Nahum N., ed., *Franz Rosenzweig: His Life and Thought* (Philadelphia: Jewish Publication Society, 1953), pp. 342-43.

76. Above, p. 176.

77. *Ibid.*

78. *Ibid.*

79. *Ibid.*

80. Above, p. 168.

81. Above, p. 173.

82. Above, p. 177.

83. Buber, *At the Turning* (New York: Farrar, Straus & Young, 1952), p. 62.

84. Herberg, *Judaism and Modern Man*, p. 274.

85. Cohen, *The Natural and the Supernatural Jew* (New York: Pantheon Books, 1962), p. 278.

86. Above, p. 170.

87. See Schoeps, *The Jewish-Christian Argument: A History of Theologies in Conflict* (New York: Holt, Rinehart and Winston, 1963), pp. 141-42.

88. See the Symposium, "The State of Jewish Belief," *Commentary*, August, 1966, pp. 118-19, 143.

89. Schulweis, *op. cit.*, p. 225.

90. See George A. F. Knight (ed.), *Jews and Christians: Preparation for Dialogue* (Philadelphia: Westminster Press, 1965), p. 173.

91. Above, p. 40.

92. Above, p. 42.

93. Shestov, *Athens and Jerusalem* (translated by Bernard Martin [Athens, O.: Ohio University Press, 1966]), p. 435.

94. Sittler, *Religious Education*, LIII (No. 2), 139.

95. Schulweis, *op. cit.*, p. 229.

96. Herberg, Discussion on "Theological Problems of the Hour," *Proceedings* of the Rabbinical Assembly of America (New York: 1949).

97. Schulweis, *op. cit.*, p. 240.

CONTRIBUTORS

BERNARD J. BAMBERGER is Rabbi of Congregation Shaaray Tefila in New York City. A former president of the Central Conference of American Rabbis, he is the author of *Fallen Angels, Proselytism in the Talmudic Period, The Story of Judaism,* and other scholarly works.

EUGENE B. BOROWITZ is Professor of Education and Jewish Religious Thought at the Hebrew Union College—Jewish Institute of Religion in New York City. He has written *A Layman's Introduction to Existentialism* and contributed to many learned journals.

SAMUEL E. KARFF is Rabbi of Sinai Temple in Chicago. He is the author of many scholarly articles and papers and serves on the faculty of Notre Dame University.

BERNARD MARTIN occupies the Abba Hillel Silver Chair of Jewish Studies and is Chairman of the Department of Religion at Case Western Reserve University in Cleveland. He is the author of *The Existentialist Theology of Paul Tillich* and *Prayer in Judaism* and the translator of Lev Shestov's *Athens and Jerusalem* and *Potestas Clavium.*

JOSEPH NAROT is Rabbi of Temple Israel of Greater Miami in

Florida. He is the author of *An Introduction to a Faith, A Preface to Well Being, A Primer for Temple Life,* and *Why I Am a Jew.* He is also chairman of the Liturgy Committee of the Central Conference of American Rabbis.

LEVI A. OLAN is Rabbi of Temple Emanu-El in Dallas and currently President of the Central Conference of American Rabbis. He is the author of *Judaism and Immortality* and has contributed many articles to scholarly journals.

JAKOB J. PETUCHOWSKI is Professor of Rabbinics and Efroymson Professor of Jewish Theology at the Hebrew Union College–Jewish Institute of Religion in Cincinnati. He has written *Ever Since Sinai* and *Zion Reconsidered* and has contributed numerous papers to learned journals.

W. GUNTHER PLAUT is Rabbi of Holy Blossom Temple in Toronto. He is the author of *The Case for the Chosen People, The Rise of Reform Judaism, The Growth of Reform Judaism,* and a number of other works on Jewish history and theology.

DAVID POLISH is Rabbi of Beth Emet the Free Synagogue in Evanston, Illinois, and a Visiting Lecturer at Garrett Theological Seminary. He is the author of *The Eternal Dissent* and *The Higher Freedom,* and co-author of *A Guide for Reform Jews.*

ALVIN J. REINES is Professor of Jewish Philosophy at the Hebrew Union College–Jewish Institute of Religion in Cincinnati. He has contributed articles to scholarly journals.

DANIEL JEREMY SILVER is Rabbi of The Temple in Cleveland. The author of *Maimonides and Maimonidean Criticism,* he is also the author of many scholarly articles and serves as editor of the *Journal* of the Central Conference of American Rabbis.

ARNOLD JACOB WOLF is Rabbi of Congregation Solel in Glencoe, Illinois. He has written *Challenge to Confirmands: An Introduction to Jewish Thinking,* edited *Rediscovering Judaism,* and contributed articles to learned journals.

DATE DUE

DEC 1 '78			
DEC 1 '78			
MAY 0 1 2000			
GAYLORD			PRINTED IN U.S.A.